Aligning Megalithic Sites of

Southern England and Carnac, France

with Groundwater Features

Aligning the Three Worlds

By

David Johnson

New York State Archaeological Association

Former Research Associate, Department of Anthropology

University of Massachusetts, Amherst

24 Manor Dr. W

Poughkeepsie, NY

12603

845-454-1860

globaldj@optonline.net

Epigraph Books
Rhinebeck, New York

Johnson dedicates this book to those who constructed these magnificent monuments.

ISBN 978-1-954744-59-2

Library of Congress Control Number 2022903083

Library and Archival Reference:
National Anthropologic and Archaeological Library, Smithsonian Institution, Washington, D.C.

Archival File Reference for Johnson's publications and research reports:
David Johnson
2018   Papers on Ceremonial Landscapes, No. 2014-14, National Anthropological Archives, Smithsonian Institution, Washington, D.C.

Photographic Credits:
David W. Johnson - throughout text
Google Earth - throughout text

Epigraph Books
22 East Market Street, Suite 304
Rhinebeck, NY 12572
(845) 876-4861
epigraphps.com

TABLE OF CONTENTS

Part 1

Introduction

Research Prior To England And France

From 1996 and 2012 I studied the correlation between areas of higher permeability / concentrated flows within the groundwater and archaeological sites in Peru and Chile. This correlation came about as a result of locating water sources for the community of Nasca, Peru. During the investigation, I located areas of high permeability which intersected the tributaries of the Rio Grande de Nasca drainage from the valley sides. Until that time, these water sources were not well known. While documenting areas of higher permeability, I realized the Nasca Lines / geoglyphs were located along them, as well as habitation, ceremonial and cemetery sites. Eventually, by comparing the location of various types of geometric geoglyphs with the geological and hydrological data, I was able to determine the function of these features. For example, along the areas of higher permeability, trapezoids mapped their course, paralleling lines of stone piles their width and spirals indicated where they curved. Collaborating with the University of Massachusetts, Amherst, Peru's Institute of National Culture and other archaeologists, this study eventually covered one thousand four hundred miles of Peru and Chile's coast and eastward into the Andes Mountains. Our data indicates inhabitants of the Atacama Desert were mapping areas of higher permeability within the groundwater as early as the Chinchorro culture, dating to 9,000 BP to the fall of the Inca Empire in the 1500's. This research is discussed in detail in my book titled Beneath the Nasca Lines And Other Coastal Geoglyphs Of Peru And Chile.

Between 2009 and 2019 I applied the same methodology used in Peru and Chile to sites throughout the United States and the results were the same. Ancestral Native Americans located areas of higher permeability within the groundwater and mapped them with surface features, such as cairns and petroglyphs, and placed their habitation, ceremonial and sacred sites along them. By placing their surface features on the areas of higher permeability and incorporating astronomical events within them, they were able to align the under, present and upper worlds. By comparing Native American Ceremonial Landscapes throughout North America, our data strongly suggests these sites share a high level of cultural uniformity among all Native American cultures during different historical periods and in diverse environments. Ceremonial Landscape features collectively function as a map of ancestral Native American movement throughout the areas we have surveyed, and very likely serve the same function throughout the Western Hemisphere. This research is discussed in my book titled Native Americans' Sacred And Ceremonial Landscapes Correlation With Groundwater.

I have also had the opportunity to apply my methodology to a selection of archaeological sites in Italy, East Africa and the Sahel in the southern Sahara Desert. In each of these regions the results were the same. In recent years, additional researchers are focusing on the association of areas of higher permeability within the groundwater and important ancient archaeological sites and features. For example, in Central

6

America, Dr. Guillermo de Anda has located caves which conduct concentrated flows of groundwater beneath Mayan temples and ceremonial sites (Gantley 2017). A team of scientists has demonstrated that archaeological sites on Easter Island are associated with freshwater sources (Brosnan 2018, DiNapoli 2018). It appears the correlation between ancient archaeological sites and areas of higher permeability within the groundwater is not unique to Native Americans. It is possible this was a universal human trait.

Although our research is ongoing within the Western Hemisphere, my attention has been drawn to other continents to determine if the alignment of ancient archaeological sites and the features within them are aligned with areas of higher permeability within the groundwater, and if this was a universal human trait at that time. Thus far, I have researched two areas in Europe, southern England and Carnac, France, which are discussed in this book. Both regions contain a concentration of megalithic sites which date to the Neolithic Period. Although researchers in these regions have discussed the correlation between megalithic sites and springs, rivers and other surface water, I am not aware of any discussions regarding the correlation between areas of higher permeability within the groundwater and these sites. Therefore, this discussion will focus on the alignment of megalithic sites in these two regions and areas of higher permeability within the groundwater. Although these sites represent a small percentage of the megalithic sites within Europe, this research provides a data base that can applied to similar sites by other researchers.

Although my research focuses on the alignment between megalithic site features and areas of higher permeability within the groundwater, it is important to keep in mind that these sites are also associated with cultural, spiritual and ceremonial concepts.

In addition to the data presented in my books and articles, the site reports from the regions my colleagues and I investigated are available in my national archival file at Smithsonian Institution's Anthropological and Archaeological Library in Washington, DC and the administrative agencies who issued research permits within their jurisdiction.

Photos credits accompany outsourced images. Those without credit were taken by David Johnson, who maintains the copyright. Anyone interested in using his photos needs to obtain his written permission. Google Earth satellite images were used throughout the text.

UTM GPS coordinates were used throughout this research.

Please keep in mind - In the figures, the width between the parallel lines with the same color represents the approximate width of an area of higher permeability. A single line represents a narrow concentrated flow.

Since these sites are thousands of years old, the structures and megalithic features present may represent only a portion of those that existed at their apex.

Please keep in mind that this research is ongoing and new datum is being added on a regular basis.

Part 2

Johnson's Methodology

The following discusses my research methodology which is followed by comments from researchers who have accompanied me during site surveys.

Before I discuss the use of dowsing, it is important to consider the following. When researchers learn that dowsing is included in my methodology, they conclude that this is the only method I use to reach my conclusions. Actually this is not the case. In addition to dowsing, geological, hydrological, archaeological and ethnographic studies are included. Within each region, Native American First Nation archaeological, spiritual, cultural and elder authorities are consulted and collaborate with this research. All of these diverse disciplines are considered prior to writing a final report. As for dowsing, I have found the most efficient way to determine an archaeological site's correlation to geological and hydrological features is using this technique. Consistently, our data corresponds with the historical documentation of ancient cultures regarding the relationship between these diverse studies. Thus, dowsing is discussed next.

An issue regarding my research is the use of dowsing, which is not generally accepted within the scientific community. During the course of this research, data from each region has continued to support a correlation existing between structures and other features constructed by ancestral Native Americans and areas of higher permeability within the groundwater. As mentioned above, the results of the South American studies in Peru and Chile are discussed in detail in my book. Throughout these investigations the same methodology has been used.

The research consists of surveying sites using dowsing rods to determine where areas of higher permeability within the groundwater are located, and if they are aligned with the Native American archaeological sites and the features associated with them. Within the bedrock, groundwater is found in permeable strata. Geological features such as faults, fractures, dikes, contacts and alluvium associated with the permeable strata can create areas of higher permeability which collect groundwater and conduct it along their length. I use two metal L shaped dowsing rods to locate areas of higher permeability. One end is contained in a plastic holder and swings freely, thus my hands do not touch the rods. The metal dowsing rods are held perpendicular to the ground and parallel to one another as I walk. When an area of higher permeability is encountered the rods cross to some extent. If they barely cross, it indicates there is a low rate of flow along the area of higher permeability. If they cross in the middle, it is moderate, and if they cross completely, it indicates a strong rate of flow. The trend and width of the areas of higher permeability are determined by crossing it several times and documenting where the rods cross. Although I admit I do not know how dowsing with metal rods works, by practicing and testing on known groundwater sources, I have come to realize it works for me, as well as others who have surveyed the same sites I have and obtained the same results. Whenever possible, I survey at least two sides of a site to determine if any areas of higher permeability intersect it. Then I follow the area(s) of higher permeability into the site and document the archaeological features associated with them, as well as those which are not. Consistently, our data indicates ancestral Native Americans placed structures and other features along areas of higher permeability. Thus far, our data indicates the ancestral Native Americans who constructed these sites were locating the same subsurface features I am documenting.

I prefer to conduct my survey prior to studying the current interpretation of the geological, hydrological and archaeological data for a region. When I began my investigation in Nasca, Peru, previous interpretations of the western Andean watershed concluded eighty percent of the runoff was through the rivers and twenty percent through the bedrock and alluvium. My investigation, followed by the University of Massachusetts study, concluded the opposite was true. Using dowsing I have been able to locate areas of higher permeability within the groundwater that are not detected by current geological and hydrological techniques. Water tables are determined by averaging the depth of groundwater in a given area using various forms of technology and well data. Narrow areas of higher permeability can go undetected using these scientific methodologies. To confirm the location of the areas of higher permeability, I am collaborating with geologists and hydrologists in each of the regions I am investigating.

When people learn that my methodology includes the use of dowsing rods, they often ask if we have found any evidence that ancient Native Americans used this technique. At this point in time, my colleagues and I have not been able to identify any archaeological evidence which indicates ancient ancestral Native Americans used some form of dowsing. However, the evidence could be present and misinterpreted, for example, in petroglyphs. It is also possible they never incorporated it into their oral tradition, and dowsing as a means to locate groundwater was lost due to conflicts, conquest, epidemics or cultural diffusion. During the course of these investigations some tribal leaders have informed me that they use dowsing, however they did not elaborate on this subject.

I realize this methodology does not follow modern archaeological methods of research, however consider the following. Perhaps ancestral Native Americans, as well as other ancient cultures throughout the world, used methods which are considered unscientific today to locate concentrated flows within the groundwater, and these techniques have been neglected in modern times. Although I use metal dowsing rods, the ancestral Native Americans could have used a variety of techniques to locate areas of higher permeability. For example, for centuries dowsing rods have been made out of forked wood sticks to locate groundwater. During the last forty years I have worked and lived with tribes in remote regions of the world whose lifestyle still resembles that of Native Americans prior to 1492 (Johnson's resumes). Many of these cultures were located in dry regions similar to the southwest. From time to time I have observed alternative techniques to locate areas of higher permeability that could have been used by ancestral Native Americans. For example, at times it is possible to hear groundwater flowing beneath the surface. In the lower Rio Grande de Nasca drainage of Peru at Usaca, residents told my colleagues and I they could hear a waterfall at night when they laid down to sleep; however, the river's surface was dry at that time. At that location, the surface and/or subsurface water flowing down the river intersects a fault which crosses it and extends deeper into the ground. Therefore, some or all of the river's flow can drain downward into the fault and follow a different course. The waterfall the people heard was the transfer of the water from the river into the fault. During the Aja Alto survey near Nasca, Peru, my colleagues and I could hear groundwater flowing beneath us along the fault we were mapping, even through there was no indication of water on the surface within the area (Johnson 2009, Chap. 2).

Northern Burkina Faso is located in the Sahel, one of the driest regions of the Sahara Desert. While working with a United Nations development project in 1992, I observed three productive wells, which were located along a 15 mile stretch of desert. I asked how they located the wells, and they introduced me to an elderly man who lived in the region and had a reputation for locating wells. He said by sitting on the ground at various locations he could sense where concentrations of groundwater are located. In 2009 during a Kenya Red Cross well project, I worked with Mohamed Roba, who told me how he taught himself to locate groundwater sources by observing various forms of vegetation and soils. Over eighty percent of his wells are successful. We tested each other's ability to locate areas of higher permeability on known and unknown water sources and had the same results. This suggests that, in addition to observing natural groundwater features such as springs, seeps, blowholes, faults, natural bedrock fractures and mineral veins, the ancestral Native Americans of the Western Hemisphere could have used a variety of methods to identify areas of higher permeability. Then they mapped the location of areas of higher permeability with surface features such as shrines, structures, petroglyphs, cairns and geoglyphs, etc.

In Chile, our data indicates the Chinchorro Culture, which inhabited one of the driest regions of the Atacama Desert as early as 9,000 B.P. (7,000 B.C.), documented areas of high permeability, which provided them with fresh water in an area where the surface water was contaminated with salt and arsenic (Johnson 2009, Chap. 6, Camarones & Chiza).

Comments Regarding Johnson's Methodology Prior To England And France

Often critics who have not accompanied me in the field suggest I can see various features from a distance and walk to them while dowsing, thus claiming the rods detected an area of higher permeability which lead me to them. However, blind surveys with other researchers who accompanied me in the field indicate the opposite is true. To test this hypothesis, I have conducted numerous blind surveys with other researchers in all of the regions I have investigated. During these surveys I am not given any information about the site or its features and location. Once in the area I apply my methodology to locate areas of higher permeability and then follow them to the site. Within the site I map the areas of higher permeability and the surface features associated with them, as well as those that are not. During all of the blind surveys we have conducted, I was able to locate the site and features associated with it successfully. The following comments represent a selection of those available regarding the results of the blind surveys we conducted.

In the fall of 2000, Dr. Steve Mabee, Department of Geoscience, University of Massachusetts, and I contacted the Navajo Nation and offered to conduct a blind survey to determine if the methodology we were using in Peru applied to Chaco sites in the southwestern United States. Then, in 2012 I returned to the Navajo Nation and have been collaborating with them since that time. In January 2014, Ronald Maldonado, Acting Tribal Historic Preservation Officer, Department of Historic Preservation, The Navajo Nation, commented:

> I was introduced to Johnson's theory regarding the correlation between areas of higher permeability and archaeological sites in the fall of 2000. He had asked to conduct a preliminary investigation of some Chaco archaeological sites within the Navajo Nation. During his visit Johnson and his colleague, Dr. Steve Mabee, Geoscience Department, University of Massachusetts, presented their data to our department and some sites were investigated. Without knowing anything about the sites, they located what they described as areas of higher permeability and followed them. The areas of higher permeability lead to archaeological features they did not know about or could see in advance.

> In 2012 Johnson contacted us and explained he was interested in changing his study area from Peru and Chile to the southwest and would like to investigate sites within our region. Thus far, permits were issued in 2012 and 2013 and he plans on returning in 2014. Johnson has investigated several sites and submitted detailed reports. His methodology is very scientific even though he incorporates dowsing. He has documented several archaeological sites and features which had not been identified prior to his investigation. In addition to our department, he is also collaborating with the Navajo Department of Water Resources.

> Johnson's research is investigating an area of archaeology which has not been thoroughly studied, and this research is helping the Navajo, as well as other Native American people, develop a more in-depth understanding of their ancient past. Please consider issuing him a permit to continue his research in your jurisdiction (Maldonado 2014).

In 2012 following a blind survey with the Hopi Nation, Max Taylor, Water Resources Technician, Hopi Tribe Water Resources Program, who conducted the blind survey with me, commented in his report:

> As we drove down State Route 264 we stopped at one spot where the rods crossed. At this location the mesa is narrow, and I knew there are springs at the base of the slope on each side of the road, however I did not tell him until he completed his test. Johnson located an area of higher permeability crossing the road. I could see what he meant about the

position of the rods when on the boundary of area of higher permeability.... At another location I had him survey the area to determine if there was an area of higher permeability since I knew there were cairns located in the area. I did not tell Johnson about this or its location. He located an area of higher permeability and began following it directly to the cairns which he could not see (Note: These cairns are very old and the purposes of the 2 markers are lost to the present day land users which are the Hopi). Along the way he also located an archaeological site I didn't know about (Taylor 2012).

Dr. Curtiss Hoffman, Department of Anthropology, Bridgewater State University, Massachusetts, who is also investigating Ceremonial Landscapes, conducted a blind survey with me in 2012. In his comments he discusses the survey and the results:

He had agreed to attempt to locate an archaeological site I know about and which he knew nothing about by locating an area(s) of higher permeability / concentrated flows using dowsing rods and following it to the site. I led him on a roundabout path through the woods around Great Hill. Actually, I led him to an entrance to the woods distant from the known Native American sacred site and let him find his way from there without guidance from me. He used his dowsing rods to locate several areas of higher permeability running off the hill. We came to the sacred site last, and without my telling him anything about it, he accurately located a concentrated flow whose edge conforms to the orientation of the stone row. He then went off downhill to find the opposite edge, and was visibly startled to discover the large split rock right at that edge! He traced the area of higher permeability on uphill, and it turns out that there are 2 others crossing the solstice sunset line, which are also marked by stones. I would say that this was a good confirmation of his method (Hoffman 2012,).

Richard Friedman, geologist and retired director of the McKinley County, New Mexico, Geographic Information Systems Center, and cultural resource archaeologist with the Chaco Protection Sites Program of the Navajo Nation Historic Preservation Department, has been collaborating with me since he conducted the first blind surveys with me. He describes the results as follows:

I spent several days in the field with David testing his theories on numerous archaeological sites on the Navajo Reservation in northwestern New Mexico. We tested sites ranging in age from early archaic to mid Pueblo III (approximately 6,000 BC to 1300 AD), with the majority of the sites being Chaco Anasazi (850 – 1125 AD) and late Basketmaker III (600-700/750 AD). I conducted numerous blind tests on locations that have not been recorded, and that are not mentioned in any report or other form of documentation. With the exception of one Chacoan Road alignment (which we now understand there is not a 100% correlation with), he located every site using his methodologies, including an isolated pecked/carved linear groove in sandstone slick rock that only 3-5 archaeologists know about. The methodology employed by David is very scientific, even though he uses dowsing, which typically has less than favorable acceptance in the scientific community. After carefully observing David for several days it became very clear that the results (dowsing rods) are not being manipulated, and that there is a very real correlation between the underground features David is mapping and archaeological site locations. When it comes to his research, I can honestly say that it's hard to fully understand and endorse it unless you have observed it in the field (Friedman 2013).

Kenneth Frye, archeological technician, retired, National Forest Service, who also worked for the BLM through a "service first" agreement, San Luis Valley Field Office, Monte Vista, Colorado, for twenty years, has also been collaborating with me since he conducted blind surveys with me. During the first survey he comments:

In 2013, I took him to a site northeast of Saguache, on private property, where a very interesting stone wall is located. Some researchers believe the wall is an ancient geoglyph in the shape of a snake or serpent. David had instructed the members of our research team at the site not to provide him with any information regarding the site. He described how he would dowse along the perimeter of the property to determine how many areas of higher permeability intersected it. Then he would follow the areas of higher permeability into the property to determine if they intersect any archaeological sites or features. Within the first half hour he located four areas of higher permeability, determined the direction they crossed the property and flagged them. All four lead him directly to four important features within the site. They included a spring and snake wall, a boulder shaped like an eagle, the high point of the site where there is a perched boulder and a large boulder which is the head of a long snake wall. Our team was amazed at how fast and accurate his calculations were (Frye 2013).

Using this methodology I have been able to predict the course of areas of higher permeability by interpreting the surface features at archaeological sites. Consistently, before entering a site I have also been able to predict which features, including petroglyphs, will be found at a site based on the characteristics of the area(s) of higher permeability I am following. During the first blind survey with Richard Henderson, Verde Valley Archaeological Center, Camp Verde, Arizona, I described and predicted the location of petroglyphs before I saw them. Henderson comments:

While driving to the first of the recommended test areas, Mr. Johnson defined his process at some length and offered a 'blind' demonstration, where I might observe his test in an area he was unlikely to be previously familiar with. The process required that Mr. Johnson hold the dowsing rods pointing to the front and initially in a parallel orientation. When nearing a concentrated flow (cf), the rods would begin oscillating and when at the cf, would cross. I asked if his process would work while in a moving vehicle, and when he said it would, I asked him to 'get out his sticks', knowing a site was not far down the road. He pulled the rods from his pack.

When Mr. Johnson said the rods were indicating that we were approaching a cf, I stopped and he got out and started walking, following the direction the rods were pointing. After a brief search, he asked that I stand where the rods indicated and again began to follow the rods. Where his rods again crossed, he noted that he was now on the other side of this cf, took GPS readings, made some notes and began a new search perpendicular to his previous line of travel which he indicated would establish a trend line. Moving some thirty meters to the side he again 'followed the rods' to a point where he again asked that I stand while he defined a new cf, perpendicular to the first.

A new trend line was defined and Mr. Johnson said, "Your site is over there," pointing to the area I knew to have a large sandstone boulder with numerous petroglyph elements. Mr. Johnson predicted that we would find among these elements, some 'squiggly' lines oriented both horizontally and vertically, defining the intersection of the two cfs. We Did! This symbology has been associated by local researchers with water, lightning or snakes (Henderson 2015).

When people read my reports and hear my presentation they find it difficult to believe the results. However, those who have conducted blind surveys with me have seen it work. This strongly suggests I am documenting the same subsurface features ancestral Native Americans located and mapped with structures and other features.

The function assigned to each feature is based on the combined research from Peru and Chile, as well as the United States and Canada, during the last twenty years. The functions discussed below were derived by comparing stone features and structures with geological and hydrological features. When a correlation is consistent from region to region and different historical periods, it is added to the list. In addition to these features, there are others which have not been associated with geological and hydrological features and are not included in this discussion. As mentioned above, many, if not all, of the features are multifunctional, while others may represent a tribal affiliation. They will be discussed at another time.

In spite of different historical periods and phases, the function of several features have remained the same throughout the sites we have investigated within North America. In Peru and Chile, geometrical shapes were used to document the flow of areas of higher permeability, and many of those found in North America have the same shape and function (Johnson 2009, Chap. 2). This suggests ancestral Native Americans were using the same basic concepts to map the location of areas of higher permeability throughout the Western Hemisphere with structures and stone features. The similarity between various stone features strongly suggests some degree of cultural uniformity existed throughout most, if not all, of the Western Hemisphere.

Interestingly, as complicated as this sounds, it is very simplistic in regard to the number of features used to map the areas of higher permeability since they are replicated from region to region. Once you know the function of several features, you can interpret them to determine the course and width of the areas of higher permeability they are mapping without using any form of dowsing. I have also demonstrated it is possible to teach others how to interpret these features. In 2012 while investigating a site in the Verde Valley in Arizona, I met two local residents, Nelson Avery and Glenn Waltrip. Neither one had a background in archaeology or hydrology, however they were interested in my research and offered to help. In the following comment they discuss the events that followed:

At the first site we visited we wanted to show David a petroglyph panel which had been shown to us during one of our mineral club's field trips. When we arrived we wanted to show David where the petroglyphs were, however he said he would find them by following the areas of higher permeability. Our interest was broadened since we had heard of "dowsing" but never had any firsthand experience with it or anyone who performed it before. We watched as David began dowsing the north end of the site and documenting areas of higher permeability within the groundwater which he said lead him to archaeological features that mapped the course of these flows. At that point it looked like he was making it up since you cannot see where the areas of higher permeability flow. Then he told us you don't have to use dowsing to locate the areas of higher permeability if you know the meaning of the various archaeological features. He offered to describe to us what he was finding and their meaning as he investigated the site. Then once we knew the function of various features we would be able to follow the areas of higher permeability by "reading" the features. This sounded intriguing and we agreed to his suggestion. The results were amazing. By that afternoon we were walking ahead of David looking for features and then describing what we thought they meant to determine if we were right. When needed, he would correct us, and we continued on. By the end of the day we couldn't wait to get to the next site to see if we could find and follow the stone features, which looked like a mess of random field stones to us when we began that morning.

The following day, as David located an area of higher permeability in one area, we located small stone cairns and circles in another location. As he followed the area of higher permeability it led him directly to us. From that point on we followed the stone features ahead of David and were able to determine the flow pattern of areas of higher permeability, as well as where they intersect one another. We were amazed at how fast we learned this, and how well it worked.(Waltrip and Avery 2014).

At this point in time, several researchers have learned this methodology and are implementing it successfully to locate Ceremonial Sites and features. For example, in 2016 Dr. Forrest Ketchin commented:

> The work we have done includes stone features and what some call "living artifacts" -- Culturally Modified Trees (CMT's) -- in the San Luis Valley of Colorado, USA. The placement of such archaeological features here has always been a bit of a mystery to archaeologists, except, of course, when the reason is unavoidably obvious, such as the presence of flowing springs or trails, or evidence of habitation.

> The placement of CMT's often seems random to the Euro-American eye, seeming to do only with the presence of the right kind of tree in the ancient territory of an American Indian Nation. Occasionally, a flowing spring, creek, trail, or habitation site is evident, but not always. I have used dowsing and some of Mr. Johnson's techniques with some interesting results that begin to explain the otherwise seemingly random placements of both stone features and CMT's. The CMT's appear to be placed in reference to underground areas of increased permeability, or 'flows'.

> In addition, dowsing these underground areas of increased permeability has led me to stone features that I would have missed otherwise, given that these also do not always occur in association with other obvious archaeological features. These include stone circles, stone spirals, cairns and possible burials, all difficult to spot in the heavily wooded and rocky area I have been investigating (Ketchin 2016).

Don Wells, who has also been investigating culturally modified trees, commented in his January 2016 newsletter:

> David Johnson, in late 2015, shared his knowledge about using dowsing rods to locate underground streams that are connected to Indian sites. David has been doing research on Indian sites in North and South America for 40 years. He has learned, over this extensive period of time, that almost all Indian artifacts, including trees, cairns, etc., and sacred sites are connected to underground streams of water. This past summer, he showed our colleague, Dr. Forrest Ketchin, in Colorado, that his techniques could be used to locate Indian Trees. We have since tested that theory on trees in Alabama and Georgia and found it to be true on these east coast trees. We have also tested it at a rock cairn site in Georgia and found it to also be true for that ancient site. The Mountain Stewards have been given permission to do an extensive survey of the Georgia rock cairn site which will begin in late January 2016 (Wells 2016).

Since our first geoscience survey of the Rio Grande de Nasca drainage with the University of Massachusetts, additional investigations have been conducted. In 2018 Dr.

David Bethune, Dr. Cathryn Ryan and Ryland Bjorndahl, Department of Geoscience, University of Calgary, Alberta, Canada, researched the geologic controls on the distribution of springs in the Ica Valley, Peru. (Bjorndahl 2018) They compared my data on one hundred and thirty-four areas of higher permeability and springs, and their association with archaeological sites and geoglyphs within the middle Ica Valley, with their data and concluded:

> Johnson et al. (2006) mapped the locations of various springs within the Ica Valley to provide the framework and information required to interpret why the springs are located there. When placed on a geologic map, each spring is located on a geologic contact between a relatively impermeable rock, and the permeable unconsolidated fluvial material of the valley bottom. They are also located on faults running through the impermeable intrusive igneous and volcanic rocks which provide the conduits for water from high elevations to reach the valley bottom where it can be discharged as springs. The geologic contact does not control the distribution of the springs as the impermeable rock is located above the permeable. Further research is needed to confirm the permeability of the Pisco Formation underlying the permeable unconsolidated material in order to determine if that impacts the distribution of the springs in the Ica Valley. Geochemical and isotopic data from one of the springs confirmed the high-altitude recharge as when compared to a high elevation sample, both were depleted $\delta^{18}O$ and δ^2H, and the EC and TDS increased as you moved to lower elevations. High altitude recharge shows that water is transported through joints, faults and fractures down to the valley bottom where it is discharged into the permeable fluvial and alluvial material. The low silica content indicates that the water does not circulate very deep as it does not experience an elevated temperature to dissolve more silica.

> Knowing the geologic controls on the distribution of these groundwater springs can provide information to the municipality of Ica and allow locals to find these springs and supplement their water usage. Ancient Nazcan and Ica people knew of these springs and utilized them as it is evident from the pottery and signs of civilization around them. Other areas of the valley surrounding Ica with similar geology may have similar springs and mapping these may provide further insight into the ground water flow system (Bjorndahl 2018).

Even if you do not believe I am mapping areas of higher permeability within the groundwater, our data strongly indicates I am mapping the same subsurface features that ancient cultures were mapping in the regions I have researched. Thus far, everyone who has accompanied me in the field, observed and independently tested this methodology, agrees that it works.

Part 3

Data Summary

During the ground surveys in southern England and Carnac, France, I utilized the same methodology I applied in Peru, Chile and the United States. Throughout these regions, megalithic sites and the features associated with them are aligned with one or more areas of higher permeability within the groundwater.

Throughout the regions my colleagues I have investigated, various types of features share specific characteristics in relation to the location of areas of higher permeability within the groundwater, in spite of being associated with different environments, cultures and historical periods. However, the terms used to describe the features vary. The following compares a selection of features and the terms used to describe them in England, France, Peru and the United States. In addition to these comparisons, others are discussed throughout the text.

1. In England, the quoits were located along one or more area(s) of higher permeability, and their width or length was equal to one of the flow's width. This was also true for dolmens in Carnac, France and culturally modified propped boulders in United States. (Figure 1 - 3)

Figure 1: Chun Quoit

Figure 2: Dolmen Er Roc'h Feutet & R 1

Figure 3: Propped glacier erratic along a concentrated flow, NY

Figure 4: Barrow / mound, Drizzlecombe, England

Figure 5: Moustoir Tumulus along M 1, Carnac, France

Figure 6: Mounds along concentrated flow, Indian Mounds Regional Park, MN

2. English mounds and barrows, French tumulus and United States mounds are very similar in construction and appearance as shown in Figures 4 through 6. These features are aligned with one or more areas of higher permeability with one of the flows crossing the center of the feature or along its length.

3. Fogous in England are located along an area of higher permeability. In the southwestern United States, kivas are also located along an area of higher permeability and often where two more intersect. (Figure 7 & 50 - 51) Both features are underground structures.

Figure 7: Kiva, CO

In spite of different terms being applied to a specific feature in different regions, once you know a feature's structural characteristics and relationship to concentrated flows within the groundwater, you can identify its function. Then, you can follow the concentrated flows by interpreting the stone features which are aligned with them. When followed, they take you from feature to feature and site to site. When you include the flow pattern of areas of higher permeability within your site survey, it helps explain why the various features are located where they are.

The following discusses various similarities and differences between sites and associated features in different regions that I have investigated.

1. Each site demonstrates a vertical alignment between the site's location, structures and other features associated with it, and areas of higher permeability within the groundwater. For example:

a. In each of these regions, our data indicates where a group of areas of higher permeability either intersect or cross one another at the same point creating a ray pattern and ponding within the bedrock, ancient cultures mapped these locations with surface features. Each of these sites share similar characteristics which indicate humans in different regions documented them in a similar way. These sites include line centers in Peru, buttes, medicine wheels and large glacier erratics in the United States and Canada, as well as Stonehenge in England. Of the sites I investigated in southern England, Stonehenge was the only site with this type of flow pattern. Examples are shown in Figures 8 - 11 and 21 .

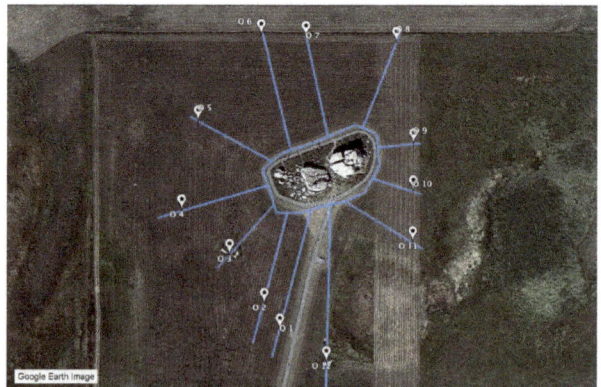

Figure 8: Line Center with several geoglyphs & concentrated flows intersecting it, Peru

Figure 9: Butte & areas of higher permeability radiating out from it, Escalone Chaco outlier site, NM

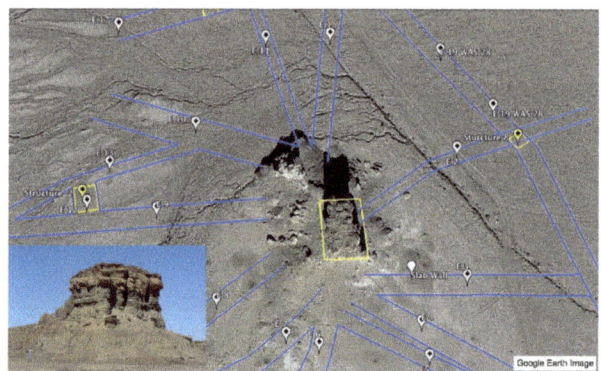

Figure 10: Medicine wheel, WY

Figure 11: Concentrated flows intersecting ponding, Okotoks Glacier Erratic Site, Alberta, Canada

b. Frequently, sites are connected to one another by areas of higher permeability and the surface features which map them. For example, in the southwestern United States, a group of Chaco great house outlier sites are connected by concentrated flows and Chaco roads as shown in Figure 12. My data from Avebury and Stonehenge suggests this was also true for these sites in England. (Figures 21 & 32) In Carnac, my data indicates the Ménec, Kermario and Kerlescan alignments are connected by concentrated flows. (Figure 80)

Figure 12: Three Chaco sites connected by Chaco roads along concentrated flows

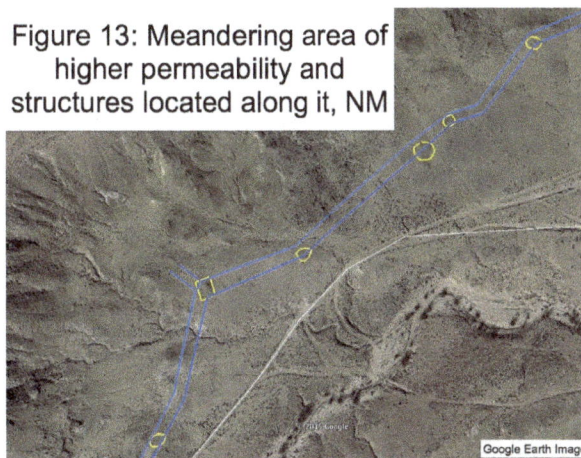

Figure 13: Meandering area of higher permeability and structures located along it, NM

c. When you compare the flow pattern of areas of higher permeability with the location of ancient man-made surface features, they correspond. For example, concentrated flows can meander as they pass through bedrock and alluvium. On the surface, archaeological features also meander since their location is dependent on the area of higher permeability's flow pattern beneath them. (Figures 13, 29 & 79)

Figure 14: Kennet Avenue with standing stones along width & trend of a concentrated flow

Figure 15: Carnac standing stone alignments

d. Consistently, in the regions I have researched, lines of paralleling stone features are located along each width boundary of a concentrated flow. These features map the trend and width of the concentrated flow. However, in different regions, various types of stone features were used along these lines and different terms are used to describe them. For example, in England lines of standing stones are called avenues and rows, while in France they are known as standing stone alignments. In Peru, lines of stone piles are described as lines and in the United States they are referred to as cairns and stone piles. Regardless of the term, they serve the same function. This can be compared to choosing a font on a computer. For example, an A in Arial, Times and Courier fonts all mean the same, even though they are shaped somewhat differently. The stone features in Figures 14 through 17 map the course and width of the area of higher permeability they are aligned with even though their style is different.

Figure 16: Stone piles along width boundary of concentrated flow, Nasca Lines, Peru

Figure 17: Cairns on width boundaries of a concentrated flow, NY

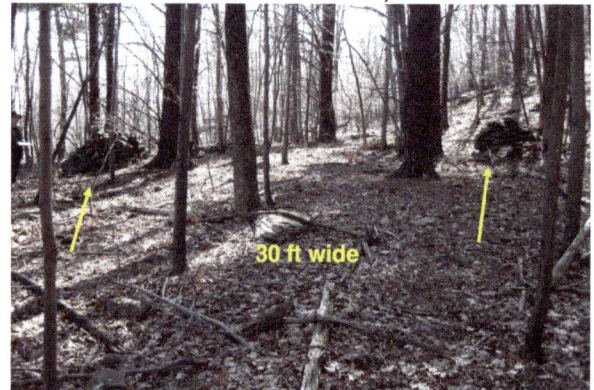

30 ft wide

e. During the time when these sites were first constructed until they were abandoned, my research strongly suggests the primary goal was to align megalithic sites, as well as, habitation and ceremonial sites, with the three worlds. Then, when an individual stood within one of these sites, they may have perceived they were aligned with the three worlds. To align a site with the three worlds, they looked for elements that were common to all three. Water is an integral component of all three worlds and is associated with life cycles, since water is life. Thus, water would have been a reasonable choice. Within the present and upper worlds, water is tangible, rain from the sky and surface water; however, as for the underworld, water is elusive. Therefore, they would have had to identify subsurface groundwater sources. My data strongly suggests it was concentrated flows / areas of higher permeability within the groundwater, even through we do not know exactly how they did this. Concentrated flows within the groundwater are controlled by geological features which were not subject to change by humans at that time, such as the use of fracking today. However, within the present world, the location of a site was flexible and at the discretion of those who constructed it. Therefore, to locate a site, certain criteria were followed. First, they mapped the concentrated flows since they are in a fixed position. Then, they located the megalithic, habitation and ceremonial sites along one or more concentrated flows, thus aligning two of the worlds. Then, their attention was drawn to the upper world. Within these sites, they observed astronomical events and aligned various features, such as stones and structures with these observations along one or more of the concentrated flows within the site. When appropriate, natural geographical components were also incorporated into observing the astronomic alignments. By first identifying the structures and stone features aligned with concentrated flows, other features which appear out of place become more apparent, and it is these features that draw one's attention to possible astronomical alignments. Examples of the correlation between areas of higher permeability, structures and astronomical events are discussed on pages 122 - 1204 and shown in Figures 21, 122 & 123.

f. Throughout the regions we investigated springs are commonly associated with ancient archaeological sites. The obvious reason one would conclude from this observation is to obtain potable water. However, many of the ancient cultures we investigated associated springs with a portal to the underworld. This is an important component of their spiritual beliefs and achieving alignment of the three worlds. Throughout the Western Hemisphere springs are sacred to ancient, as well as contemporary, Native Americans. They serve as a way to communicate with their ancestors in the underworld, as well as a passage of emergence from the underworld. Interestingly, many of the springs throughout southern England are referred to as sacred springs. Springs have been revered by cultures throughout the various historical periods, as well as by religions. However, with that said, their spiritual context changed as modern religions, such as Christianity, replaced earlier beliefs which focused on Mother Earth.

g. In Peru, Chile, the United States and Canada, habitation sites were located along areas of higher permeability. In southern England, some of the small family habitation units were located on concentrated flows, while others were not. This could be due to the historical period they are associated with. If the practice of aligning the three worlds was an important concept to them, habitation units were specifically located along the concentrated flows within the groundwater. If it was not, they located them wherever it was prudent. It is also possible the location of family habitation units was not restricted to being located along the concentrated flows within the groundwater. (Figures 50 - 52)

h. The ancient archaeological sites share a commonality which may be expressing a universal human trait. In addition to the regions my colleagues and I have investigated, researchers in other regions are finding the same alignment between areas of higher permeability within the groundwater, ancient archaeological sites and the features associated with them.

2. Within these regions, regional centers have been associated with unusual geological and / or hydrological features. For example:

a. Saqsaywaman is a large complex situated above Cusco which has one of the most unique geological features in the Western Hemisphere, if not the world. In 1978, the Geological Society of America Bulletin published an article titled "The Extraordinary Striated Outcrop at Saqsaywaman, Peru" by Tomas Feininger. In the article, he explains how the outcrop was formed: "The andesite reached the Earth's surface along an eruptive fissure. The first materials ejected were hot but solid blocks which built an elongated, steep-sided mound. Later, viscous lava was extruded though the crest of the mound and flowed down its flanks. The stretching of the lava during flowage caused its surface to become striated, analogous to the striations on the surface of pulled taffy." In geological terms, this outcrop is also referred to as a mullion structure, which is defined as "consisting of a series of parallel columns composed of folded bedrock. The morphology of the outcrop is so remarkable that even the most casual observer is at once

Figure 18: The Mullion, Cusco, Peru

awed." (Feininger 1978). (Figure 18) My colleagues at the Geoscience Department of the University of Massachusetts and I examined this feature and came to the same conclusion. Cusco and Saqsaywaman were the political and spiritual focal points of the empire. For example, during the winter solstice the Inca ruler, along with the mummies of past rulers which were carried to the site, went and sat on the mullion to ask the spirits and their ancestors for guidance (Johnson 2009, Chap. 7 & 2019).

b. Within the strata beneath Chaco Canyon, New Mexico, there are important regional sandstone aquifers which include the Point Lookout Sandstone, Gallup Sandstone, Dakota Sandstone and Westwater Canyon Member of the Morrison Formation (Martin 2005). "Recharge occurs in and adjacent to outcrop areas at the western and southern margins of the San Juan Basin. Most groundwater in the Gallup sandstone flows northeasterly toward the basin

Figure 19: Stone's ground water flow chart for Chaco Canyon

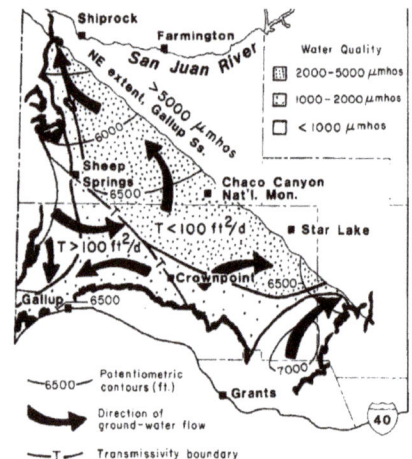

center, then moves northwestward and discharges into the San Juan River in the vicinity of the four corners." (Stone 2006). (Figure 19) The great houses in Chaco Canyon are located where the Gallup aquifer's flow turns from northeast to the northwest at the center of the San Juan Basin. The largest Chaco structures are the great houses located within Chaco Canyon, and all are located along areas of higher permeability, for example, Pueblo Bonito in Figure 20. Chaco roads radiate outward to distant outlier sites.

24

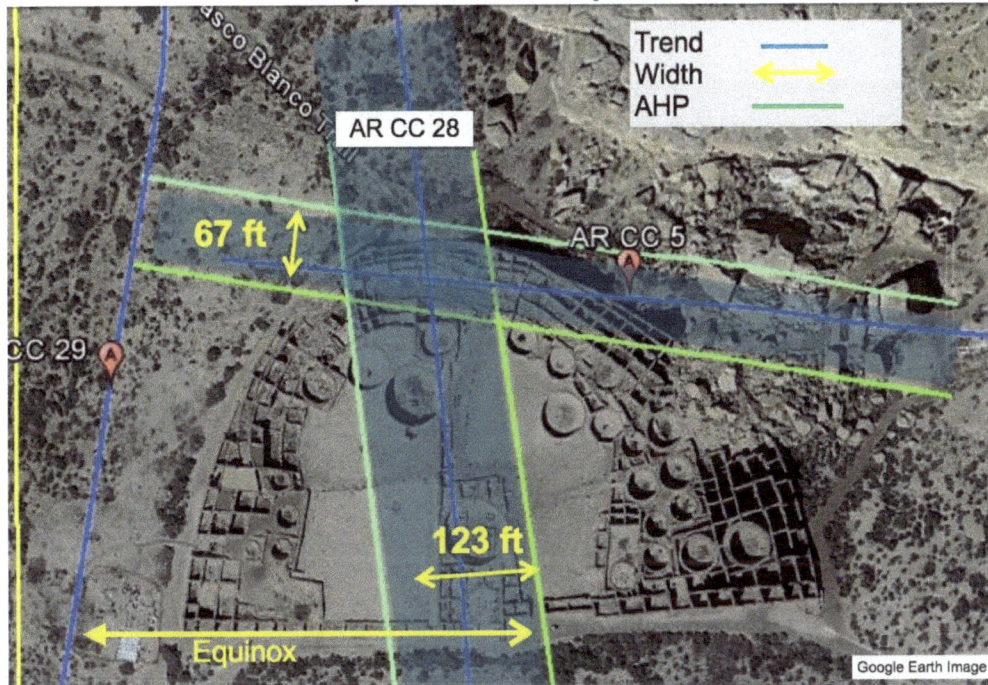

Figure 20: Width & trend of areas of higher permeability at Pueblo Bonito & equinox, Chaco Canyon, NM.

c. The area of higher permeability flow patterns I documented at Avebury, England, are very unusual when compared to all the other English sites I researched, as well as, sites in the regions my colleagues and I have investigated. For example, A 1's width increases before it intersects A 10, which is much wider, and then narrows on the other side of the site. Also, A 8 branches from A 1 along the south side of the site and then merges with A 1 on the north side. Although this has been documented at other sites, it is unusual when you consider A 8's location next to the intersection of A 1 and A 10. The location of the surviving standing stones indicate the people who constructed this site were aware of these underground flow patterns and constructed the site according to them. For example, basically half of the Avebury circle / henge follows the flow pattern of A 8. The tallest standing stones are located where A 1 and A 10 intersect. (Figure 35) Like Cusco and Chaco Canyon, Avebury is the focal point of a large complex.

d. The sheer magnitude of the existing concentration of standing stones and areas of higher permeability within a relatively small area at Ménec and Kermario strongly suggest these sites were important culturally and spiritually to the people who constructed them. Throughout the regions I have researched, I have not documented another site where a group of concentrated flows parallel one another within a linear, narrow confined area like they do at these sites. The mining map of Brittany (Geological Formations Of The Main Mines In Brittany 2020) indicated a northeast-southwest trending fault crosses this area, and it

25

appears as though these two sites may be aligned with it. Normally, I locate a concentrated flow along a fault, however, at these two sites there is a group of them along the projected trend of the fault. Also, the number, size and close proximity of the standing stones is unlike other sites I have researched. It is possible other sites like these existed in the regions I have investigated which have been destroyed, however, of the existing sites, Ménec and Kermario are unusual. (Figures 78 - 79, 85, 93 & 98) Although I did not find any reference which indicated these sites were an important regional center, their unusual characteristics strongly suggest they were.

For a more comprehensive discussion of stone features, petroglyphs, pictographs, culturally modified trees and other features associated with mapping areas of higher permeability within the groundwater, refer to my publications.

Comparing Dates

Prior to discussing this issue, it is important to mention that most of the stone features, such as cairns, effigy walls and circles, within the United States and Canada have not been thoroughly investigated to determine their age or cultural affiliation. Most non-native archaeologists still do not recognize them as Native American archaeological features. Therefore, the dates provided for these features are based on our data and the limited number of sites which have been investigated by other researchers.

Another point to consider is the initial research in southern England targeted Neolithic, Bronze and Iron Age megalithic sites. In Carnac, France, Neolithic sites dating to 5,500 to 6,500 B.P. were investigated. I did not have time to research earlier sites which may or may not be present at these locations. Therefore, I cannot comment on how far back they were locating sites on areas of higher permeability.

Within the United States, my colleagues and I have associated Paleo sites with areas of higher permeability dating to 12,000 B.P., however we have not been able to verify if the stone features are contemporary to the site. The earliest stone features we documented were in the southwest and are associated with Archaic diagnostic artifacts dating to around 6,000 B.P.. Then, around 5,000 B.P., there is an increase in the number of stone features which are associated with artifacts from that period. In Peru, the Nasca Lines date from around 2,400 B.P. to 1,200 B.P. and stone features continued into the Inca Period (Johnson 2009, Ch. 2, p. 7).

In England, the megalithic stone features that I researched are associated with the Neolithic, Bronze and Iron Ages. The earliest stone features were solitary standing stones which began to appear around 6,500 B.P.. Then around 6,000 B.P. tombs and dolmens begin to appear. Around 5,000 B.P. the grouping of several standing stones in lines and circles begins, for example Stonehenge. (WIKIPEDIA) While the use of these stone features appears to have subsided in England during the Roman Period, Native Americans continued to use them until they encountered western European cultures and religions during the seventeenth through nineteenth centuries.

When you compare the dates from the regions my colleagues and I have investigated, it suggests the associations between cultural beliefs, areas of higher permeability and megalithic sites in England and France and the United States began to increase after 6,000 BP. Although we have investigated only a few regions, this data at least gives us something to work with. We many never know where this concept originated, and in which directions it spread. Since similar megalithic sites exist throughout the world, this could be a universal human trait during the late Neolithic Period.

Part 4

Southern England

During September 2018 I investigated several sites in southern England from Stonehenge to Land's End, Cornwall. I am sure my critics will point out that numerous megalithic and ancient habitation sites exist throughout the British Isles, thus my survey represents only a small percentage of the whole. The purpose of this initial investigation was to research another region of the world which has a concentration of sites containing a variety of megalithic features to determine if they are associated with areas of higher permeability within the groundwater.

Prior to traveling to England, I contacted various supervising organizations such as the National Trust, as well as, various archaeologists who are currently investigating some of the sites I chose. In my inquires I mentioned I use dowsing. I also mentioned that my methodology does not require any excavations or collecting artifacts. Interestingly, none of them responded. While conducting some of the site surveys I discussed my research with various staff who were on duty, including park rangers and security, and none of them objected to my research since I was not disturbing anything. Another interesting point was site accessibility. In the United States, most of the land is posted and one has to obtain permission from the owner or supervising agency to enter it. In southern England, every site I surveyed had public access right of ways, which was evident by the number of people hiking along them. All of the landowners I met did not object to me entering their land as long as I did not disturb their crops or livestock. In addition to this, The United Kingdom's National Grid Reference Index is accessible to the public through the internet and contains all the GPS coordinates for the archaeological sites I investigated (ARCHI 2018). Thus, I conducted the surveys.

I prefer to survey a site prior to researching it. This way I am not influenced by other researchers' data. Then, after completing my research, I compare my data with their data. This is why I was not aware of some of the features at various sites. In some cases, the features were buried, destroyed or altered. This approach is beneficial since it builds attributes of a blind survey into my research. The percentage of features I locate that I cannot see or know about helps me determine the accuracy of my methodology.

Since I do not know of anyone else who has presented data on the correlation between stone features and areas of higher permeability in England using this methodology, I have included all the data I documented. This way other researchers can expand upon it as they wish. I have included a brief description of each site which was taken from WIKIPEDIA. All of their citations are listed under references.

Site Surveys

Since Stonehenge and Avebury are both complexes consisting of a group of sites with a variety of stone features, I will discuss them first to show their relationship to areas of higher permeability within the groundwater.

Stonehenge

Stonehenge encompasses a large area with numerous features. Due to time restraints only a portion of the site was surveyed. However, the survey provided interesting data which helps explain why various features were placed where they are. As discussed below, all of the stone features, mounds and the cursus were located along one or more concentrated flows which either intersect or cross one another.

Stonehenge Circle

Figure 21: Stonehenge, concentrated flows & solstice

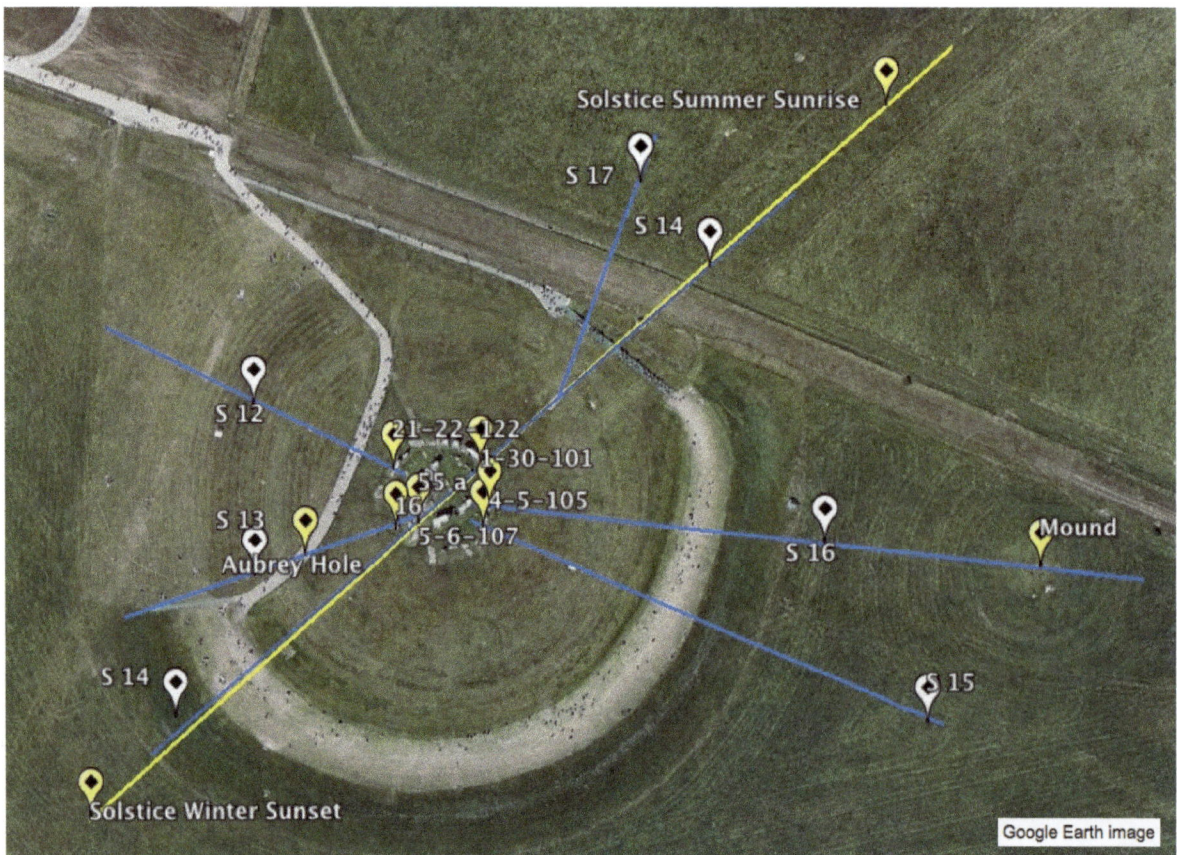

WIKIPEDIA describes Stonehenge Circle as follows:

It consists of a ring of standing stones, with each standing stone around 13 feet (4.0 m) high, 7 feet (2.1 m) wide and weighing around 25 tons. The stones are set within earthworks in the middle of the most dense complex of Neolithic and Bronze Age and monuments in England, including several hundred burial mounds.[1] Archaeologist believe it was constructed from 3000 BC to 2000 BC. The surrounding circular earth bank and ditch, which constitute the earliest phase of the monument, have been dated to about 3100 BC. Radiocarbon dating suggests that the first bluestones were raised between 2400 and 2200 BC,[2] although they may have been at the site as early as 3000 BC.[3][4][5] (WIKIPEDIA 2018)

Since this is the most iconic megalithic site in England, it was the first site I investigated. Due to access restraints and a large number of tourists, this survey was limited to the pathway around the feature. As I circled the megalithic stone circle I located six concentrated flows which intersected it, and they were labeled S 12 through S 17. (Figure 21)

S 12 - 15 ft / 4.5 m wide which is basically the width of vertical stones 21 and 22. Its trend was 294° NW from the outer ring to a stone located at 582010.16 m E, 5670388.08 m N. It is possible that S 12 and S 16 are the same concentrated flow which crosses the site. This cannot be determined without entering the ring. (Figure 22)

Figure 22: Stones 21, 22, 122 & S 12

S 13 - 9 ft / 2.7 m wide which is basically the width of stone 16. Aubrey Hole, which is identified by a round marker on the pathway at 582009.00 m E, 5670352.00 m N, is centrally located along the flow's trend. S 13 appears to intersect the center and does not cross the site.

S 14 - 16 ft / 4.87 m wide and crosses the site at approximately 50° NE. Stones 55 and 1-30-101 are located along it. The markers for summer solstice sunrise and winter solstice sunset are located along this concentrated flow. Interestingly, although the trends of S 12 and S 15 are not located along the winter solstice sunrise and summer solstice sunset axis, the two points where this axis intersects the outer ring of Stonehenge appears to be where S 12 and S 15 intersect it (Wood 1978).

S 15 - 18 ft / 5.48 m wide which is basically the width of cap stone 107 and the width of stones 5 and 6. Its trend is 112° SE, and the stone located at 582089.09 m E, 5670350.21 m N is centrally located on it.

S 16 - 38 ft / 11.6 m wide and trends outward at 96° E from stones 4-5-105 to the mound located at 582228.48 m E, 5670352.02 m N. The mound appears to be equal to the width of S 16.

S 17 - 16 ft / 4.87 m wide and intersects S 4 at 582085.79 m E, 5670397.95 m N where there are two large stones. Since it was taken within a short distance, its trend appears to be approximately 21° NE.

Ponding - Consistently, at other sites which have concentrated flows intersecting a single location, there is subsurface ponding which is identified by the central circle or a stone pile (Johnson 2019). Since I could not enter Stonehenge's the inner stone circle, I could not confirm if there is ponding.

Other sites with areas of higher permeability intersecting the same location include line centers, buttes with rays, medicine wheels and large glacier erratic sites (Johnson 2009, 2019 and Papers on Ceremonial Landscapes 2018). (Figures 8 - 11) These sites share several characteristics with Stonehenge as follows: (Figure 21)

1. Several areas of higher permeability intersect the same location.

2. The location is mapped by specific surface features.

3. The surface features can consist of man-made and culturally modified natural features.

4. Each feature is associated with other features within the area.

5. Man-made surface features are aligned with geological and hydrological features.

6. When combined, these features often constitute a complex.

7. One or more cultural phases are associated with the site.

Stonehenge Cursus

WIKIPEDIA describes Stonehenge Cursus as follows:

> The Stonehenge Cursus (sometimes known as the Greater Cursus) is a large Neolithic cursus monument on Salisbury plain, near to Stonehenge in Wiltshire, England. It is roughly 3 kilometers (1.9 mi) long and between 100 meters (330 ft) and 150 meters (490 ft) wide.

Excavations in 2007 dated the construction of the earthwork to between 3630 and 3375 BCE,[3] several hundred years before the earliest phase of Stonehenge in 3000 BC.

Figure 23: Cursus & S 1

Radiocarbon dating of a red deer antler pick discovered at the bottom of the western terminal ditch suggests that the Stonehenge Cursus was first constructed between 3630 and 3375 BCE. It is just under 3 km long, and is roughly 100 m wide. Because of a slight difference in the alignment of its north and south ditches, it widens to a point nearly 150m near its western end. It is roughly aligned east-west and is oriented toward the sunrise on the spring and autumn equinoxes. There is a (later) Bronze Age round barrow inside the western end of the enclosure, and a large Neolithic long barrow was constructed at its east terminal. The Stonehenge Riverside project excavated the remains of the long barrow in 2008 to determine if the barrow predated, or was contemporary with the cursus itself. The ditches of the cursus are not uniform and vary in width and depth. The eastern ditch is fairly shallow, as is the southern ditch – being only 0.75m deep and 1.8m wide at the top. At the western terminal, the ditch is 2m deep and 2.75m wide.

Like most cursus, its function is unclear, although it is believed to be ceremonial. The length of the cursus, running roughly east west, crosses a dry river valley known as Stonehenge Bottom. This may have been a winterbourne during the Neolithic era. If so, this would give it similar characteristics to other cursus, such as the Dorset Cursus, and it may be related to a ceremonial function. It has also been suggested that the Stonehenge Cursus acts as a boundary between areas of settlement and ceremonial activity.[4] The cursus is also aligned on the equinox sunrise which rises over the eastern long barrow.[5] Two artificial pits have been found near the east and west ends of the curses. It has been found that lines of sunrise and sunset at midsummer through these pits are aligned with Stonehenge.[6] (WIKIPEDIA 2018)

Upon arriving at the visitor center, I began dowsing in the parking lot where I located an area of higher permeability which was 146 ft / 44.5 m wide and labeled it S 1. (Figures 23 - 25) Then, following it eastward, I documented it where it crossed a road or pathway. Its trend took me to the western end of the cursus. Then, as I investigated Woodhenge, I realized S 1 passed immediately south of this site. The trend of S 1 was ground surveyed at the following GPS coordinates:

1. Where it intersects the visitor parking lot at 579820.96 m E, 5670791.10 m N

2. Along the trail at 580510.58 m E, 5670983.86 m N

3. At 580717.89 m E, 5671052.41 m N which is the western end of the cursus.

4. At 581712.17 m E, 5671133.37 m N which is north of mounds 44 and 45.

5. Its trend was projected between 581712.17 m E, 5671133.37 m N and 584436.97 m E, 5671525.13 m N which is where the Cookoo Stone is located at 584444.00 m E, 5671554.00 m N.

6. Immediately southwest of Woodhenge at 584774.21 m E, 5671503.80 m N where it curves slightly.

7. Where it crosses Fargo Road at 584942.87 m E, 5671498.63 m N

8. Its trend was projected eastward from Fargo Road, the white lines in the Google Image.

When you include the projected course of S1 with the area ground surveyed, it covers a distance of 2.61 mi / 4.20 km, and its width averaged between 146 ft / 44.5 m by the visitor center parking lot and 195 ft / 59.4 m at the Cookoo Stone. (Figure 27) When you take into consideration the concentrated flows which either intersect or cross S1, as well as, those which were not surveyed, the variance in the widths is reasonable. Frequently, stone features are located along an area of higher permeability, however with the exception of the trench, very few exist along the cursus. Since the cursus was constructed more than 5,000 years ago, it is possible S1 was wider at that time. Another factor is variables within the concentrated flows which intersect or cross S 1 as discussed below.

The cursus is also aligned on the equinox sunrise which rises over the eastern long barrow.[5] (WIKIPEDIA 2018) We have also documented concentrated flows which align with astronomical events and are mapped with stone features in North America.

Concentrated Flows Intersecting S 1 And The Cursus

It is important to mention that I only had time to survey the south side of S 1 and the cursus. Therefore, additional areas of higher permeability may be intersecting the north side.

Figure 24: Mounds 54, 55, 56 & S 1 - 4

During the S 1 ground survey, twelve concentrated flows were documented which either intersect or cross it. Along the cursus, S 2 - 4 and S 6 - 11 intersected S 1. D 3, D 4 and W 1 are discussed under Woodhenge. (Figures 23 - 27)

S 2 - It intersects S1 at 580855.05 m E, 5671038.95 m N, and S 2 was 53 ft / 16 m wide. There is a white circular feature on each width boundary of S 2 where it intersects S 1. Mound 56 is centered on S1 and the trend of S 2. I did not cross S 1 to determine if S 2 crosses S 1. Based on the trend of S 2, mound 55 is also located along it. The diameter of mound 56 is listed as 82 ft / 25 m and mound 55 is 190 ft / 58 m. Thus, neither of these two mounds are the same width as S 1 or S 2.

S 3 and S 4 - They branch from S 18 at mound 54 which is located at 580969.00 m E, 5670998.00 m N. Then, after a short distance S 3 and S 4 intersect S1. There are white stones / chalk markers on or near the width boundaries of both S 3 and S 4. S 3 was 15 ft / 4.57 m wide, and S 4 was 20 ft / 6 m wide.

S 18 - I did not measure the width of S 18 at mound 54 since I did not know if the public had access to that location.

These areas of higher permeability either contribute or draw water from S 1.

I did not investigate the area where the Fargo Hengiform and mounds 50 through 53 are located since mounds 43 through 47 were one of the main areas I wanted to survey.

Great Cursus Barrow Burial Mounds

WIKIPEDIA describes Great Cursus Barrow Burial Mounds as follows:

> The Cursus Barrows is the name given to a Neolithic and Bronze Age round barrow cemetery located mostly south of the western end of the Stonehenge Cursus. The cemetery contains around 18 round mounds scattered along an east-to-west ridge, although some of the mounds are no longer visible. (WIKIPEDIA 2018)

During this survey I knew about mounds 43 through 47 since I could see them. I was not aware of mound 48 until after I returned home and conducted the research on these features. It is important to mention that when I compared the diameters of these mounds in Google Earth with those given in WIKIPEDIA's references, there was a difference of approximately eight meters. In this report, I used Google Earth measurements for these mounds since they are closer to mine and appear to be more accurate. (Figure 25)

Seven areas of higher permeability were associated with these mounds. They were labeled S 5 - S 11 of which S 6 - S 11 intersect S 1. I did not have time to determine if they crossed S 1.

Figure 25: Mounds 43 - 48 & concentrated flows

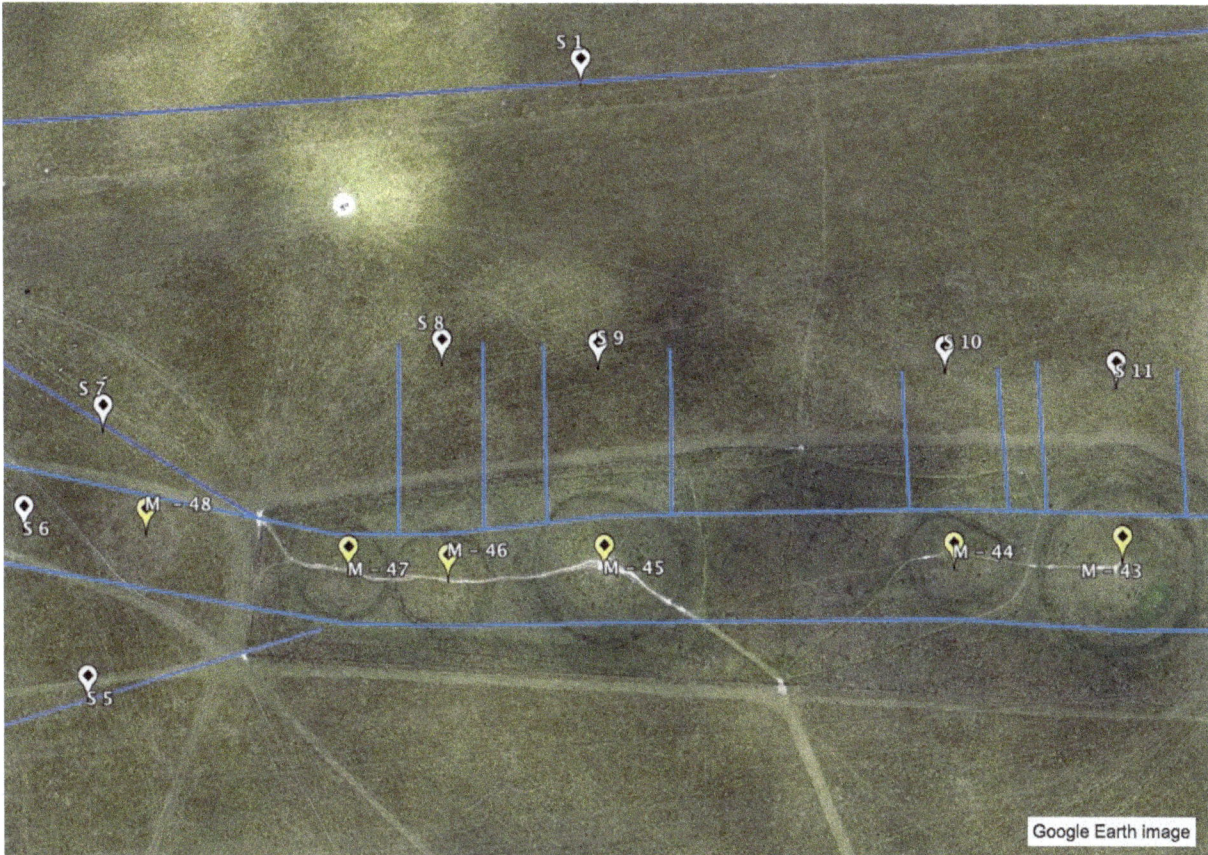

S 6 - The six mounds are located along the trend of S 6 and where S 5 and S 7 - S 11 intersect it. S 6 intersects S 1 near 581034.37 m E, 5671051.37 m N, and it averaged 100 ft / 30.48 m wide.

Although I did not have time to ground survey each area of higher permeability to where it intersected S 1 and the cursus, I followed them to where I could make a reasonable projection as to where they intersected S 1.

Mound 48 - It is located along S 6 and after S 5 and S 7 intersect mound 47 and S 6.

Mound 47 - At this mound, S 5 and S 7 intersect S 6 on the west side. Mound 47 is approximately the width of S 6. S 7 branches from S 6 and intersects S 1 near 581334.18 m E, 5671079.01 m N. Following the trend of S 5 lead me to mound 50.

Mound 46 - S 8 intersects S 6 and mound 46. The width of S 8 is approximately the diameter of mound 46, which appears to be 98.4 ft / 30 m.

Mound 45 - S 9 intersects S 6 at mound 45. The width of S 9 is approximately the diameter of mound 45, which appears to be 147.6 ft / 45 m.

Mound 44 - S 10 intersects S 6 at mound 44 which consists of two barrow mounds. The width of S 10 is approximately equal to the combined diameter of these mounds, which appears to be 108 ft / 33 m.

Mound 43 - S 11 intersects S 6 at mound 43. The width of S 11 is approximately the diameter of mound 43, which appears to be 164 ft / 50 m.

Along the cursus, nearby mounds were approximately equal to the width of one of the areas of higher permeability they are located on. This is also true for the great cairns and mounds I documented in the United States (Johnson 2009, 2019 and Papers on Ceremonial Landscapes 2018).

An English cursus, like the coastal geoglyphs of Peru and Chile, map the course of primary areas of higher permeability within a given area and can extend for miles. Often, they are the main water contributor to other concentrated flows which branch from them. By constructing surface features along these concentrated flows, each feature is connected to the other. (Johnson 2009, 2019 and Papers on Ceremonial Landscapes 2018)

Both Woodhenge and the Durrington Walls are connected to Stonehenge and the cursus by intersecting concentrated flows. Therefore, they are discussed next.

Woodhenge

WIKIPEDIA describes Woodhenge as follows:

Woodhenge is a Neolithic Class II henge and timber circle monument within the Stonehenge World Heritage Site in Wiltshire, England. Pottery from the excavation was identified as being consistent with the grove ware style of the middle Neolithic, although later Beaker shards were also found. So, the structure was probably built during the period of cultural similarities commonly known as the Beaker. The Beaker culture spans both the Late Neolithic and Britain's Early Bronze age and includes both the distinctive "bell beaker " type ceramic vessels for which the cultural grouping is known as well as other local styles of pottery from the Late Neolithic and Early Bronze Age. While construction of the timber monument was probably earlier, the ditch has been dated to between 2470 and 2000 BC, which would be about the same time as, or slightly later than, construction of the stone circle at Stonehenge.[8] Radiocarbon dating of artifacts shows that the site was still in use around 1800 BC.[9] (WIKIPEDIA 2018)

Two concentrated flows were associated with Woodhenge. (Figure 26)

Figure 26: Woodhenge, W 1 & W 2

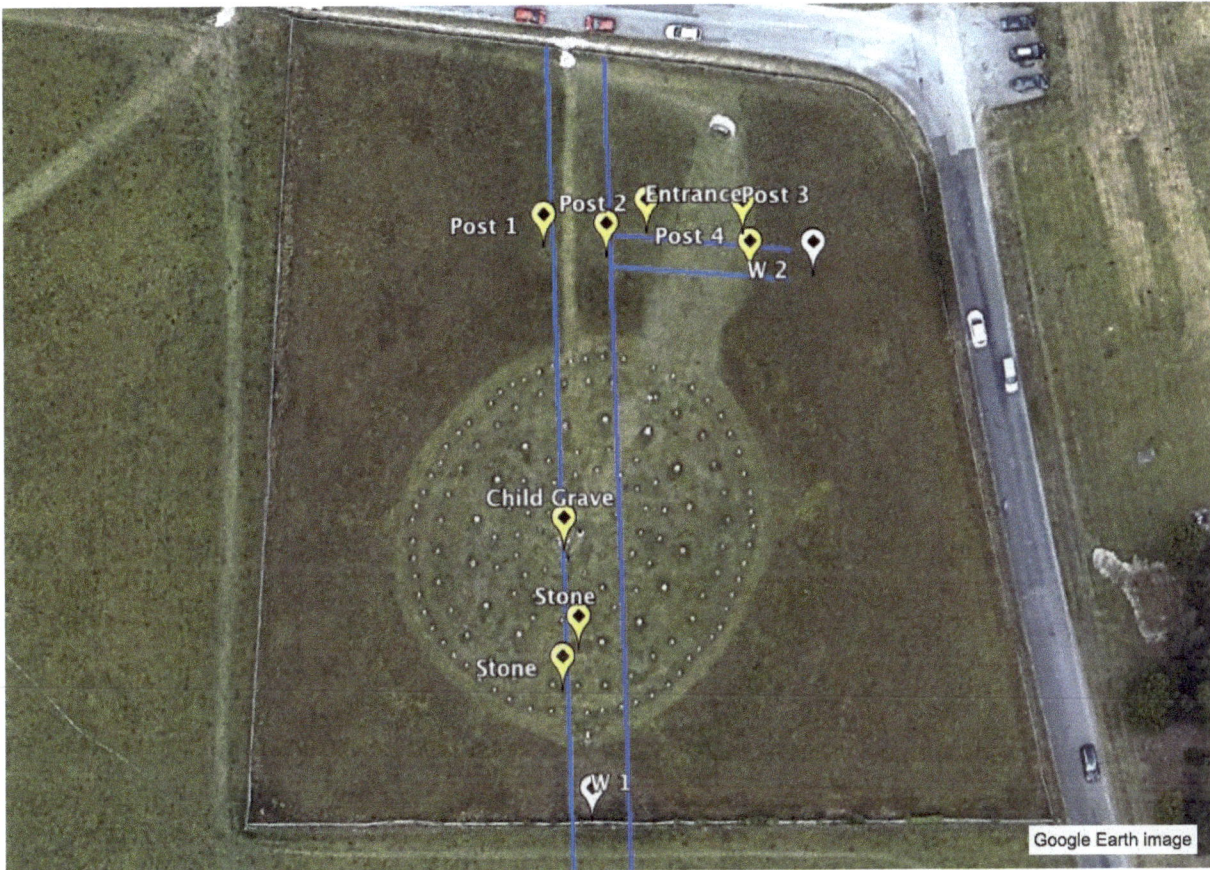

W 1 - It crosses the site in a north-south direction and was 24 ft / 7.3 m wide with posts 1 and 2 on each of its width boundaries. W 1 intersects S 1 but does not cross it.

W 2 - It was 12 ft / 3.65 m wide with posts 3 and 4 on each of its width boundaries, and its trend was 94° E. Post 2 is centrally located on W 2 and where W 2 and W 1 intersect.

When you compare the intersection of W 1 and W 2 at the four posts, they are basically aligned with the entrance to Woodhenge which is located between posts 1 and 2 and 3 and 4.

The following features are located along W 1:

1. The west side of the entrance to Woodhenge is located along W 1.

2. The child's grave is located along the west width boundary of W 1.

3. The two stone holes are located along W 1.

4. W 1's trend crosses through the middle of Woodhenge.

5. W 1 intersects S 1, thus connecting it to other stone features located along S 1, as well as, the other concentrated flows that intersect it.

Near Woodhenge D 3 and D4 intersect S 1. (Figure 27)

D 3 - It intersects S 1 at 584469.57 m E, 5671499.11 m N and was 87 ft / 26.5 m wide trending at 48.5º NE .

D 4 - It branches from S 1 at 584906.56 m E, 5671463.01 m N and was 55 ft / 16.7 m wide trending at 175º S.

Figure 27: D 3 & D 4 intersecting S 1 near Woodhenge

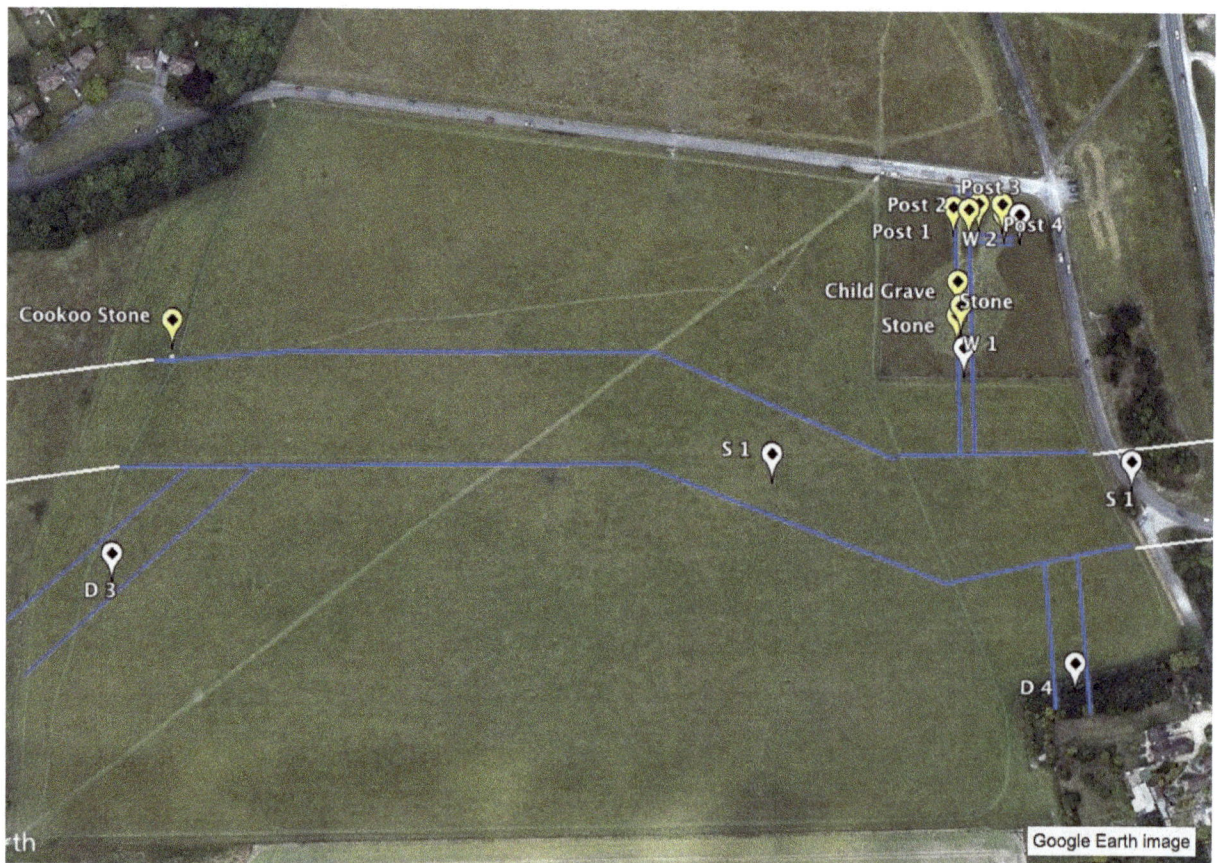

This Woodhenge is similar to the Cahokia, Illinois, Woodhenge which I also surveyed. Both are incorporated into a major cultural complex, located on one concentrated flow and are associated with astronomical alignments (WIKIPEDIA 2018, Johnson Papers on Ceremonial Landscapes 2018).

Durrington Walls

WIKIPEDIA describes Durrington Walls as follows:

Durrington Walls is the site of a large Neoliithic settlement, and later henge enclosure, located in the Stonehenge World Heritage Site. It lies 2 miles (3.2 km) north-east of Stonehenge in the parish of Durrington, just north of Avebury. Between 2004 and 2006, excavations on the site by a team led by the University of Sheffield revealed seven houses. It has been suggested that the settlement may have originally had up to 1000 houses and perhaps 4,000 people, if the entire enclosed area was used. The period of settlement was about 500 years, starting sometime between c.2800 and 2100 BC.[3]

It may have been the largest village in northern Europe for a brief period.[4][5][6] At 500 metres (1,600 ft) in diameter, the henge is the largest in Britain and recent evidence suggests that it was a complementary monument to Stonehenge.[7] (WIKIPEDIA 2018)

Figure 28: Durrington Walls & D1

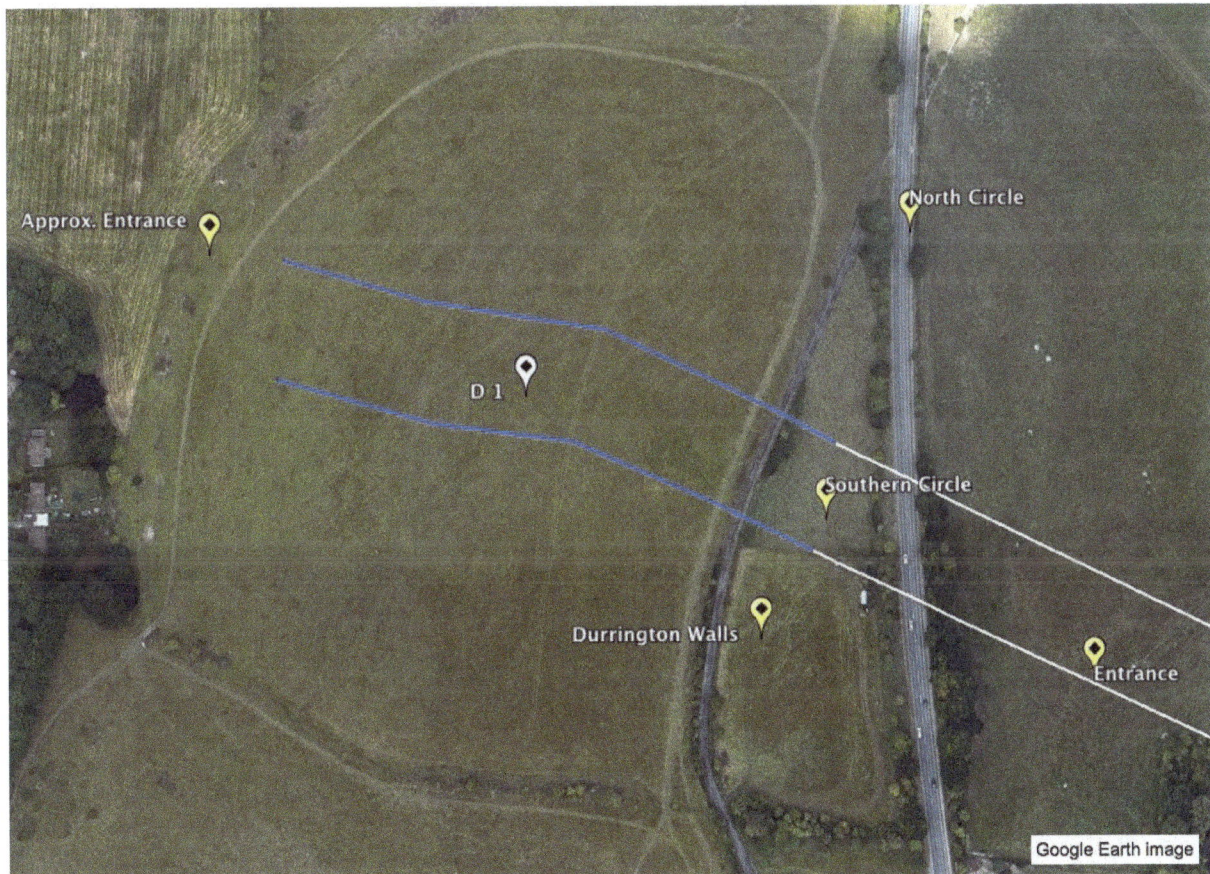

Although I did not have time to survey the entire site, I located one area of higher permeability which crossed it. (Figure 28) D 1 was 163 ft / 49.6 m wide on average and curves as it crosses the site from 296° NW to 286° NW. When projected to the southeast, it appears to intersect S 1 near 585547.19 m E, 5671598.11 m N. D 1 flows through what appears to be the center of the Durrington Walls which enclosed the Neolithic community.

The following features are located along D 1:

1. The southeast entrance of the community is nearly centered on D 1.

2. The northwest entrance is along the northern width boundary of D 1.

3. The southern circle appears to be centrally located on D 1.

Based on the trend of the areas of higher permeability I ground surveyed, and the data from other sites I have researched, it appears all of the various features within the Stonehenge, Woodhenge and Durrington Walls complex are connected to one another by one or more concentrated flows within the groundwater (Johnson 2009, 2019 and Papers on Ceremonial Landscapes 2018).

The Avebury Complex

During this survey I was able to investigate the following sites within the Avebury complex: Avebury Stone Circle, Sanctuary Stone Circle, West Kennet Long Barrow, Silbury Hill and Longstone Cove. Prior to my research, other researchers have indicated these sites are connected by various stone features including stone rows known as avenues. The areas of higher permeability I documented at these sites indicate they are all connected by one or more concentrated flows within the groundwater. This complex has the same characteristics as other cultural centers such as Cahuachi, Peru, and Chaco Canyon, New Mexico which are discussed in Johnson's previous books. (Johnson 2009, 2019 and Papers on Ceremonial Landscapes 2018) (Figure 29)

WIKIPEDIA describes Avebury Complex as follows:

Avebury is a Neolithic henge monument containing three stone circles, around the village of Avebury in Wiltshire, in southwest England. One of the best known prehistoric sites in Britain, it contains the largest megalithic stone circle in the world. It is both a tourist attraction and a place of religious importance to contemporary pagans.

Constructed over several hundred years in the Third Millennium BC,[1] during the Neolithic, or New Stone Age, the monument comprises a large henge (a bank and a ditch) with a large outer stone circle and two separate smaller stone circles situated inside the centre of the monument. Its original purpose is unknown, although archaeologists believe that it was most likely used for some form of ritual or ceremony. The Avebury monument is a part of a larger prehistoric landscape containing several older monuments nearby, including West Kennet Long Barrow, Windmill Hill and Silbury Hill. (WIKIPEDIA 2018)

Figure 29: Avebury Complex

Although the map only highlights the well-known features of Avebury, the whole area contains an abundance of lesser sites relating to the Neolithic and Bronze-Age periods. The Ridgeway, which skirts the side of the Sanctuary, was one of the main trade routes in the British Isles at that time. Without visiting the area, it is difficult to fully appreciate the awesome scale of the monuments as they relate to the surrounding landscape.

A number of springs exist in the area of Avebury which must have had great significance to the builders of the monuments. Midway between Silbury Hill and the West Kennet Long Barrow, Swallowhead Spring is marked prominently on the older maps shown below. Many visitors to the area still make a pilgrimage to this revered place on the stream that feeds the River Kennet. In recent years it has become a repository for a variety

41

of "offerings". Unfortunately some of the less bio-degradable can give this picturesque spot the appearance of a rubbish tip on occasions. (WIKIPEDIA 2018)

In the 4th millennium BCE, around the start of the Neolithic period in Britain, British society underwent radical changes. These coincided with the introduction to the island of domesticated species of animals and plants, as well as a changing material culture that included pottery. These developments allowed hunter-gatherers to settle down and produce their own food. As agriculture spread, people cleared land. At the same time, they also erected the first monuments to be seen in the local landscape, an activity interpreted as evidence of a change in the way people viewed their place in the world.[12] (WIKIPEDIA 2018)

The Kennet Avenue

I began my survey at the southern end of the double row of megalithic standing stones which is referred to as Kennet Avenue. (Figures 14, 30 & 31) This stone row connected Avebury Stone Circle with Sanctuary Stone Circle.

Figure 30: A 2 - A 6, A 1 & Kennet Avenue

This is a magnificent double row of large standing stones which extends from Avebury southward for .63 mi / 1.01 km. I followed it from the southern most surviving stones located on each side of the road at 580297.80 m E, 5697197.86 m N into Avebury. The following observations were made:

1. The paralleling standing stones are located along the width boundaries of A 1 which averaged 50 ft / 15 m wide along this distance. This width corresponds to my measurement at the time of the survey and the measurement taken in Google Earth; however in WIKIPEDIA, according to their references, the width is 82 ft / 25 m wide. Since the discrepancy is 32 ft / 9.75 m, I used my measurement from the ground survey and Google Earth.

2. Along this distance A 1 meanders, and the paralleling rows of standing stones follow the trend of the concentrated flow. The double row of standing stones in England, paralleling cairns and stone piles in the United States and paralleling stone lines in Peru all have the same function, which is mapping the width and trend of the area of higher permeability they are located on (Johnson 2009).

Figure 31: Kennet Avenue standing stones on width boundaries of a concentrated flow

3. Along this section six areas of higher permeability intersect A 1. (Figure 31) Each intersection is indicated by a stone adjacent to the double standing stone row, and also indicates the trend's flow as follows:

A 2 - intersects A 1 at 579974.88 m E, 5697660.85 m N and is 12 ft / 3.65 m wide trending at 67° NE. There is a stone located at 579986.86 m E, 5697666.84 m N on the east side of the road which is located along the trend of A 2.

A 3 - intersects A 1 at 579993.22 m E, 5697641.02 m N and is 15 ft / 4.57 m wide trending at 70° NE. There is a stone located at 580004.00 m E, 5697649.00 m N on the east side of the road which is located along the trend of A 3.

A 4 - intersects A 1 at 580004.54 m E, 5697625.30 m N and is 12 ft / 3.65 m wide trending at 60° NE. There is a stone located at 580016.53 m E, 5697630.28 m N on the east side of the road which is located along the trend of A 4.

A 5 - intersects A 1 at 580032.40 m E, 5697580.99 m N and is 10 ft / 3 m wide trending at 65° NE. There is a stone located at 580043.31 m E, 5697589.21 m N on the east side of the road which is located along the trend of A 5.

A 6 - intersects A 1 at 580044.34 m E, 5697563.95 m N and is 12 ft / 3.65 m wide trending at 65° NE. There is a stone located at 580058.00 m E, 5697568.00 m N on the east side of the road which is located along the trend of A 6.

A 7 - intersects A 1 at 580091.30 m E, 5697502.31 m N and is 12 ft / 3.65 m wide trending at 66° NE.

Avebury Circle

Within the Avebury henge the pattern of areas of higher permeability becomes very complex. (Figure 32) The following concentrated flows were documented:

Figure 32: Concentrated flows A 1, 8 - 10 & Avebury Circle

A 1 - widens at 579709.56 m E, 5697999.77 m N. Its expanding width is mapped by a line of standing stones along its western width boundary to where A 8 intersects it on the north side of the site. A row of smaller standing stones located at 579698.27 m E, 5698045.04 m N map the eastern width boundary of A 1. Then the large standing stones located at 579666.94 m E, 5698164.79 m N indicate where A 1 and A 10 intersect. The stone located at 579631.74 m E, 5698271.96 m N indicates where the eastern width boundary of A 1 continues. (Figure 32)

A 8 - Within the Avebury henge at 579726.37 m E, 5697957.16 m N, there are two large standing stones on each width boundary of A 1, which also indicate where A 8 branches from A 1. (Figure 33) Then for .3 mi / .49 km, A 8's trend curves forming a half circle which is paralleled by the henge to where it merges with A 1 at 579605.45 m E, 5698255.15 m N. Along this distance A 8's western boundary is mapped with a row of large standing stones. A 8 averaged 36 ft / 10.97 m wide along this distance. Although this pattern of branching from and then merging with the same concentrated flow appears to be unusual, I have documented this type of pattern at sites throughout the regions I have researched.

Figure 33: Intersection of A 1 & A 8

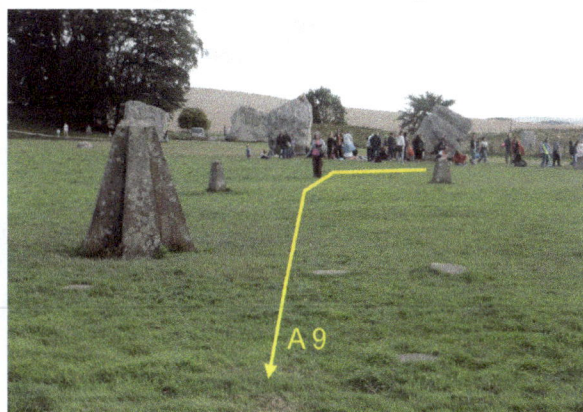
Figure 34: Stones along A 9

A 9 - branches from A 1 at 579705.71 m E, 5698028.91 m N where there are a few small stones located along its width boundaries. (Figure 34) Then it merges with A 10 at 579713.64 m E, 5698163.68 m N where there is a large standing stone. Where it branches from A 1, it was 18 ft / 5.48 m wide, and where it intersects A 10 it was 75 ft / 22.86 m wide.

A 10 - intersects A 1 at 579677.62 m E, 5698185.14 m N. At this location, A 10's width is indicated by the two large standing stones located at 579666.69 m E, 5698166.28 m N and 579690.02 m E, 5698211.63 m N. (Figure 35) A 10 is the widest area of high permeability I documented at Avebury. It was 163 ft / 49.6 m wide where it intersects A 1 at 579677.62 m E, 5698185.14 m N and 185 ft / 56.8 m wide where it intersects the Avebury henge on the east side of the site. At this location there are two large stones on each

Figure 35: Standing stones at intersection of A 1 & A 10

45

width boundary of A 10, which are located at 579806.59 m E, 5698231.11 m N on the north width boundary and at 579835.29 m E, 5698183.09 m N on the south side.

The historical drawings of Avebury indicate there were two stone circles located within the henge. It appears the south stone circle was located where A 9 branches from A 1. The north stone circle appears to have been located where A 1, A 9 and A 10 intersect one another. (Figure 32)

Avebury is an outstanding example of the diverse functions of standing stones. While the double row defined the width and trend of a concentrated flow, for example A 1 and A 8, others identified where two areas of higher permeability intersect, for example A 1 and A 10.

Sanctuary Stone Circle

WIKIPEDIA discribes Sanctuary Circle as follows:

The Sanctuary is a prehistoric site on Overton Hill located around 5 mi / 8 km west of Marlborough in the English County of Wiltshire. Four concentric rings of post holes, and two outer rings of standing stones were first noted in 1648, and were drawn by William Stukeley in 1723, shortly before it was largely destroyed by a local farmer.[1] Excavation in 1930 re-identified the location of the 58 stone sockets and 62 post-holes, the locations of which are now marked with concrete blocks.[2] It is part of a wider Neolithic landscape which includes the nearby sites of Silbury Hill, West Kennet Long Barrow and Avebury, to which the Sanctuary was linked by the 82 ft / 25 m wide and 8 mi / 2.5 km long Kennet Avenue. It also lies close to the route of the prehistoric Ridgeway and near several Bronze Age barrows.

The first stage of activity at the site, some time around 3000 BC, consisted of a ring of eight wooden posts 4.5 metres (15 ft) across, with a central post, presumed to be a round hut.[2] Within 200 years the first ring was enlarged to 6m and a second ring was added, also of eight posts, but this time 11.2 metres (37 ft), perhaps creating a large hut or an enclosure. [4] Phase three, some time in the later Neolthic, a third ring of 33 posts were added, in a circle 21 metres (69 ft) across, and at the same time an inner stone circle of 15 or 16 sarsen stones was introduced alongside what was by that point the middle ring, making an almost solid wall of stones and posts.

The final phase was of 42 sarsen stones forming a boundary ring 40 metres (130 ft) across, which replaced all the timber structures.[4] This may have been built at a similar time to the Avebury stone circle, and had an entrance way that led into the Kennet Avenue, two parallel lines of

stones running the 2.5 kilometres (1.6 mi) from The Sanctuary to Avebury.
[2] (WIKIPEDIA 2018)

Figure 36: Sanctuary Stone Circle & concentrated flows S 1 - 3

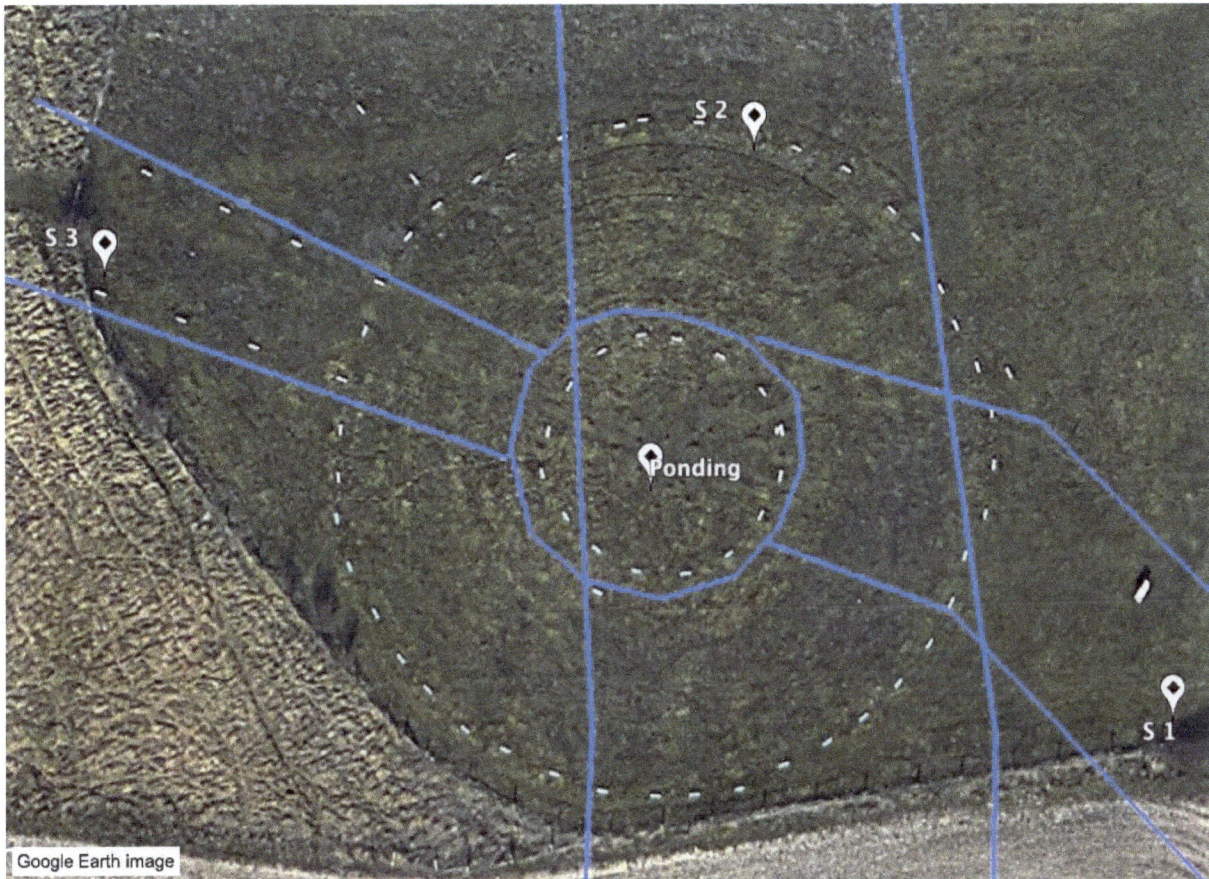

I dowsed around Sanctuary Stone Circle and located three areas of higher permeability intersecting it as follows: (Figures 36 & 37)

S 1 - intersects the site from the southeast trending on average at 312° NW while curving into the stone circle. It was 40 ft / 12 m wide where it intersects the outer circle. It also intersects the mound located at 581348.00 m E, 5696140.00 m N.

S 2 - crosses the stone circle along a north-south trend, and the average width was 83 ft / 25 m wide. Based on my calculations, the center circle is not centrally located on S 2. Consistently, when concentric circles, mounds and standing stone circles are located where two or more areas of higher permeability intersect one another, the intersection is centered within the circle(s). In Figure 36 my calculations indicate the center of the circles is offset to the west of the intersecting flows. This could have happened during the reconstruction in 1930. S 2 also trends towards mound 8 which is located south of the site.

47

S 3 - intersects the stone circle from the northwest at 118° SE and was 25 ft / 7.6 m wide, which is the width between the two rows of paralleling standing stones that are located along each width boundary.

As mentioned above, Kennet Avenue extended 8 mi / 2.5 km from Sanctuary to Avebury. I did not have time to determine which area of higher permeability extending northward from the Sanctuary Stone Circle intersects A 1 and Kennet Avenue.

In addition to these concentrated flows, the following observations were documented: (Figure 37)

S 4 - 77 ft / 23.4 m wide trending at 20° NE while curving slightly. It extends from mound 1 northward, and mounds 2 through 5 are located along it.

S 5 - S 4 and S 5 could be the same concentrated flow.

S 6 - Its trend was projected based on mound 6.

Figure 37: Sanctuary Stone Circle features & S 1 - 4

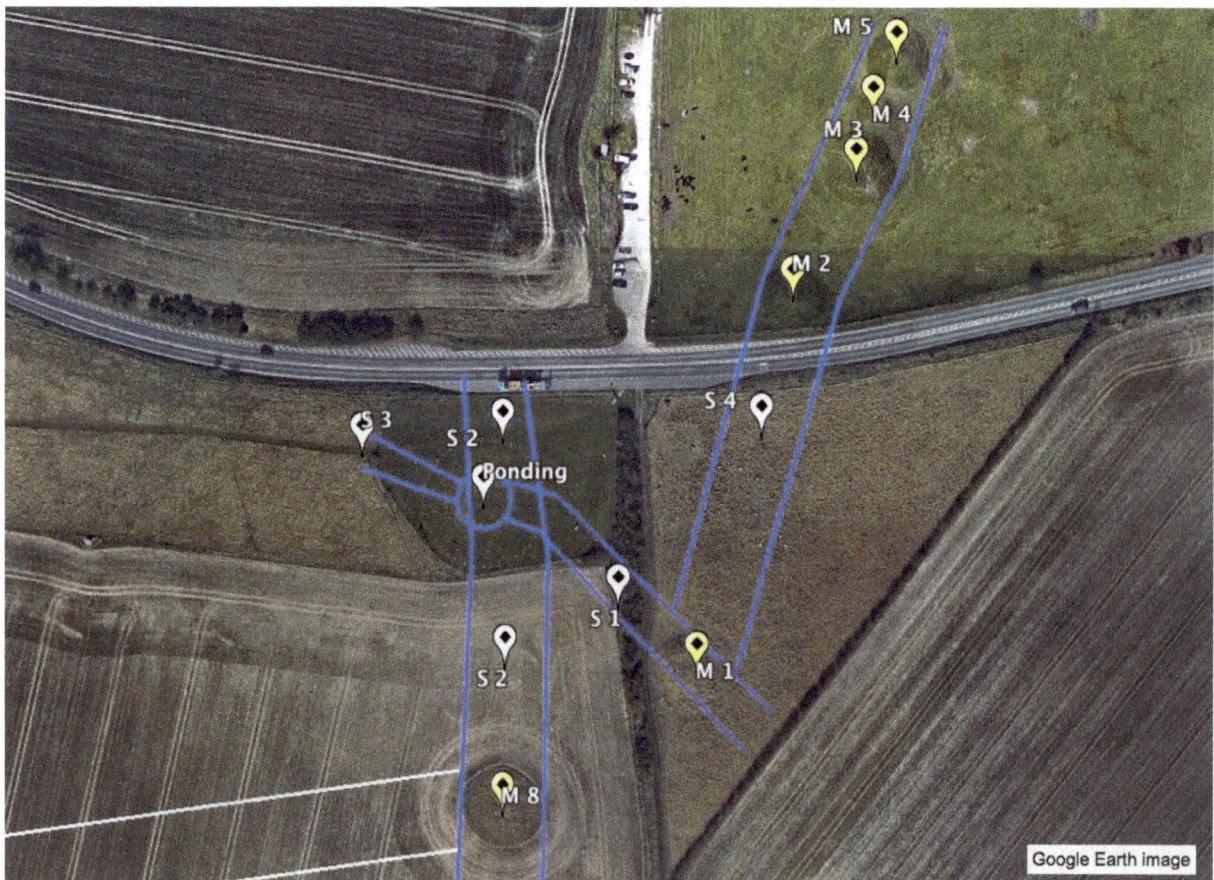

Based on the features associated with Sanctuary Stone Circle, although it is smaller than the Stonehenge Circle, it served the same function and has the same characteristics as line centers, buttes with rays, medicine wheels and large glacier erratics with rays which are discussed in Johnson's previous books. (Johnson 2009, 2019 and Papers on Ceremonial Landscapes 2018)

Silbury Hill

WIKIPEDIA discribes Sanctuary Circle as follows:

Silbury Hill is a prehistoric artificial chalk mound near Avebury in the English county of Wiltshire. It is part of the Stonehenge, Avebury and Associated Sites UNESCO World Heritage Site. At 39.3 metres (129 ft) high,[1] it is the tallest prehistoric man-made mound in Europe[2] and one of the largest in the world; similar in size to some of the smaller Egyptian pyramids of the Gisa Necropolis.[3]

Silbury Hill is part of the complex of Neolithic monuments around Avebury, which includes the Avebury Ring and West Kennet Long Barrow. Composed mainly of chalk and clay excavated from the surrounding area, the mound stands 40 metres (131 ft) high[4] and covers about 5 acres (2 ha). The hill was constructed in several stages between c.2400–2300 BC[5] and displays immense technical skill and prolonged control over labour and resources. Archaeologists calculate that it took 18 million man-hours, equivalent to 500 men working for Kennet15 years (Atkinson 1974:128) to deposit and shape 248,000 cubic metres (324,000 cu yd) of earth and fill. Euan W. Mackie asserts that no simple late Neolithic tribal structure as usually imagined could have sustained this and similar projects, and envisages an authoritarian theocratic power elite with broad-ranging control across southern Britain.[6]"

The base of the hill is circular and 167 metres (548 ft) in diameter. The summit is flat-topped and 30 metres (98 ft) in diameter. A smaller mound was constructed first, and in a later phase much enlarged. The initial structures at the base of the hill were perfectly circular: surveying reveals that the centre of the flat top and the centre of the cone that describes the hill lie within a metre of one another.[7] There are indications that the top originally had a rounded profile, but this was flattened in the medieval period to provide a base for a building, perhaps with a defensive purpose.[8]

The first clear evidence of construction, dated to around 2400 BC[9] consisted of a gravel core with a revetting Kerb of stakes and sarsen boulders. Alternate layers of chalk rubble and earth were placed on top of this: the second phase involved heaping further chalk on top of the core, using material excavated from a series of surrounding ditches which were progressively refilled then recut several metres further out.[5] The step surrounding the summit dates from this phase of construction, either as a precaution against slippage,[10] or as the remnants of a spiral path ascending from the base, used during construction to raise materials and later as a processional route.[11][9] (WIKIPEDIA 2018)

Figure 38: Silbury Hill

Figure 39: Silbury Hill & S 1 - 4

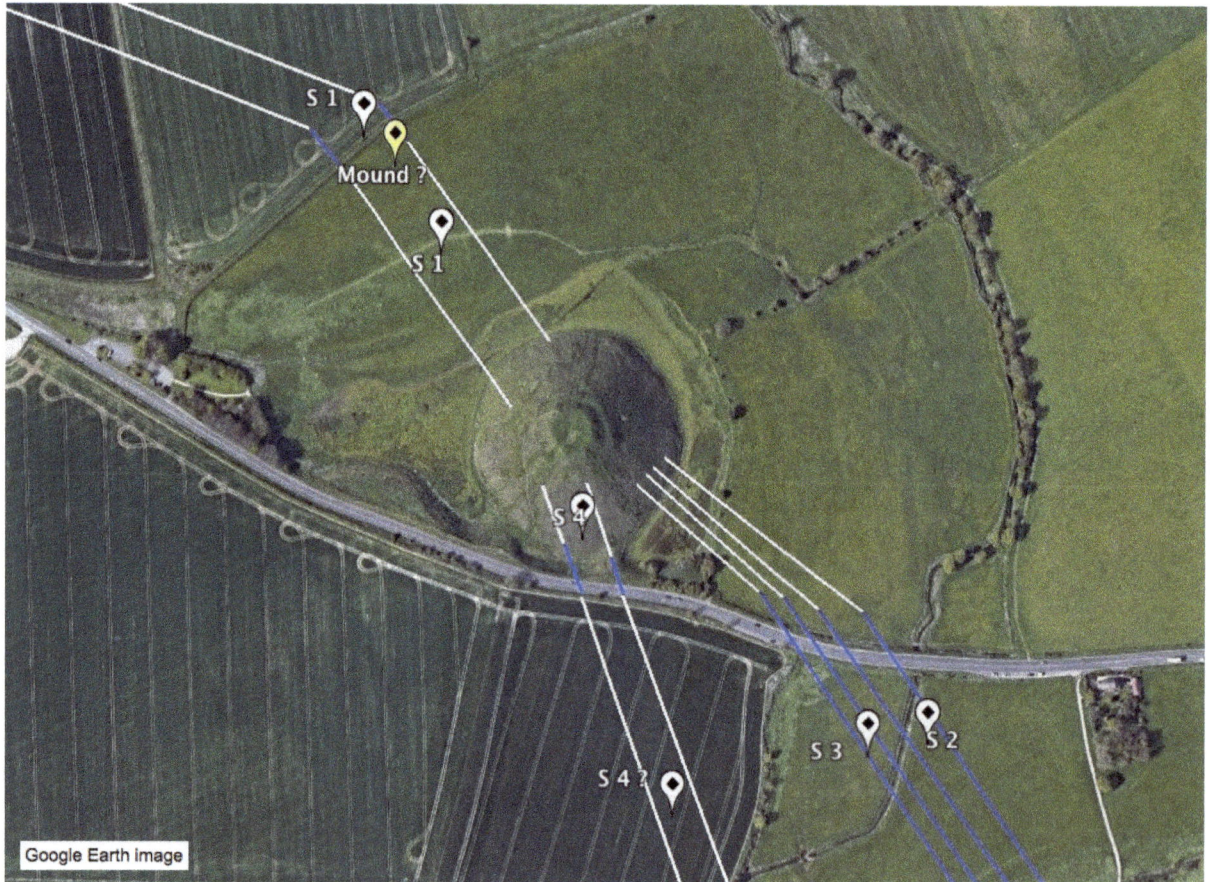

Following the public access trail which circles Silbury Hill, I located four areas of higher permeability which intersect the mound: (Figures 38 & 39)

S 1 - 158 ft / 48 m wide along the trail. Due to the field and site closure, S 1's trend was taken within a very short distance and is not representative of its overall course. However with that said, it intersects the mound. When I projected the trend of L 1 taken at Longstone Cove, which is nearby, it trends towards the mound. It is possible that L 1 and S 1 are the same concentrated flow.

After S 1 intersects the mound, it branches into three concentrated flows labeled S 2 through 4. All three were documented along the trail which is adjacent to the road, and S 2 and 4 along the trail to the West Kennet Long Barrow.

> S 2 - documented at 579668.91 m E, 5696548.08 m N along the road and at 579938.01 m E, 5696173.50 m N along the trail to the West Kennet Long Barrow. It was 80 ft / 24.3 m wide trending at 145° SE.

> S 3 - documented at 579619.99 m E, 5696549.82 m N along the road and at 579948.16 m E, 5696095.46 m N along the trail to the West Kennet Long Barrow. It was 42 ft / 12.8 m wide trending at 145° SE.

> S 4 - documented at 579474.23 m E, 5696576.35 m N along the road. Although the trend was taken within a short distance, it appears to intersect the rectangular feature located at 579694.72 m E, 5696014.07 m N. It was 102 ft / 31 m wide trending at 159° SE.

When the trends of S 2 thought S 4 are projected, all three intersect K 1 near West Kennet Long Barrow.

The intersection of S 1 through S 4 suggests that Silbury Hill was intentionally constructed where four concentrated flows intersect.

West Kennet Long Barrow

WIKIPEDIA describes West Kennet Long Barrow as follows:

> Archaeologists classify it as a chambered long barrow and one of the Seven-Cotswold tombs. It has two pairs of opposing transept chambers and a single terminal chamber used for burial. The stone burial chambers are located at one end of one of the longest barrows in Britain at 328 ft /100 m: in total it is estimated that 15,700 man-hours were expended in its construction. The entrance consists of a concave forecourt with a facade made from large slabs of sarsen stones which were placed to seal entry.

> The construction of the West Kennet Long Barrow commenced about 3600 BC, which is some 400 years before the first stage of Stonehenge, and it was in use until around 2500 BC. The mound has been damaged by indiscriminate digging, but archaeological excavations in 1859 and 1955-56 found at least 46 burials, ranging from babies to elderly persons. The bones were disarticulated with some of the skulls and

long bones missing. It has been suggested that the bones were removed periodically for display or transported elsewhere with the blocking facade being removed and replaced each time. Recent re-analysis of the dating evidence suggests that the 46 people all died within 20 – 30 years of each other, and that the tomb was open for 1,000 years. (WIKIPEDIA 2018)

Figure 40: West Kennet Long Barrow & K 1

Figure 41: West Kennet Long Barrow & K 1 - 2

I circled the barrow and located two concentrated flows which intersect it. (Figures 40 & 41)

L 1 - The barrow's length and width are located along L 1. L 1 was 81 ft / 24.6 m wide across the barrow's eastern entrance. L 1's trend was 81º E along the barrow, however it curves to 238º SW just beyond its western end. When L 1's trend is projected eastward, it appears to intersect S 2 and mound 8 just south of Sanctuary Stone Circle.

L 2 - It intersects the barrow and L 1 at 579924.94 m E, 5695903.29 m N and was 62 ft / 18.89 m wide trending at 352° N. L 2 intersects S 3 near 579898.17 m E, 5696151.78 m N.

Additional barrows and mounds are discussed below.

Longstone Cove Standing Stones

WIKIPEDIA discribes Longstone Cove Standing Stones as follows:

> The Longstones are two standing stones, one of which is the remains of a prehistoric "cove" of standing stones....Two stones are visible, known as 'Adam' and 'Eve' although the latter is more likely to have been a stone that formed part of the Beckhampton Avenue that connected with Avebury. Adam is the larger of the two stones, weighing an estimated 62 tons, and along with three others formed a four-sided cove. The cove had been open on its south eastern side which faced towards the nearby South Street barrow 130 m away. The other stones were destroyed in the post-medieval period by a local landowner. (WIKIPEDIA 2018)

Figure 42: Longstone Cove & L 1

Figure 43: Longstone Cove standing stones

I circled the two standing stones and located one area of higher permeability which I labeled L 1. (Figures 42 & 43) L 1 was 100 ft / 30.48 m wide trending at 97° E on the west side of the two stones and 131° SE on the east side. Even though WIKIPEDIA comments the larger stone, called Adam, had fallen over and was incorrectly re-erected in 1912, it is located on the width boundary of L 1. I dowsed along both width boundaries of L 1 from the road on the eastern side of the field to the fence line on the west side and did not locate any additional concentrated flows intersecting L 1. Maps of the area indicate these stones were most likely part of the Beckhampton Avenue /

standing stone row which connected with Avebury. Perhaps an intersecting concentrated flow crosses or intersects L 1 just west of the stones.

As mentioned above, the trend of L 1 suggests it intersects S 1 at Silbury Hill. Interestingly, mentioned above, "The cove had been open on its south eastern side which faced towards the nearby South Street Barrow 130 m away." This is the direction of L 1's trend.

Based on the surface features within this complex, researchers had concluded these sites were connected to one another. When you include the areas of higher permeability, they support this hypothesis.

Hillforts

Some of the hillforts had two or more areas of higher permeability intersecting them, for example, Oldbury Castle, Maiden Castle and Old Sarum.

Oldbury Castle

Figure 44: Oldbury Castle & O 1 - 3

WIKIPEDIA describes Oldbury Castle as follows:

Oldbury Castle "is the largest Iron Age hill in south-eastern England.[1] It was built in the 1st century BC by Celtic British tribes on a hilltop west of Lghtham, Kent, in a strategic location overlooking routes through the Kentish Weald. The fort comprises a bank and ditch enclosing an area of about 50 hectares (120 acres), with entrances at the north-east and south ends." "Within the interior several pits and possible building foundations survive. At least two entrances were constructed, on the north-east and southern ends of the hillfort.[3] A spring is located near the center of the site." It is unusual since it has an earthen rampart crossing the interior in a north south direction and researchers are uncertain regarding its function. (WIKIPEDIA 2018)

I circled the site's ramparts and located three areas of higher permeability which crossed it: (Figures 44 & 45)

O 1 - 57 ft / 17.37 m wide in the northwest corner of the site and near the modern monument. It trends southeasterly at 135° SE while meandering slightly to where it merges with O 2 and O 3 at 574430.32 m E, 5697224.74 m N.

O 2 - 30 ft / 9.14 m wide in the northeast corner of the site along one of the earthen ramparts at 574395.63 m E, 5697569.92 m N. From this location its trend curved from southeastward to southwestward to where it merges with O 1 and O 3 at 574430.32 m E, 5697224.74 m N. (Figure 45)

O 3 - It extends southward from where O 1 and O 2 intersect one another at 574430.32 m E, 5697224.74 m N and was 95 ft / 28.9 m wide.

Figure 45: Small mound where O 1 - 3 intersect

The following features are associated with these concentrated flows:

1. The eastern earthen ramparts follow the eastern width boundary of O 2.

2. The earthen rampart crossing the site near the middle in a north-south direction follows the western width boundary of O 1.

3. The northeast entrance is located along O 2.

4. The southern entrance is located along O 3.

5. Although I do not know the exact location of the spring, based on the description mentioned above, it appears to be located along O 1.

Maiden Castle

Figure 46: Maiden Castle, M 1 & 2

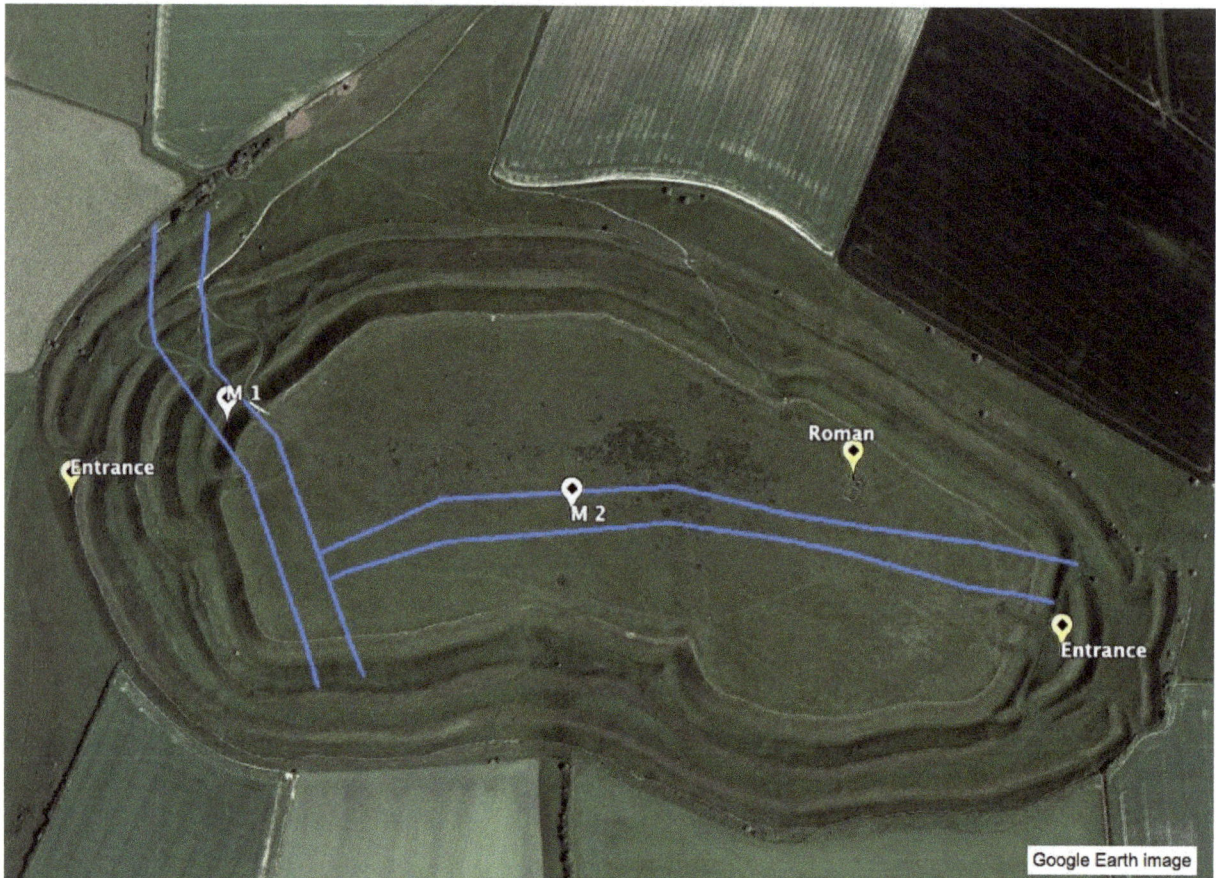

WIKIPEDIA describes Maiden Castle as follows:

The earliest archaeological evidence of human activity on the site consists of a Neolithic causewayed enclosure and bank barrow around 4,000 BC. In about 1800 BC, during the Bronze Age, the site was used for growing crops before being abandoned. Maiden Castle itself was built in about 600 BC; the early phase was a simple and unremarkable site, similar to many other hillforts in Britain and covering 6.4 hectares (16 acres). Around 450 BC it was greatly expanded, during which the enclosed area was nearly tripled in size to 19 ha (47 acres), making it the largest hillfort in Britain and, by some definitions, the largest in Europe. At the same time, Maiden Castle's defenses were made more complex with the addition of further ramparts and ditches. Around 100 BC, habitation at the hillfort went into decline and became concentrated at the eastern end of the site. It was occupied until at least the Roman period, by which time it was in the territory of the Durotriges, a Celtic tribe. After the Roman conquest of Britain in the 1st century AD, Maiden Castle appears to have been abandoned, although the Romans may have had a military presence on the site. In the late 4th century AD, a temple and ancillary buildings were constructed. In the 6th century AD the hill top was entirely abandoned and was used only for agriculture during the medieval period. (WIKIPEDIA 2018)

Two areas of higher permeability were located within the earthen ramparts of Maiden Castle and labeled M 1 and M 2: (Figure 46)

M 1 - crosses the western end of the hillfort and averaged 150 ft / 45.7 m wide trending at 158° S while meandering slightly. It is possible that M 1 trends to the mound located at 537216.51 m E, 5616849.95 m N. The western entrance is located immediately west of the western width boundary of M 1.

M 2 - 125 ft / 38 m wide trending east-west while meandering slightly as it crosses the length of the site near the center. It intersects M 1 near 537161.25 m E, 5615959.20 m N and the northern side of the east entrance at 537815.46 m E, 5615955.08 m N.

Old Sarum

WIKIPEDIA describes Old Sarum as follows:

Old Sarum is the site of the earliest settlement of Salisbury in England. Located on a hill about 2 miles (3 km) north of modern Salisbury, the settlement appears in some of the earliest records in the country. The great monoliths of Stonehenge and Avebury were erected nearby and indications of prehistoric settlement have been discovered from as early as 3000 BC. An Iron Age hillfort was erected around 400 BC, controlling the intersection of two native trade paths and the Hampshire Avon. The site continued to be occupied during the Roman period, when the paths became roads. The Saxons took the British fort in the 6th century and later used it as a stronghold against marauding Vikings. The Normans constructed a motte and bailey castle, a stone curtain wall, and a great cathedral. A royal palace was built within the castle for King Henry I and was subsequently used by Plantagenet monarchs. This heyday of the settlement lasted for around 300 years until disputes between the Sheriff of Wiltshire and the Bishop of Salisbury finally led to the removal of the church into the nearby plain. As New Salisbury grew up around the construction site for the new cathedral in the early 13th century, the buildings of Old Sarum were dismantled for stone and the old town dwindled. Its long-neglected castle was abandoned by Edward II in 1322 and sold by Henry VIII in 1514. (WIKIPEDIA 2018)

Figure 47: Old Sarum & S 1 - 3

I circled the royal palace / inner castle and located three areas of higher permeability, S 1, 2 and 3, which intersect near the center: (Figure 47)

S 1 - 84 ft / 25.6 m wide and meandered sharply as it crossed the south side of the site in a southern direction, as shown in Figure 47.

S 2 - 69 ft / 21 m wide trending at 135° SE to where it intersects S 1 and S 3 at 583695.01 m E, 5660895.69 m N. S 2 crosses the cathedral; however, this structure is not orientated along the trend of S 2.

S 3 - 57 ft / 17.37 m wide where it intersects S 1 and S 2 at 583695.01 m E, 5660895.69 m N; however, it widened to 105 ft / 32 m near the outer wall at 583680.37 m E5661052.24 m N. It crosses the northern section of the site at 171° SE while meandering slightly.

One of WIKIPEDIA's references comments, "Holinshed noted that the hill was "very plentifully served with springs and wells of very sweet water";[28] excavation has discovered numerous wells (including one within the Norman keep) but suggests that they were so deep as to make their use more cumbersome than carting water uphill from the rivers." (WIKIPEDIA 2018) The sign by the well comments, " this was the main source of water in the castle, apart from what drained off the lead roofs. The original depth of the well shaft is unknown, but it may have been more than 70 meters, approximately 230 feet. The well is located at 583701.00 m E, 5660878.00 m N within the keep and on the eastern width boundary of where S 1 through S 3 intersect.

Some of the hillforts had one area of higher permeability crossing it, for example, Chun Castle and Castle an Dinas (St Clumb).

Castle an Dinas (St Clumb)

Figure 48: Castle an Dinas & C 1

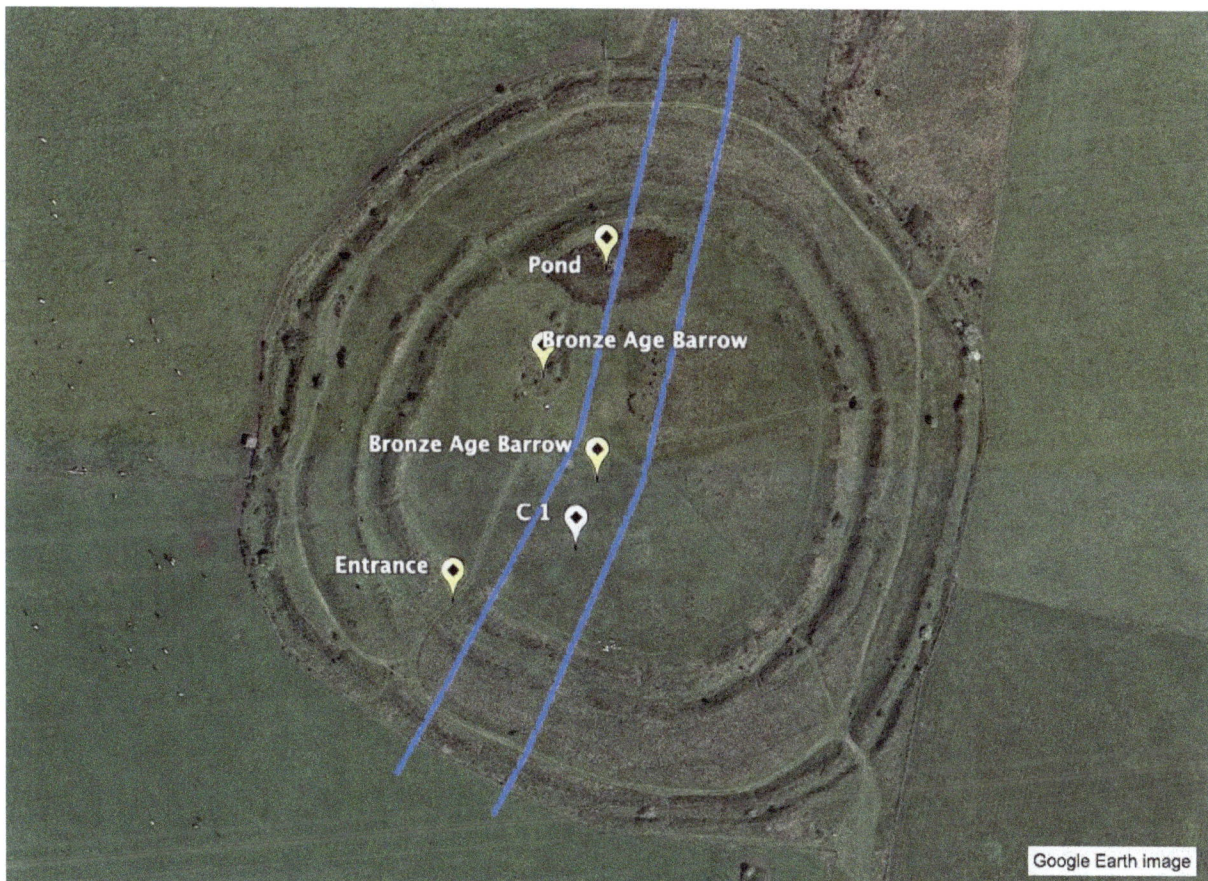

WIKIPEDIA describes Castle an Dinas (St Clumb) as follows:

Castle an Dinas is an Iron Age hillfort at the summit of Castle Downs near St Columb Major in Cornwall, and is considered one of the most important hillforts in the southwest of Britain. It dates from around the 3rd to 2nd century BCE and consists of three ditch and rampart concentric rings, 850 feet (260 m) above sea level. (WIKIPEDIA 2018)

There are two Bronze Age barrows in the central enclosed area and these may be traces of the first human use of this hill, although recent surveys have suggested that there is a leveled-off platform between the outer and inner banks and ditches which may represent the traces of even earlier (Neolithic) use. The main entrance lies on the south-west side, and the gateway had a cobbled surface. There is a wet, marshy area inside the enclosed area, suggesting that it might once have contained a well, making it possible to live on the site. (Cornwall Heritage 2018)

I located only one area of higher permeability within this site. (Figure 48)

C1 - crosses the site in a north-south direction while curving slightly to the southwest along the southern end of the site. It was 78 ft / 23.77 m wide along the north rampart and 116 ft / 35.35 m at the southern end.

Within the ramparts the following features were associated with C 1:

1. The pond, which may have been a well, is located along the western half of C 1's width.

2. Of the two Bronze Age barrows, the one in the center is located on C 1.

3. The southern entrance is located along the western width boundary of C 1.

Chûn Castle

WIKIPEDIA describes Chun Castle as follows:

Chûn Castle is a large Iron Age hillfort (ringfort).[1] The fort was built about 2,500 years ago, and fell into disuse until the early centuries AD when it was possibly re-occupied to protect the nearby tin mines. It stands beside a prehistoric trackway that was formerly known as the Old St Ives Road and the Tinners' Way.

The purpose of the fort is speculated to be for protection of tin and copper gathered in the tin-rich locality of what is now Pendeen, with its Geevor Tin Mine, and surrounding villages. Iron and tin slags were found within the castle, near the well. It overlooks many miles of ocean, the Celtic Sea, to the north, and overlooks the only land route to this peninsula (West Penwith) to the south. Therefore, not only its structure but its location suggest a much more actively militaristic function.

The well, within the inner walls, is of note as it once had a stairway leading to the water, water which remains to this day even during dry spells. Locals used the well water until the 1940s for domestic purposes and some for superstitious reasons, viz. the endowment of perpetual youth. Neopagans still make pilgrimages to the site on religiously significant days. (WIKIPEDIA 2018)

Figure 49: Chûn Castle & C 1

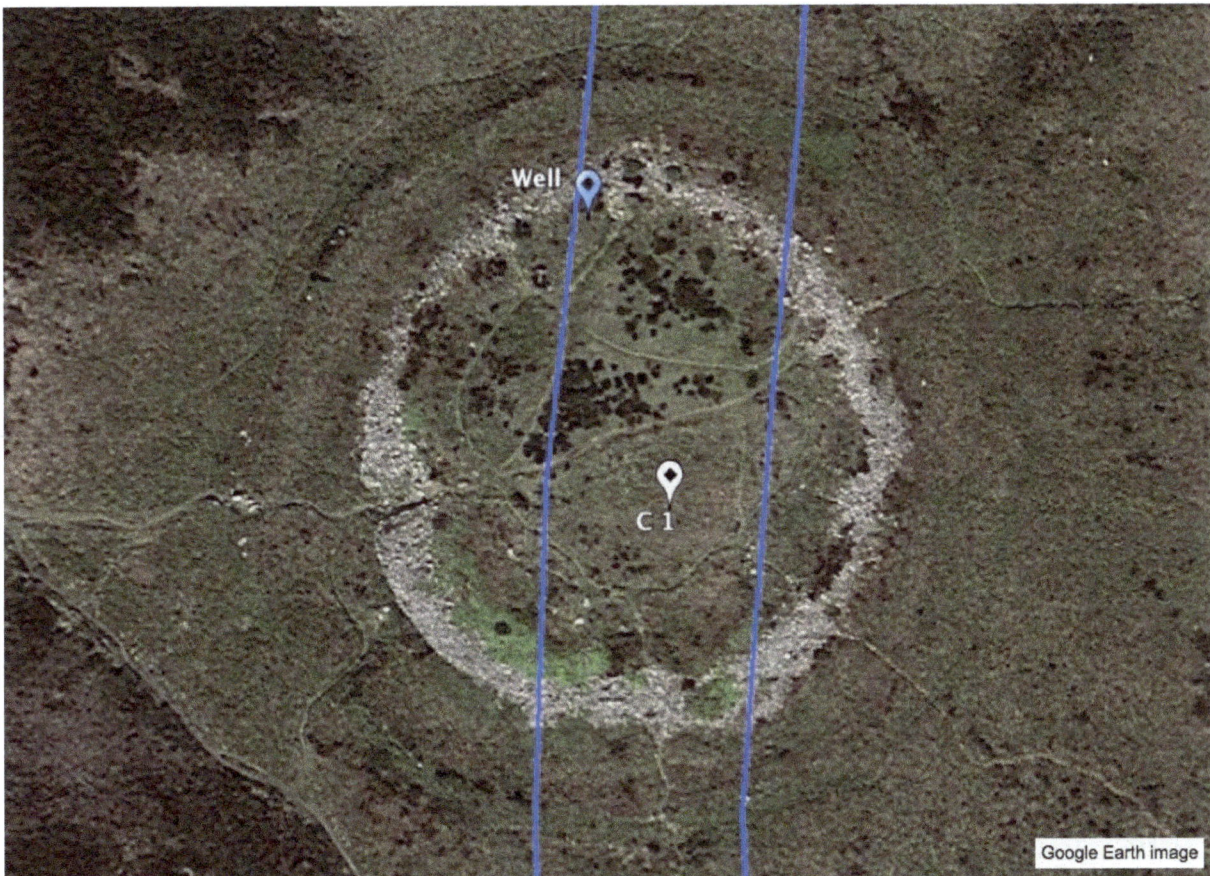

I circled the hillfort and located only one concentrated flow which crossed it. (Figure 49)

C 1 - 75 ft / 22.86 m wide and crosses the site in a north-south direction. The well is located adjacent to the western width boundary of C 1.

All of the hillforts I surveyed were located on one or more areas of higher permeability and most had known wells associated with them. Near some of these sites there are other hills which appear to be equally suitable for a hillfort, however, they were not used for this purpose. Although I did not investigate the other hills due to time restraints, it is possible they do not have a concentrated flow(s) crossing beneath them. Therefore, they did not locate a hillfort on them.

Iron Age Villages and Fogous

During the research in Peru, Chile and the United States, habitation, ceremonial and burial sites were consistently located along one or more areas of higher permeability, which is discussed throughout my site reports (Johnson 2009 and Papers on Ceremonial Landscapes 2018). This was also true for similar sites in southern England. It is important to note that within the sites I investigated in the Western Hemisphere, the earliest structures were located along the area(s) of higher permeability which crossed the site. Then, as the area along the flow(s) began to fill up, additional structures were located as close as possible to the concentrated flow(s). Based on the data from England, it appears this is also true for these sites.

Fogou

A fogou is defined as follows:

A fogou or fougou[1] (pronounced "foo-goo") is an underground, dry-stone structure found on Iron Age or Romano-British-defended settlement sites in Cornwall. The original purpose of a fogou is uncertain today. Colloquially called vugs, vows, foggos, giant holts, or fuggy holes in various dialects,[2] fogous have similarities with souterrains or earth-houses of northern Europe and particularly Scotland, including Orkney. Fewer than 15 confirmed fogous have been found. (WIKIPEDIA 2018)

Although I only investigated two fogous, both were located along a concentrated flow and remind me of kivas in the southwestern United States. (Figures 7 & 50 - 51) A kiva is an underground room used by the Puebloan Native Americans for religious rituals and meetings. All of the great kivas and many of the smaller ones I investigated are located along at least one area of higher permeability (Johnson 2019).

In England, most sites contain multiple occupations ranging from the Neolithic period to modern times. All of the pre-Roman villages and large habitation sites I ground surveyed were associated with one or more areas of higher permeability. I did not investigate sites dating from Roman to present.

Carn Euny and Chysausrer Iron Age Villages are examples of communities which were located on one or more areas of higher permeability. In addition to these, others are mentioned under other headings.

Carn Euny Iron Age Village

WIKIPEDIA describes Carn Euny as follows:

Carn Euny is an archaeological site on the Penrith peninsula in Cornwall, England, United Kingdom with considerable evidence of both

Iron Age and post-Iron Age settlement.[2] Excavations on this site have shown that there was activity at Carn Euny as early as the Neolithic period. There is evidence that shows the first timber huts there were built about 200 BC, but by the 1st century BC, these had been replaced by stone huts. The remains of these stone huts are still visible today.

Figure 50: Carn Euny, E 1 & E 2

Carn Euny is best known for the well-preserved state of the large Fogou, an underground passageway, which is more than 65 feet (20 metres) long. This fogou runs just below the surface of the ground and is roofed with massive stone slabs. Although the exact purpose of these fogous is still a mystery, possibilities include storage, habitation, or ritual. The site was abandoned late in the Roman period.

Traces of human activity in Carn Euny have been detected from the early Neolithic period. The first settlement of wooden huts was around 200 BC. In the 1st century BC these were replaced by stone huts, the remains of which are still visible. At this time, the people of Carn Euny lived from agriculture, livestock, trade, and perhaps Tin mining. The houses were of a type with enclosed courtyards. The most important structure of the site is

63

certainly the fogou (Cornish for *cave*), a man-made underground passage which is covered with massive stone slabs. Fogous can be found in other places in the UK and Ireland, and are known more generally as souterrains. Their purpose is unclear. The fogou of Carn Euny is in particularly good condition and consists of a 20 m long corridor, with a side passage that leads to a round stone chamber with a collapsed roof, and a small tunnel which may be a second entrance.[5] West of the settlement are a pair of ancient wells. (WIKIPEDIA 2018)

Within Carn Euny, E 1 crosses the center of the site in a north-south direction and was 43 ft / 13 m wide as shown in Figure 50.

I only investigated one of the wells which is located near 311610.00 m E, 5553371.00 m N. The well is located on E 2, which was 15 ft / 4.57 m wide and the depth to water was about 6 ft / 1.8 m.

The following features were associated with these flows:

1. The village is centrally located on E 1.

2. The fogou is centrally located on E 1.

3. The well is centrally located on E 2. The trend of E 2 indicates it merges with E 1 at the north end of the site.

Chysauster Iron Age Village

WIKIPEDIA describes Chysauster Iron Age Village as follows:

Chysauster Ancient Village is a late Iron Age and Romano-British village of courtyard houses in Cornwall, England. The village included eight to ten houses, each with its own internal courtyard. To the south east is the remains of a fogou, an underground structure of uncertain function.

Chysauster village is believed to have been inhabited from about 100 BC until the 3rd century AD;[3] it was primarily agricultural and unfortified and probably occupied by members of the Dumnonii tribe. The village consists of the remains of around 10 courtyard houses, each around 98 ft / 30 m in diameter.[2] Eight of the houses form two distinct rows,[2] and each house had an open central courtyard surrounded by a number of thatched rooms.[4] The houses have a similar layout. The buildings are oriented on an east-west axis, with the entrance facing east. [3] The walls survive to heights of up to 3 metres. A field system in the vicinity attests to the site's farming connections.

To the south of the settlement is an underground passage of a type known locally as fogou. The fogou at Chysauster was originally recorded as running well over 52.5 ft / 16 m in length but was blocked up in the late 20th century for safety reasons.[2] It was recorded around 1847 by Henry Crozier who described it as a "voe or sepulchral chamber".[2] (WIKIPEDIA 2018)

Figure 51: Chysauster Ancient Village & C 1

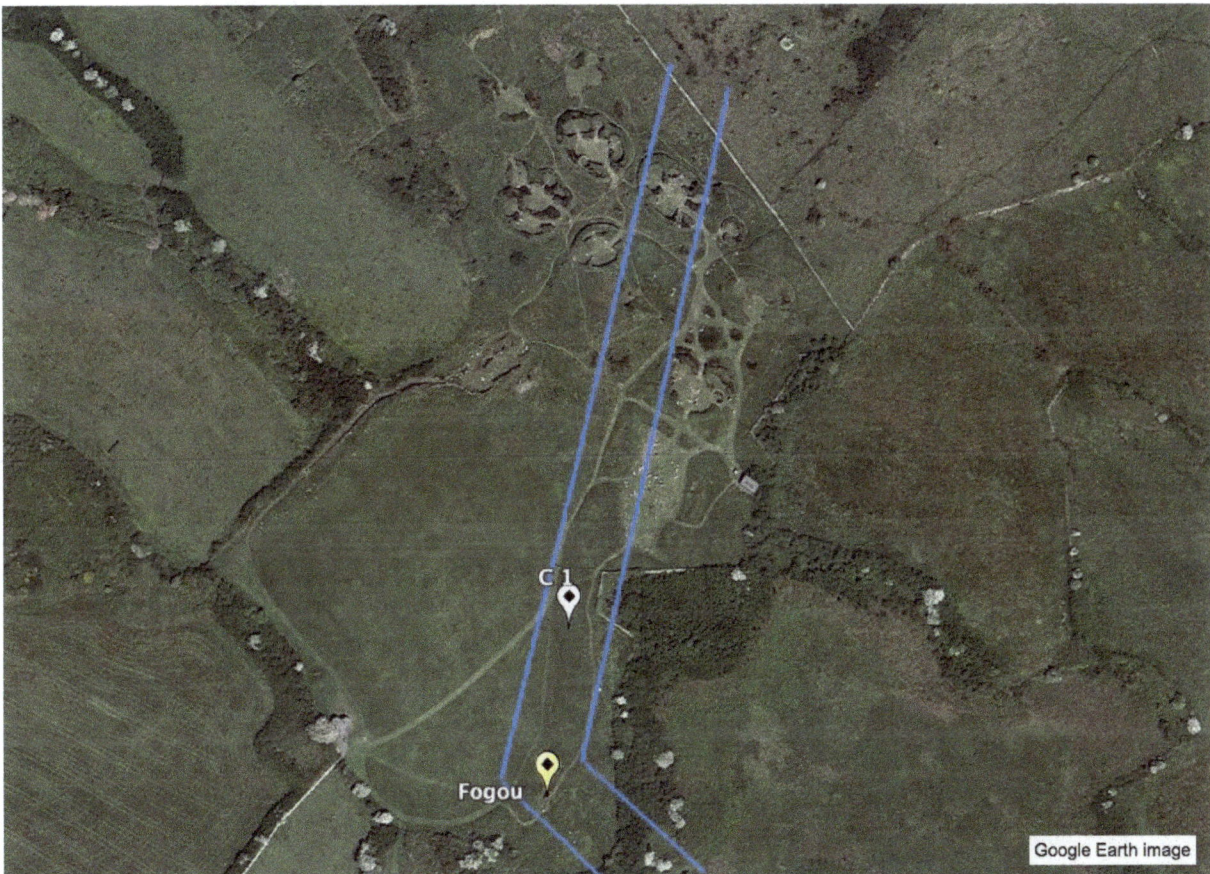

Before I discuss this survey, I need to mention that I arrived at the site within an hour of the closing time. Therefore, the survey includes only the area indicated by the trend of C 1. I did not survey the field along the west side of the access trail between the structures and the entrance. Therefore, there may be additional concentrated flows within that area. Another point is, according to one of the staff, there may have been additional habitation structures near the fogou. (Figure 51)

C 1 - 70 ft / 21.3 m wide and crossed the northern portion the site where the structures are located at 193° SW. Then, by the fogou it turns southeast at 130° SE.

The following features were associated with this flow:

1. C 1 crosses near the center of the northern section of the site.

2. The entrance to the fogou, and possibly the structure itself, is basically centered on C 1.

Habitation Enclosure Sites

During the ground surveys some of the sites contained stone wall enclosures with small structures located along the perimeter. These features appear to be an isolated farm or group of farms. (Cunliffe 1991, p. 45.). While some of them were located on one or more areas of higher permeability, others were not. These structures were the only ones that were not consistently located on one or more areas of higher permeability. I have included Sharpitor Northeast, Down Tor and Drizzlecombe as examples.

Sharpitor Northeast

Figure 52: Sharpitor Northeast & enclosures 1 & 2

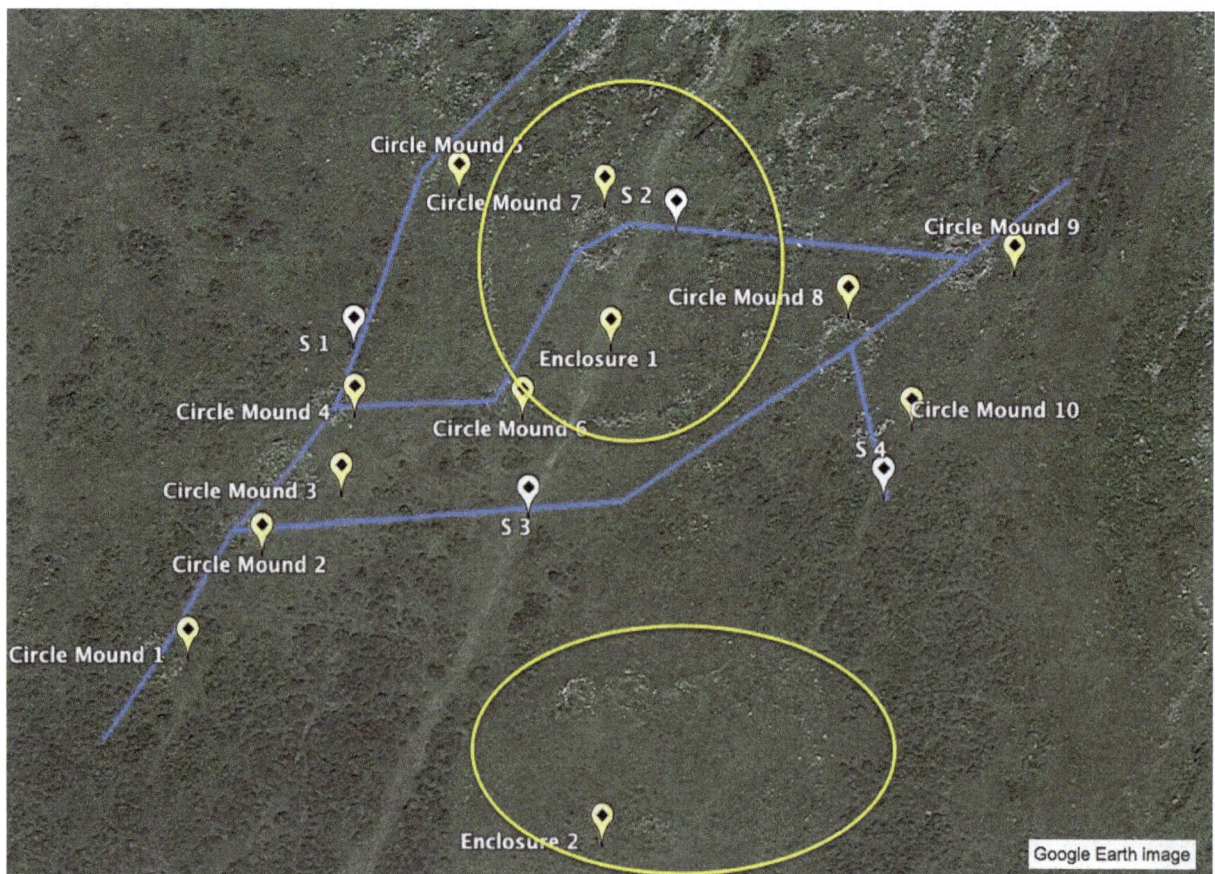

Along the north side of the B3212 highway, approximately 3.5 mi / 5.64 km northeast of Yelverton, there is a group of mounds located at 426962.00 m E, 5597176.00 m N which also contain stone wall enclosures. Two are shown in Figure 52 and labeled Enclosure 1 and 2. They are within 180 ft / 54.8 m of one another and enclose approximately the same area. Enclosure 1 has mound 7, which is a large saucer / ring shaped mound, located within it and concentrated flow S 2 crosses through it. However, enclosure 2 appears to have six or seven structures along the wall's northern perimeter, and they are not associated with a concentrated flow.

Down Tor

Figure 53: Down Tor circular wall & D 1

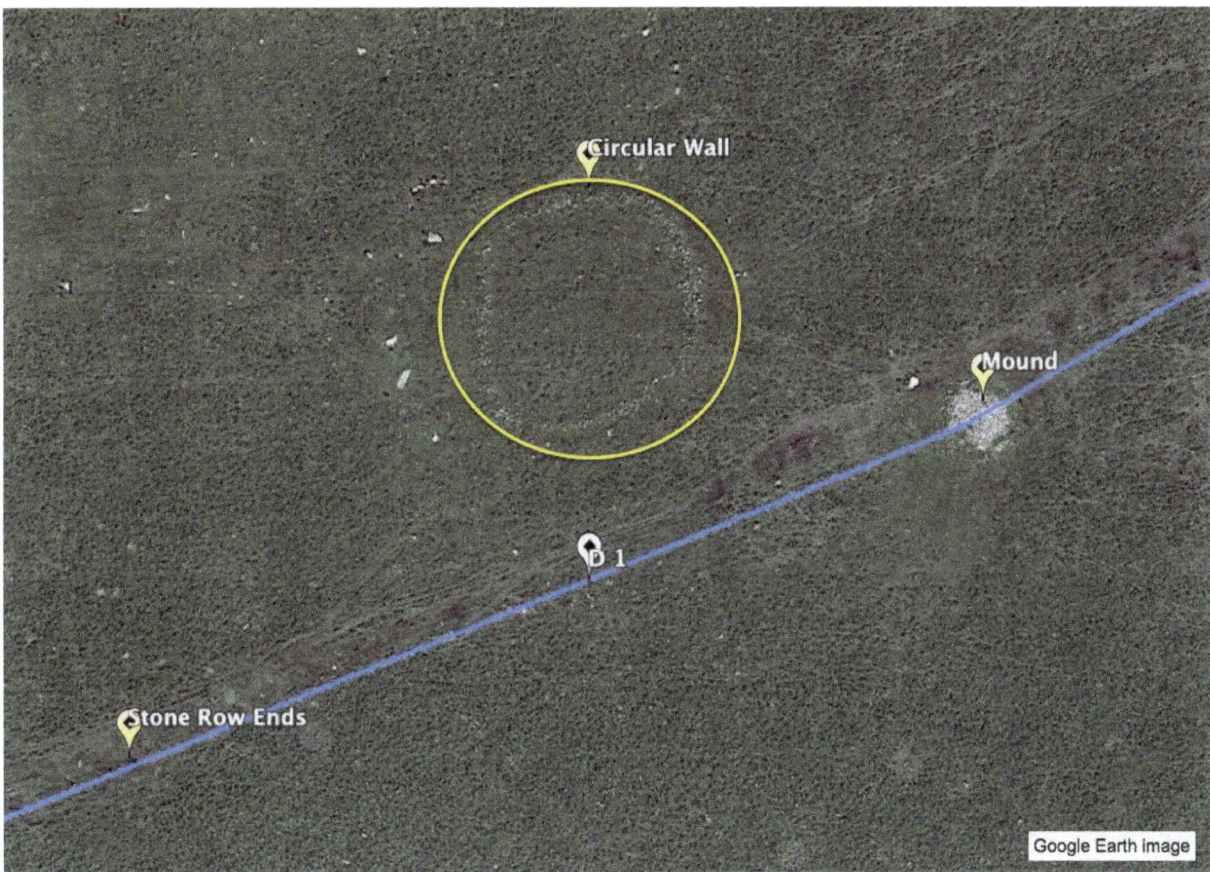

At this site there is a stone row, stone circle and standing stones, as well as a large stone circular enclosure. (Figure 53) The enclosure is located just north of the main concentrated flow, D 1, and a round mound. All the other features I documented at this site were associated with D 1 and the concentrated flows which intersected or crossed it. However, the stone enclosure is not associated with a concentrated flow, nor does it appear to have a structure associated with it. I circled it three times to make sure.

Drizzlecombe

Figure 54: Drizzlecombe enclosures 1 & 2

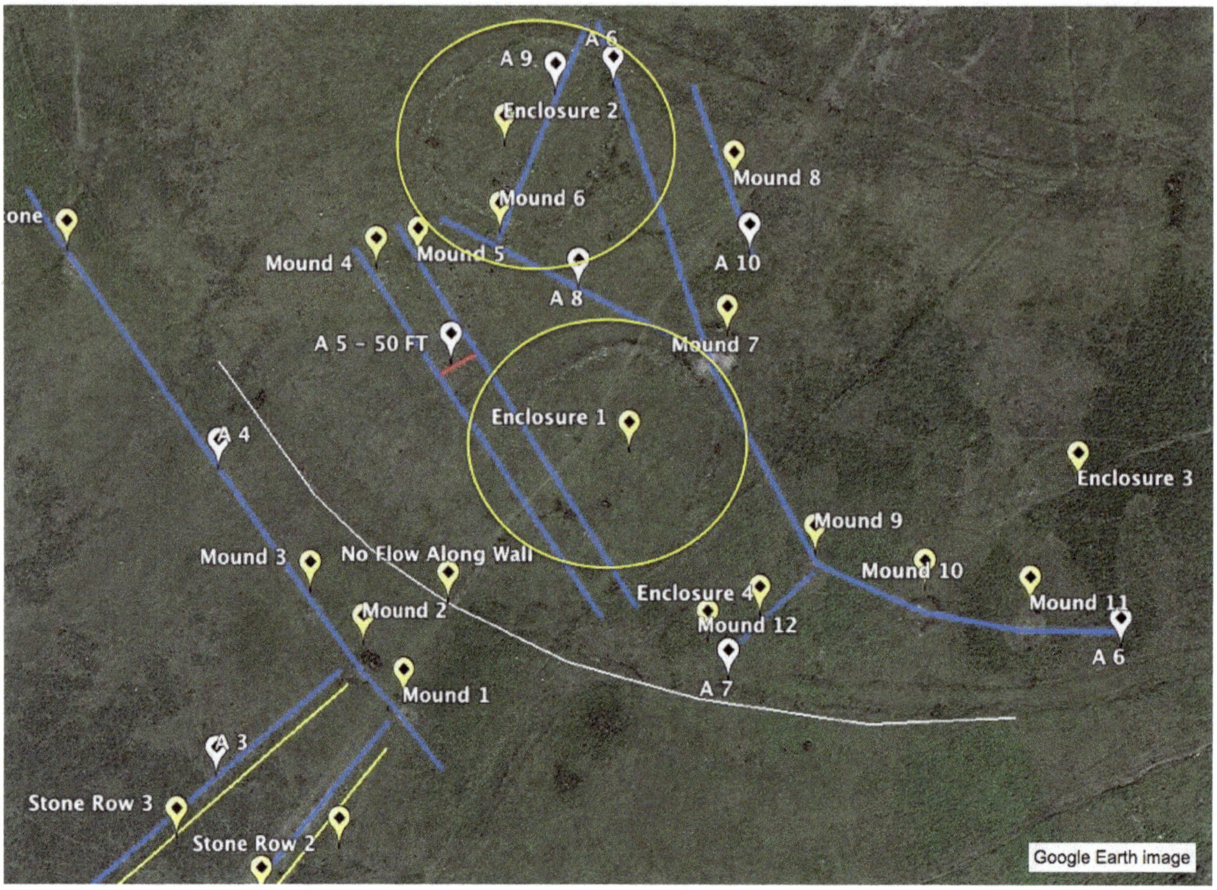

At this site, enclosure 1 has three areas of higher permeability which touch its outer perimeter. A 5 crosses the southern edge of the enclosure, and A 6 and A 8 intersect mound 7 located on the northeast side of the enclosure. (Figure 54)

At enclosure 2, three concentrated flows touch the enclosure. A 9 crosses the enclosure and intersects A 8 at mound 6 along the southern perimeter. On the north perimeter, A 9 intersects A 6.

It is possible these enclosures may have been used for various activities; however, they are the only stone features which are not consistently located along one or more areas of higher permeability. If anyone has additional information regarding this type of feature, please contact me.

Stone Circles

Stone circles consist of standing stones of various heights forming a circle(s). Some also have a tall standing stone in the middle. As I investigated the stone circles in

England, I kept thinking how similar they are to Native American medicine wheels and other features with intersecting areas of higher permeability in the United States.

Stone circles were investigated throughout the survey region, and all were located on one or more areas of higher permeability. Nearby stone features were located on concentrated flows which connected them to the stone circles, for example, Woodhenge, Avebury and Sanctuary stone circles discussed above. In addition to these, the following included additional varieties.

Boscawen-Un Circle

Figure 55: Boscawen-Un Circle & B 1

WIKIPEDIA describes Boscawen Un Circle as follows:

Boscawen-Un is a Bronze Age stone circle close to St Buryan in Cornwall, UK. It consists of 19 upright stones in an ellipse with another, leaning, middle stone just south of the centre. There is a west-facing gap in the circle, which may have formed an entrance. The elliptical circle has diameters 24.9 and 21.9 metres (82 and 72 ft).

69

The stone circle consists of a central standing stone encircled by 19 other stones, including 18 made of grey granite and one of bright quartz, which describe an ellipse with axes of 24.9 m and 21.9 m. The position of the quartz stone in the southwest may indicate the likely direction of the full moon during the solstice. At the northeastern edge of the stone circle are two stones in the ground, one of which has an feet or axe petroglyph. These engravings are unusual in the United Kingdom, though they can also be observed on some of the stones at Stonehenge. The rock art is only fully illuminated around the summer solstice sunrise, although there is some illumination around the summer sunset. The circle has been aligned with the winter solstice sun rises from the Lamorna Gap. [5] (WIKIPEDIA 2018)

There is a wide gap in the west of the circle, which suggests the loss of stones. However this gap may represent, as with the nearby Merry Maidens, an entrance. The central stone is 2.7 m long, but because of its strong inclination to the north-east, the tip is only 2.0 m above the ground. It is thought by some researchers that the central stone embodies the phallic male principle and the quartz stone represents the female powers of the ring.[4] (WIKIPEDIA 2018)

I dowsed around the circle and located only one concentrated flow. B 1 was 20 ft / 6 m wide trending north-south across the center of the circle. (Figure 55)

Down Tor Stone Circle

I circled the Down Tor stone circle and located only one area of higher permeability which crossed it. (Figures 56 & 68) D 1 was 13 ft / 3.96 m wide trending at 68.5° NE. However, it was different from the others I investigated since the circle defined a circular area of groundwater ponding which had the same diameter as the circle. There is a depression in the center of the circle which could have been the location of a standing stone which has been removed, or it could be a spring. I could not find any information on this depression. The tall standing stone on the northeast side of the circle and the double stone row are centrally located on D 1.

Figure 56: Down Tor Stone Circle & D 1

Merry Maidens Stone Circle

WIKIPEDIA describes the Merry Maidens Stone Circle as follows:

This is a late neolithic stone circle. The circle, which is thought to be complete, comprises nineteen granite megaliths. The stones are approximately 1.2 metres high, with the tallest standing 4.6 ft / 1.4 m. They are spaced three to 13 ft / 4 m apart with a larger gap between the stones on the east side. The circle is approximately 78.7 ft / 24 m in diameter. To the south is another stone which suggests a possible north-south orientation. In earlier times there was another stone circle located 200 metres away, but this had been destroyed by the end of the 19th century. (WIKIPEDIA 2018)

Figure 57: Merry Maidens Circle & M 1 & 2

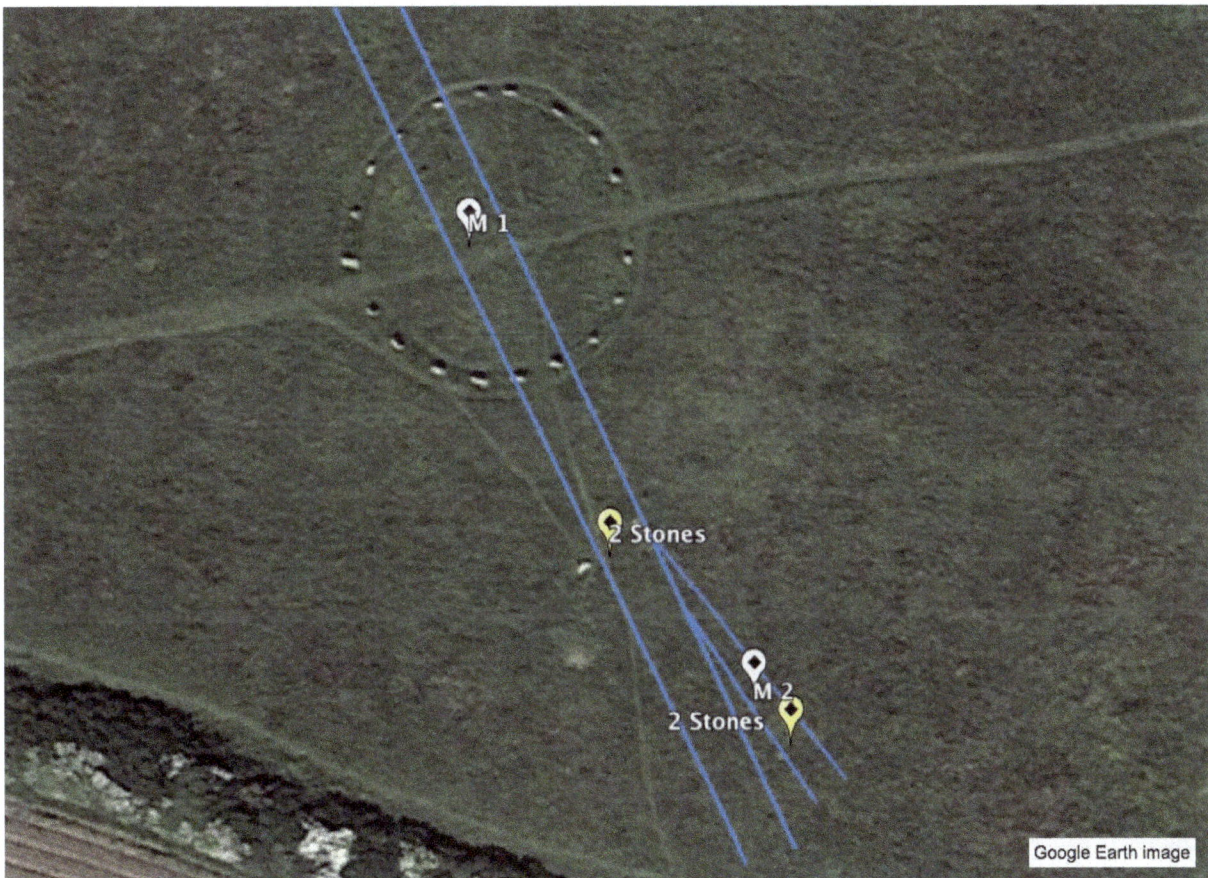

The following areas of higher permeability were associated with this site. (Figure 57)

M 1 - 16 ft / 4.87 m wide trending at 154° SE through the center of the circle

M 2 - 8 ft / 2.4 m wide trending at 140° SE, and it intersects M 1 at 314740.00 m E, 5549056.00 m N where there are two stones.

Features associated with M 1 and M 2:

1. M 1 crosses through the center of the circle.

2. Stones along the circle are located along the east and west width boundaries of M 1.

3. The two stones located at 314740.00 m E, 5549056.00 m N are on the east and west width boundaries of M 1 where M1 and M2 intersect one another.

4. The nearby destroyed stone circle mentioned above may have been located along one of these two concentrated flows.

Hurlers Three Stone Circles

Figure 58: Hurlers Three Stone Circles & H 1

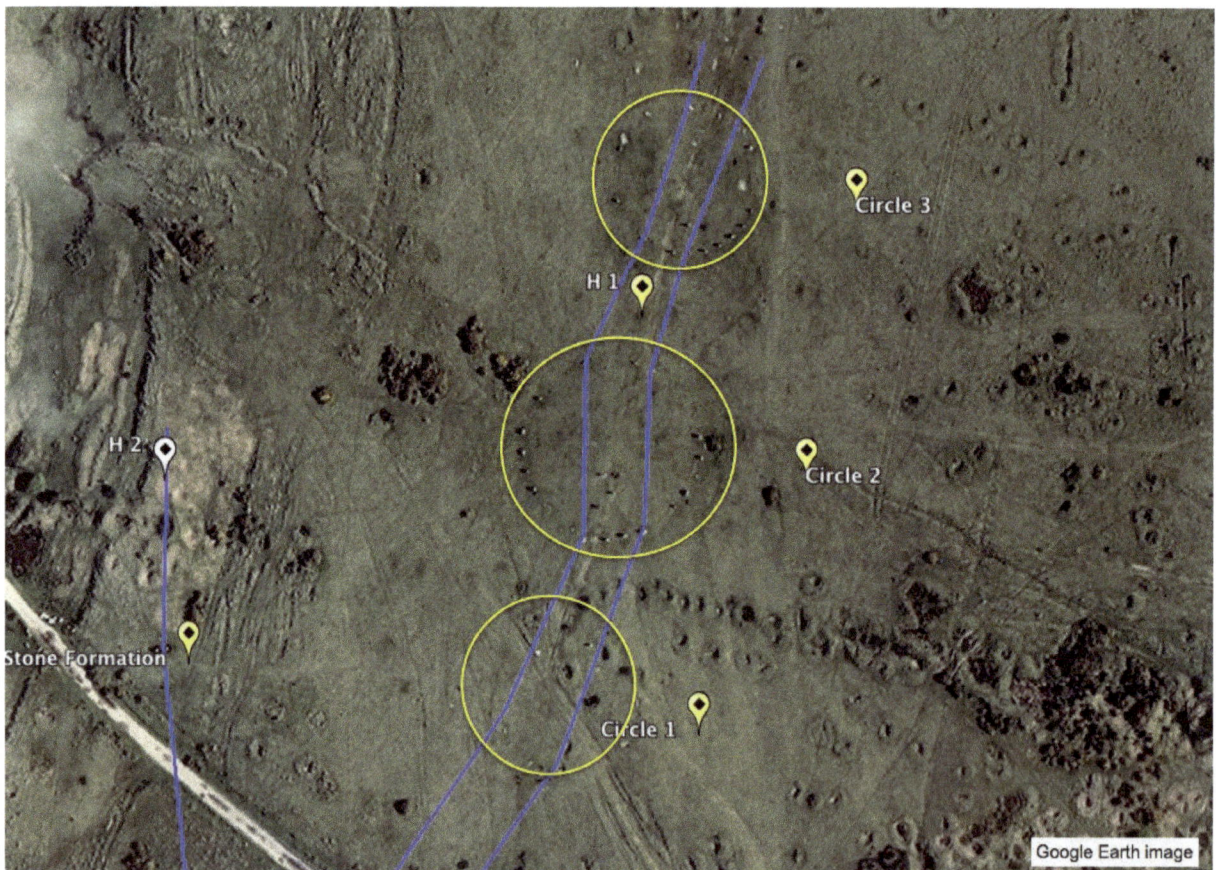

WIKIPEDIA describes the Hurlers Three Stone Circles as follows:

The Hurlers comprises three stone circles that lie on a line from SSW to NNE, and have diameters of 35 metres (115 ft), 42 metres (138 ft) and 33 metres (108 ft). The two outer stone circles are circular. The middle

72

circle, the largest is slightly elliptical. The survival of the southern stone circle, which now contains nine stones, has been most precarious: only two of the remaining stones are upright and the other seven are partially covered with soil.[5] In the middle circle 14 stones survive out of 28.[5] The stones show clear traces of being hammered smooth.[5] The northern stone circle contained around 30 standing stones, from which 15 are still visible.[5] (WIKIPEDIA 2018)

I circled the three stone circles and located only one area of higher permeability. (Figure 58)

H 1 - 40 ft / 12 m wide along the northern circle, 52 ft / 15.8 m wide along the middle circle and 56 ft / 17 m wide along the third circle. Its trend meanders slightly while averaging 21° NE as it crosses through the center of each circle. In North America I have also documented 2 or more medicine wheels on the same concentrated flow. The stone circles are not located in a straight line. At this location, H 1 meanders, and the three stone circles are located along H 1 to document its curving trend.

As mentioned above, although these stone circles are smaller than the Stonehenge circle, they served the same function and share similar characteristics with line centers, buttes with rays, medicine wheels and large glacier erratics with rays.

Standing Stones

At nearly every site one or more standing stones were associated with it. As mentioned above, the remaining standing stones represent only a fraction of those that existed during the sites' apex. The surveys included sites with only one or two standing stones, as well as single and double rows. As discussed above, Avebury is an outstanding example of a variety of standing stone features and functions. The following discusses some additional standing stones sites and their association with area(s) of higher permeability.

1. Individual Standing Stones - Several were the width of the narrow concentrated flow they are located on. For example:

   Boswens Standing Stone - It was the width of the concentrated flow which was only 3 ft / .91 m wide. (Figure 59)

   Trelew Standing Stone - The stone was narrower than concentrated flow T 1 which was 18 ft / 5.48 m wide trending at 82° NE.

   Men Gurta Standing Stone - M 1 which was 12 ft / 3.65 m wide trending at 3° N. The standing stone was half the width of M 1 and centrally located on it. The mounds located nearby are also located along concentrated flows.

Figure 59: Boswens Standing Stone & S 1 both 3 ft wide

Figure 60 : Drift Stones & D 1

20 ft

Piper Standing Stones - They are located by Merry Maidens Circle. These two stones are located 300 ft / 91.44 m apart trending at 318º NE and are centered on P 1 which was 9 ft / 2.74 m. The southern Piper stone (1) was nearly the width of P 1.

2. Two Standing Stones - When two are next to one another, it indicates the width of the concentrated flow. For example:

Piper Standing Stones at Hurlers - They are located along H 2 which was 10 ft / 3 m wide trending at 357º N while curving very slightly. The width between the outer edges of both standing stones is the same as the width of H 2.

Drift Stones - They are located along D 1 which was 20 ft / 6 m wide trending at 223.5º SW. The distance between the stones' outer edges is approximately the same width as D 1. (Figure 60)

3. Single and Double Stone Rows - At Avebury, discussed above, the width of the stone row equalled the width of the concentrated flow while following its trend. (Figures 30, 32 - 35, 43, 59 - 61) However, at other locations, although the stone row followed the trend, its width did not equal the width of the concentrated flow. For example:

Figure 61: Drizzlecombe stone row 1 & A 1

Drizzlecombe Stone Rows - Two of the stone rows are located along A 1, and the third is located along A 3. (Figure 61) All of the low and tall standing stones along these rows were centered on the concentrated flows they are associated with. A 1 and A 3 were both 25 ft / 7.62 m wide, while the stone rows were only a few feet wide.

<u>Down Tor Standing Stone</u> - While D 1 was 14 ft / 4.26 m wide, the stone row was only a few feet wide. (Figure 56)

Quoit

Quoits / dolmens consist of standing stones supporting a cap stone. These features correspond to propped boulders and culturally modified glacier erratics in the United States and Canada. (Johnson 2009, 2019 and Papers on Ceremonial Landscapes 2018)

Carwynnen Quoit

WIKIPEDIA describes Carwynnen Quoit as follows:

Carwynnen Quoit is one of an ancient and rare group of monuments, and can be found at Carwynnen in Cornwall. It is a portal dolmen belonging to the Neolithic period, possibly 5000 years old, one of the few Cornish portal dolmens to be found outside the Penrith peninsula. It is situated on a gentle west-facing slope between two small tributaries to the Red River. The dolmen stands to a height of 4.9 ft / 1.5 m with a capstone measuring approximately 10.8 ft / 3.3 m long by 2.5m wide and 0.098 ft / 0.3m thick, and weighs approximately 10 tons.(WIKIPEDIA 2018)

Although at least one of the supporting stones may not be in its original position, the others appear to be based on the reconstruction's description. (Figure 62)

C 1 - 7 ft / 2 m wide trending at 126° SE. In the United States and Canada, propped boulders frequently have three supporting stones which create a triangle, and the length of the triangle corresponds to the trend of the concentrated flow. Although one of the stones supporting this quoit may not be in its original position, the three of them form a triangle and its length corresponds to the trend of C1.

Figure 62: Carwynnen Quoit

Lanyon Quoit

WIKIPEDIA describes Lanyon Quoit as follows:

Lanyon Quoit currently has three support stones which stand to a height of 4.9 ft / 1.5 m.[2] These bear a capstone which is 18 ft / 5.5 m long,[3] and which weighs more than 12 tonnes.[4] In the 18th century the quoit had four supporting stones and the structure was tall enough for a person on horse back to ride under. On 19 October 1815, Lanyon Quoit fell down in a storm.[5] Nine years later enough money was raised by local inhabitants to re-erect the structure, under the guidance of Captain Giddy of the Royal Navy. One of the original stones was considered too badly damaged to put back in place, thus there are only three uprights today and the structure does not stand as high as it once did.[4] The reconstruction also placed the structure at right angles to its original position.[4] The quoit lies at the north end of a long barrow 85.3 ft / 26 m long and 39.37 ft / 12 m wide.[6] The barrow, which is covered by grass and bracken, is damaged and its outline is difficult to see.[3] At the south end of the barrow are some more large stones which may be the remains of one or more cists.[3] (WIKIPEDIA 2018)

Figure 63 : Lanyon Quoit, other features and concentrated flows

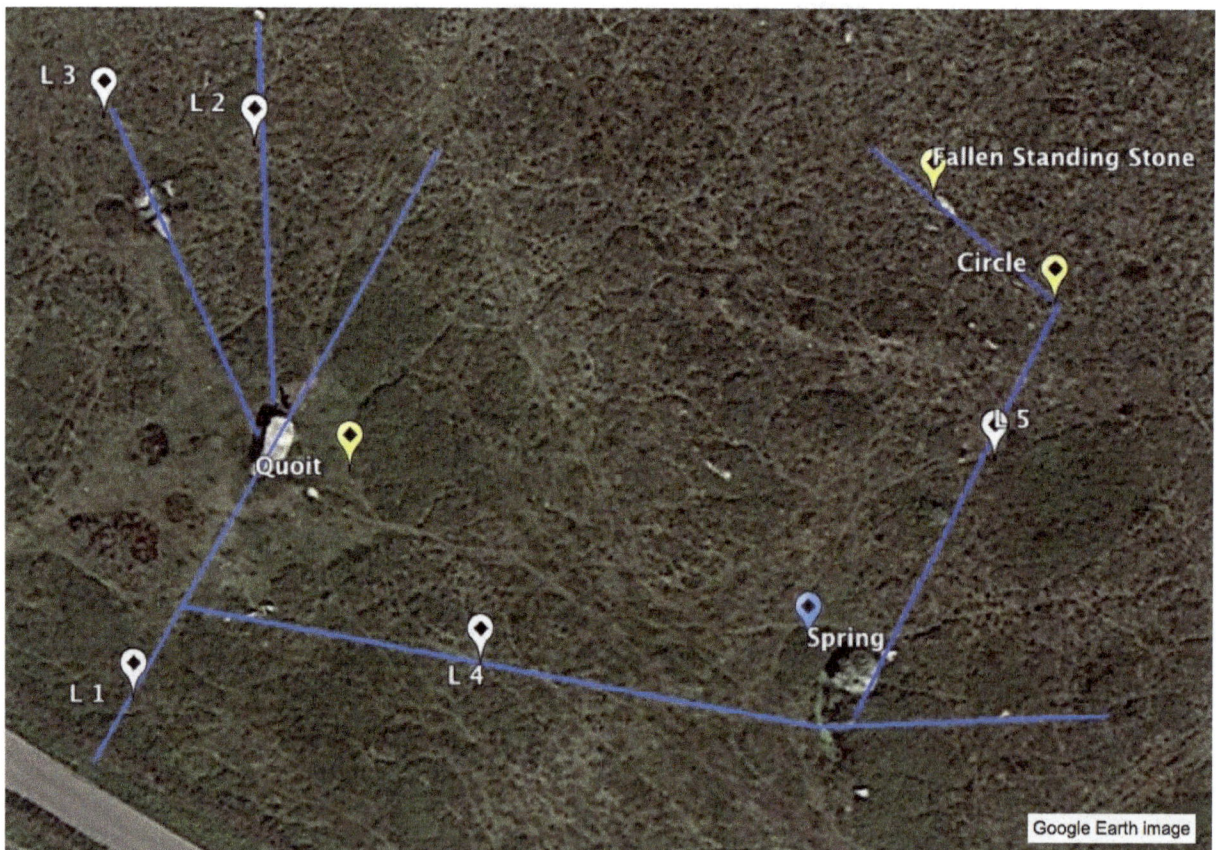

Even though its reconstruction modified its appearance, its association with areas of higher permeability and standing stone features is significant. The quoit is

associated with five areas of higher permeability, additional stone features and a spring. (Figures 63 & 64) I did not locate the long barrow during the survey. I am sure that I would have located additional stone features and concentrated flows if I had time to expand the survey.

Figure 64: Lanyon Quoit where L 1 - L 3 intersect

Figure 65: Spring where L 4 & 5 intersect by white boulder, Lanyon Quoit

The following areas of higher permeability were associated with this site:

L 1 - 15 ft / 4.57 m wide trending at 30° NE

L 2 - 7 ft / 2 m wide trending at 357° NW

L 3 - 9 ft / 2.74 m wide trending at 335° NW

L 4 - 15 ft / 4.57 m wide trending at 100° E to the spring and then curving to 87° E. (Figure 65)

L 5 - 12 ft / 3.65 m wide trending at 27° NE from the spring and then curving to 309° NW

The following features were associated with the areas of high permeability:

1. The quoit is located along the trend of L 1, and where L 2 and L 3 intersect L 1.

2. There is a stone pile / mound where L 4 intersects L 1.

3. The spring is located where L 5 intersects L 4.

4. There is a large boulder on the north side of the spring which is located on L 5. Then where L 5 curves there is a stone circle. From there, L 5 trends towards, what appears to be, a fallen standing stone located at 314377.94 m E, 5558270.13 m N.

When you add the areas of higher permeability to this site, you can clearly see how all of the stone features are connected to one another, and why they are located where they are.

Chûn Quoit

Figure 66: Chûn Quoit, Q 1 & Q 2

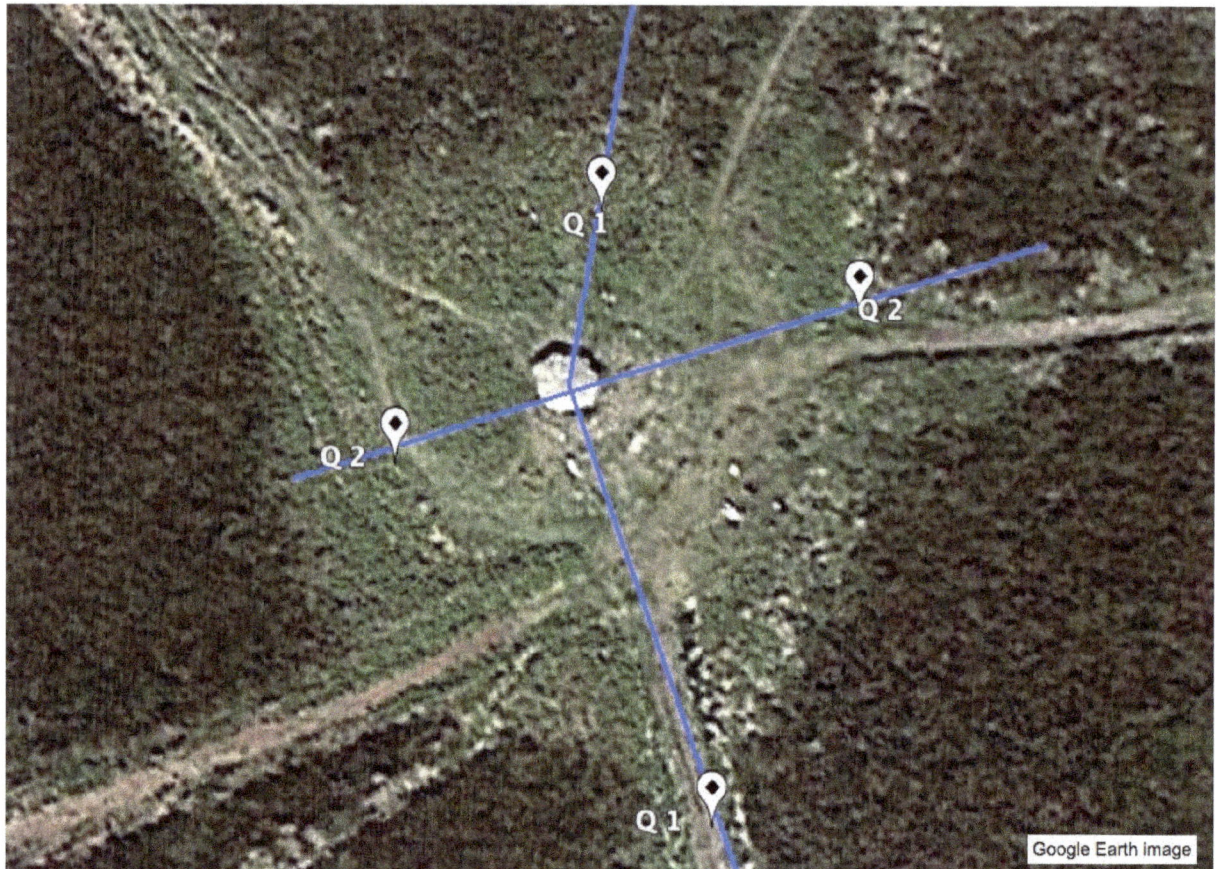

WIKIPEDIA describes Chun Quoit as follows:

Chûn Quoit is one of the best preserved of all Neolithic quoits . As with the other quoits, the quoit was probably covered by a round barrow (35 ft in diameter), of which much evidence abounds. It was a closed chamber and its mushroom-domed capstone measures 3.3 m (11 ft) by 3 m (10 ft), with a maximum thickness of 0.8 m (2 ft 7 in). There is a cup mark on top of the capstone. It is supported about 2 m (7 ft) from the ground by four substantial slabs.[1] There is evidence of an entrance passage to the south-east within the mound area. The site was examined in 1871 but no significant finds were made.

In the vicinity of Chûn Quoit there are many other megalithic and archaeological sites as Lanyon Quoit, Mulfra Quoit, Mên-an-Tol and Mên Scryfa. The rocky outline of Carn Kenidjack marks the position of midwinter sunset away to the south-west. This is the only dolmen in West Penrith to retain its capstone 'in situ' – others have been re-settled. It is believed to have been built around 2400 BC, two millennia before the neighbouring Chun Castle. (WIKIPEDIA 2018)

Two areas of high permeability cross one another at the quoit: (Figures 66 & 67)

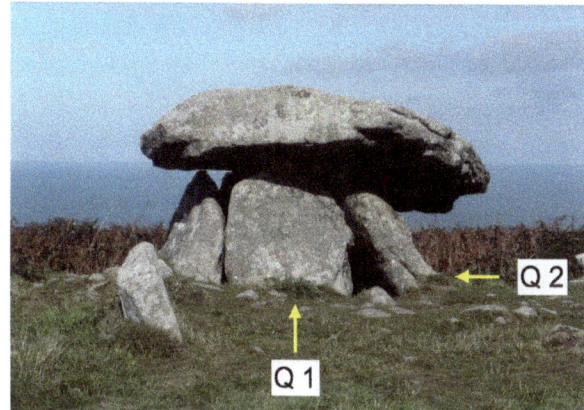

Figure 67: Chûn Quoit, Q 1 & Q 2

Q 1 - 10 ft / 3 m wide trending at 340° NW south of the quoit and curving to 10° NE on the north side.

Q 2 - 8 ft / 2.4 m wide trending at 253° SW.

The two supporting standing stones on the north and south sides are aligned with Q1. The two supporting standing stones on the east and west sides are aligned with Q 2.

With the exception of Carwynner Quoit, the others were located where areas of high permeability intersect one another and were associated with other stone features.

Stone Rows

WIKIPEDIA defines a stone row as follows:

A stone row (or stone alignment), is a linear arrangement of upright, parallel megalithic standing stones set at intervals along a common axis or series of axes, usually dating from the later Neolithic or Bronze Age.[1] Rows may be individual or grouped, and three or more stones aligned can constitute a stone row. (WIKIPEDIA 2018)

A variety of stone rows were surveyed, and all were located on one or more areas of higher permeability. The stone rows of southern England, paralleling stone lines in Peru and paralleling stone piles and cairns in the United States and Canada map the trend of the area of higher permeability they are located along. In some cases, they also map the width of the concentrated flow. (Johnson 2009, 2019 and Papers on Ceremonial Landscapes 2018) For example, the ones in Avebury which are discussed above. Other examples include the following:

Avebury Stone Rows

They are discussed above.

Drizzlecombe Stone Rows

WIKIPEDIA describes Drizzlecombe Stone Rows as follows:

There are three principal stone rows each with an associated barrow and terminal menhir. Most of the artifacts are on the southwest slope of Harbor Hill. The tallest menhir, which at 14 ft (4.3 m) high is the largest on Dartmoor, was re-erected by Sabine Baring-Gould, R. Hansford Worth and others in 1893.[1][2]" (WIKIPEDIA 2018)

Drizzlecombe is located on the western side of Dartmoor, about 4 miles (6.4 km) east of the village of Yelverton, to the west of the upper reaches of the River Plym. Nearby is the large but damaged cairn known as *Giant's Basin*; many of its stones were removed by warreners to build their rabbit-warrens at Ditsworthy, lower down the river. Higher up the slope and overlooking these monuments is a village of stone hut circles, akin to the one at Grimspond. To the north-east lie the extensive remains of Eylesbarrow tin mine and north-west is the concentric Yellowmead stone circle . The area also includes the Neolithic Dartmoor Kistvaens, or tombs. (WIKIPEDIA 2018)

This is a large complex site with several concentrated flows and stone features associated with it. This discussion only includes the stone rows and the features associated with the areas of higher permeability I documented.

Within the survey area as shown in Figures 54, 61 & 68, I located ten areas of higher permeability, however the three stone rows were only located along two of the flows, A 1 and A 3. All the others were associated with mounds and barrows.

A 1 - 25 ft / 7.62 m wide trending at 49° NE between two tall standing stones located at 429901.01 m E, 5592970.91 m N and 430010.18 m E, 5593066.36 m N and along stone row 1. Then, from the last GPS coordinate it curves slightly to 40° NE and stone row 2, with the standing stone and mound 1 located along it. The stone rows were only a few feet wide and did not equal the width of A 1.

A 3 - 25 ft / 7.62 m wide trending at 51° NE from the tall standing stone located at 429975.17 m E, 5593097.64 m N and mound 2. The stone row was only a few feet wide and did not equal the width of A 1.

Down Tor Stone Row

Only one stone row was investigated at Down Tor, and five areas of higher permeability were associated with it.

Figure 68: Drizzlecombe Stone Rows

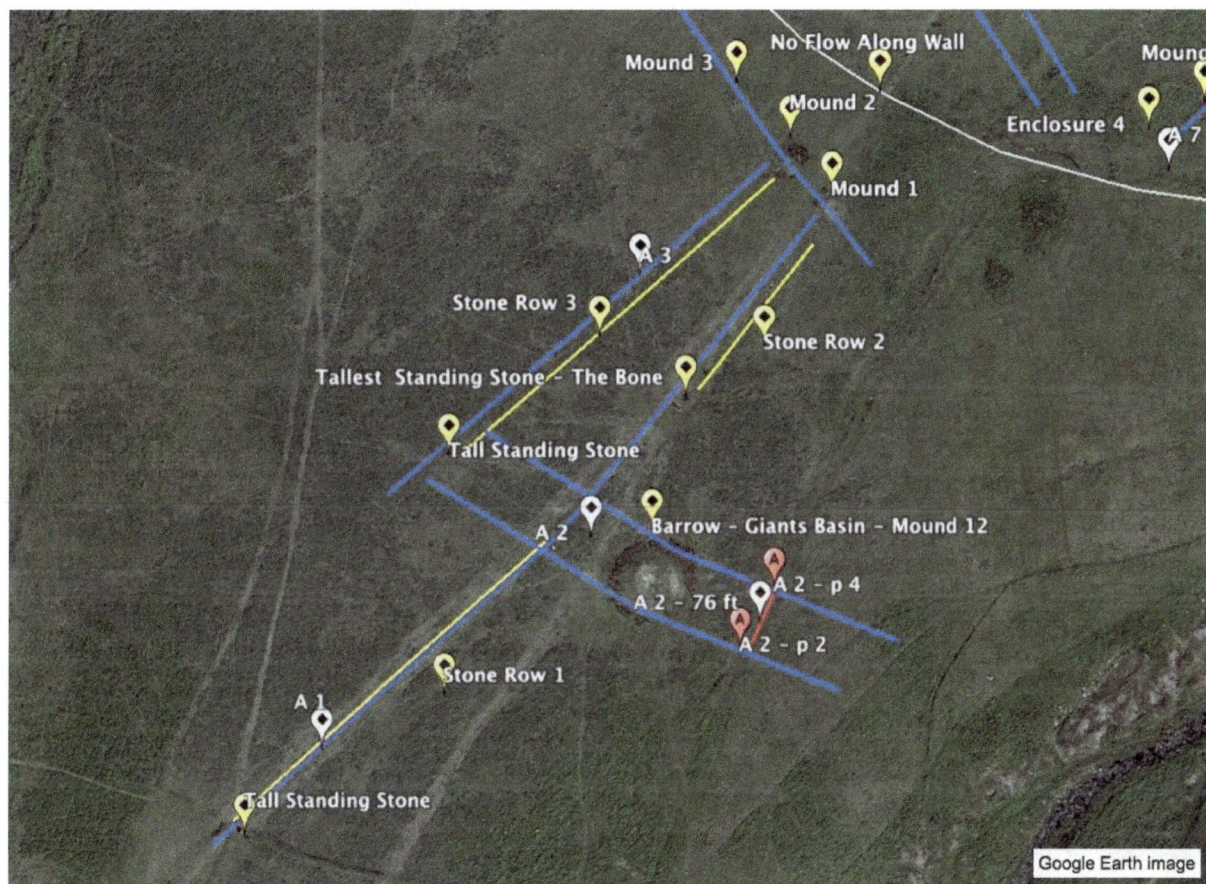

D 1 - The stone row is located along a concentrated flow which I labeled D 1. (Figures 56 & 69) D1 was 14 ft / 4.26 m wide trending at 68.5° NE to the mound located at 430009.60 m E, 5595565.96 m N and then curves slightly to 60.5° NE. The stone row extends for .22 mi / .35 km along D 1. Along the stone row three areas of higher permeability cross D 1, and one intersects D 1 as follows:

D 2 - 18 ft / 5.48 m wide trending at 316° NW and crossed D 1 at 429582.30 m E, 5595403.08 m N. At this location there is a small boulder on each side of the stone row which is located along D 2's trend. At 429537.99 m E, 5595451.65 m N there is, what appears to be, a very small mound which could be natural. At this location D 2 turns to 24° NE, and there is a group of very small mounds along it. Interestingly, the one located at 429558.00 m E, 5595496.00 m N extends across the width of D 2.

Figure 69: Down Tor Stone Row & D 1 - D 5

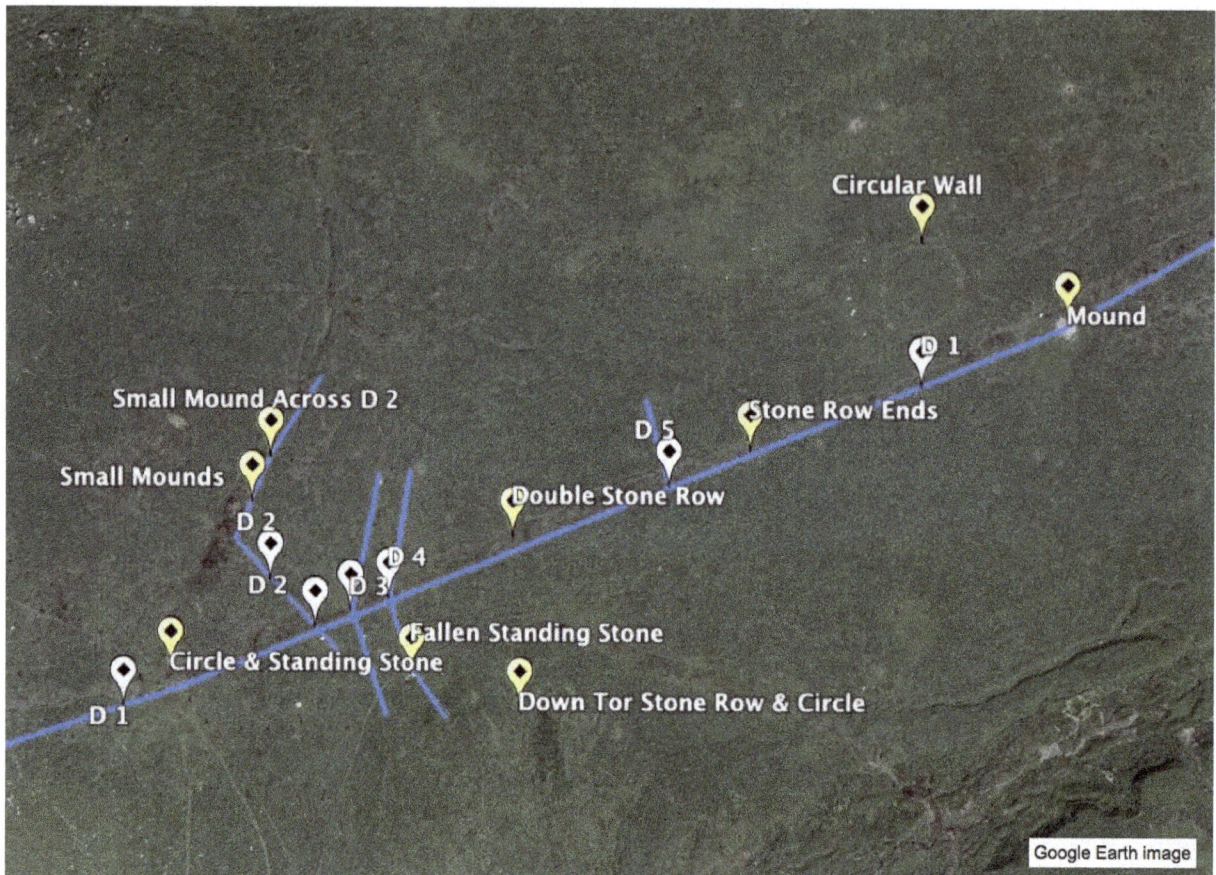

D 3 - 6 ft / 1.8 m wide where it crossed D 1 at 429602.00 m E, 5595412.00 m N. On the south side of the stone row, D 3 trends at 341° NW along a scattered row of stones / boulders which can be seen in Google Earth. On the north side of D 1, it trends at 12° NE, and the boulder located at 429620.08 m E, 5595481.82 m N is on it.

D 4 - 12 ft / 3.65 m wide where it crossed D 1 at 429624.00 m E, 5595418.00 m N. On the south side of the stone row and adjacent to it, there is a large boulder, and D 4 trends at 161° SE to, what appears to be, a large fallen standing stone located at 429637.88 m E, 5595377.95 m N. Then it curves to 144° SE. On the north side of the row, it trends at 188° NE.

D 5 - 14 ft / 4.26 m wide trending at 345° NW, and it intersects D 1 at 429784.31 m E, 5595477.31 m N, but does not cross it.

Although the stone rows at these two sites are not equal to the width of the area of higher permeability, they map the trend. It appears as though, in addition to mapping the areas of higher permeability, the stone rows guide you to the other features associated with these sites. Again, this corresponds to the function of the linear coastal geoglyphs and lines of stone piles and cairns along concentrated flows in the western Hemisphere.

Holed Stone

Mên-An-Tol

WIKIPEDIA describes Men-an-Tol as follows:

The Mên-an-Tol consists of three upright granite stones: a round stone with its middle holed out with two standing stones to each side, in front of and behind the hole. When seen at an angle from one side, the stones form a three-dimensional "101". The two side stones are both about 1.2 metres high. The westernmost stone was moved and brought into a straight line with the other two stones sometime after 1815.[1] The holed stone is roughly octagonal in outline. It is 1.3 metres wide and 1.1 metres high; the circular hole is 0.5 m in diameter.[1] The only other holed stone in Cornwall of this type is the Tolven Holed Stone which can be seen in a garden near Helston.

There is one other standing stone nearby, and six recumbent stones, some of which are buried.[1] A cairn exists as a low stony mound just to the southeast. There are two other early Bronze Age barrows or cairns between 120 and 150 metres to the north.[1]

The Mên-an-Tol is thought to date to either the late Neolithic or early Bronze Age. The holed stone could originally have been a natural occurrence rather than deliberately sculpted.[1] The distribution of the stones around the site has led to the suggestion that the monument is actually part of a stone circle.[1] If so, then it is likely that the stones have been rearranged at some point, and the two standing stones either side of the holed stone may have been moved from their original positions.[1] It has also been suggested that the holed stone could have been a capstone for the nearby cairn before being moved to its present position.[1]

In 1749 the site was first archaeologically investigated by William Borlase, who also drew a plan. This shows that the megaliths were not in a line like today, but formed an angle of about 135°. Borlase also reported that farmers had taken away some stones from the area. From him comes the first written record of the myths and rituals.[2] In the 19th Century the local antiquary John Thomas Blight published several drawings of the site, and made the first suggestion that the stones could be the remains of a stone circle.[3] In 1872 William Copeland Borlase, a descendant of the earlier Borlase, gave a more detailed description of the area.[4] In 1932 Hugh O'Neil Hencken wrote the first modern archaeological report. He believed that the position of the stones was not the prehistoric arrangement, but had been significantly changed. He also thought that the holed stone might be part of a destroyed tomb. He was even told that local farmers with back or limb complaints would crawl through the hole to relieve their pain.[5]

In 1993, the Cornwall *Historic Environment Service* published a detailed report with the latest research results. They suggested that the standing stones

Figure 70: Mên-an-Tol, M 1 & M 2

originated from a stone circle which consisted of 18 to 20 stones. The holed stone, however, could be part of a nearby portal tomb. It also possible that the holed stone stood at the center of the stone circle and served to frame specific points on the horizon. Such a use of a holed stone is not known in other sites,[6] although the nearby stone circle of Boscawen-Un does have a central standing stone. (WIKIPEDIA 2018)

Figure 71: Mên-an-Tol, M 1 & M 2

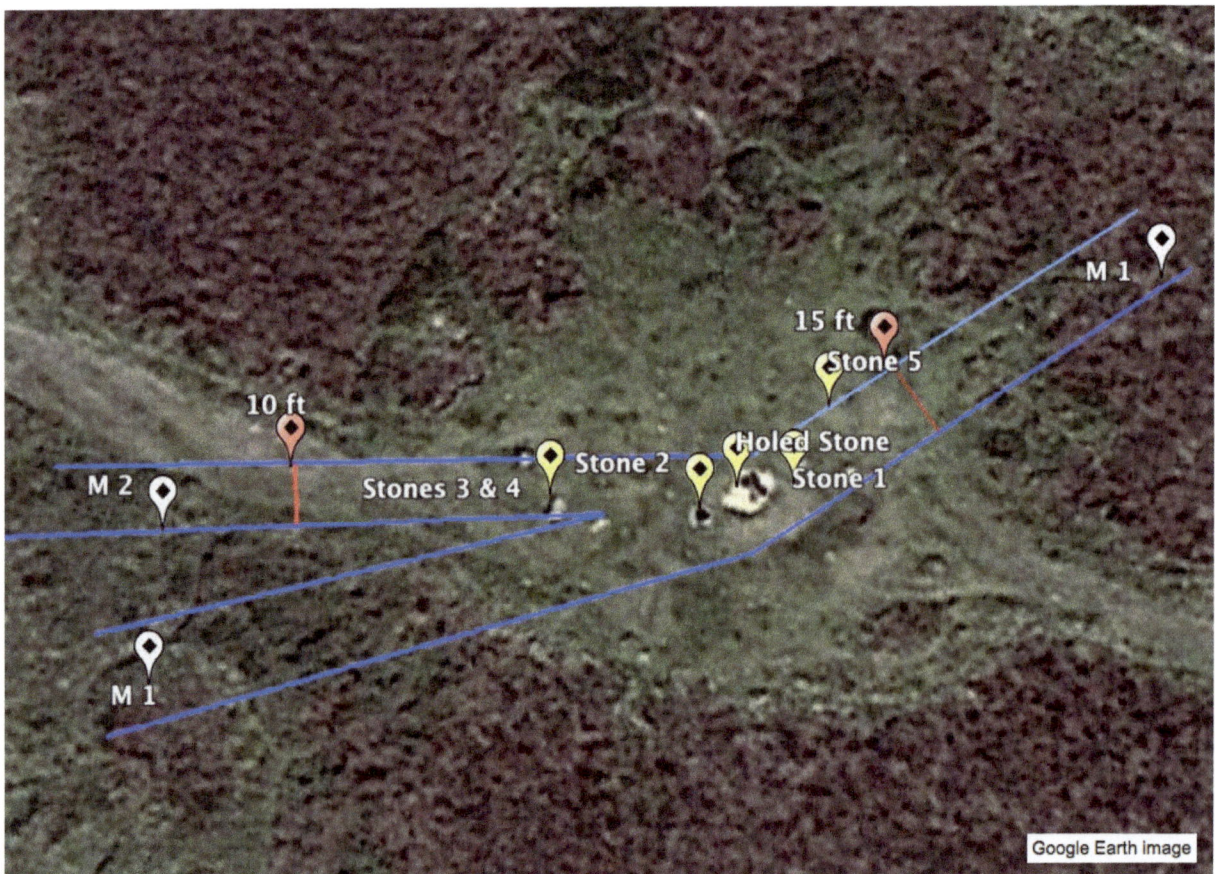

I circled the feature and located two areas of higher permeability which intersected it and labeled them M 1 and M 2. (Figures 70 & 71)

M 1 - 15 ft / 4.57 m wide. On the east side of the holed stone it trends at 238° SW and then curves to 255° SW on the south side.

M 2 - 10 ft / 3 m wide trending at 269° SW and intersects M 1 at the holed stone.

My data indicates the following:

1. When you compare my data with the plan drawn by William Borlase in 1749, it is possible that the western standing stone, stone 2, was located on M 2 rather than M 1 at that time.

2. The holed stone is centrally located where M 1 and M 2 intersect.

3. Stone 1, on east side of the holed stone, is centrally located on M 1.

4. Stones 3 and 4 are located along the width boundaries of M 2.

5. Stone 5 is located on the north width boundary of M 1.

Based on these correlations, the stones were specifically placed to map the intersection of M 1 and M 2. The holed stone and quoits appear to have the a similar function.

Figure

Unfortunately, I only had time to investigate one figure; however, the results were interesting.

Cerne Abbas Giant

WIKIPEDIA describes Cerne Abbas Giant as follows:

The Giant is located just outside the small village of Cerne Abbas in Dorset. The figure depicts a naked man and is of colossal dimensions, being about 55 metres (180 ft) high and 51 metres (167 ft) wide. It is cut into the steep west-facing side of a hill known as Giant Hill[2] or Trendle Hill.[3][4] Atop the hill is another landmark, the Iron Age earthworks known as the "Trendle" or "Frying Pan".[5] The figure's outline is formed by trenches cut into the turf about 0.6 metres (2 ft 0 in) deep, and filled with crushed chalk .[2] In his right hand the giant holds a knobbled club 37 metres (121 ft) in length,[6] and adding 11 metres (36 ft) to the total height of the figure.[7] A line across the waist has been suggested to represent a belt.[8] Writing in 1901 in the *Proceedings* of the Dorset Natural History and Archaeological Society, Henry Colley March noted that: "The Cerne Giant presents five characteristics: (1) It is petrographic ... It is, therefore, a rock carving ... (2) It is colossal ... (3) It is nude. ... (4) It is ithyphallic ... (5) The Giant is clavigerous. It bears a weapon in its right hand.[9]

A 1996 study indicated some features have changed over time, concluding that the figure originally held a cloak in its left arm and stood over a disembodied head.[10] The former presence of a cloak was corroborated in 2008 when a team of archaeologists using special equipment determined that part of the carving had been allowed to be obliterated. The cloak might have been a depiction of an animal skin, giving credence to the theory that the giant was a depiction of a hunter, or alternatively, Hercules with the skin of the Nemean Lion over his arm.[11] In 1993, the National Trust gave the Giant a "nose job" after years of erosion had worn it away.[12][13]

The Giant has been described as "renowned for its manhood",[14] "markedly phallic",[7] "sexually explicit"[15] and "ithyphallic".[16] The Giant sports an erection, including its testicles, some 11 metres (36 feet) long, and nearly the length of its head.[17] It has been called "Britain's most famous phallus";[18] one commentator noted that postcards of the Giant were the only indecent photographs that could be sent through the English Post Office.[19] However, this feature may also have changed over time. From a review of historical depictions of the figure, it has been identified that the Giant's current large erection is, in fact, the result of merging a circle representing his navel with a smaller penis during a 1908 re-cut: the navel still appears on a late 1890s picture postcard.[20] (WIKIPEDIA 2018)

At the time of this investigation, a fence enclosed the figure and hillfort. I walked around the fence and located two areas of higher permeability which cross this area. They were labeled G 1 and G 2. Therefore, I could not follow either flow across this area. Within the enclosure, the trend of G 1 and G 2 were projected based on their trend outside of the enclosure. Therefore, where G 1 and G 2 actually cross one another may be more in line with the figure than indicated by my drawing. (Figure 72)

G 1 - averaged 68 ft / 20.7 m wide trending at 73° NE.

G 2 - averaged 43 ft / 13 m wide 14° NE.

My data indicates the following:

1. The figure is just off the center of where G 1 and G 2 cross one another.

2. The figure is in line with the trend of G 1.

3. The left arm extension, head and middle of the club are located along the trend of G 2.

4. The hillfort henge / rampart is basically the width of G 1.

Figure 72: Cerne Abbas Giant, G 1 & G 2

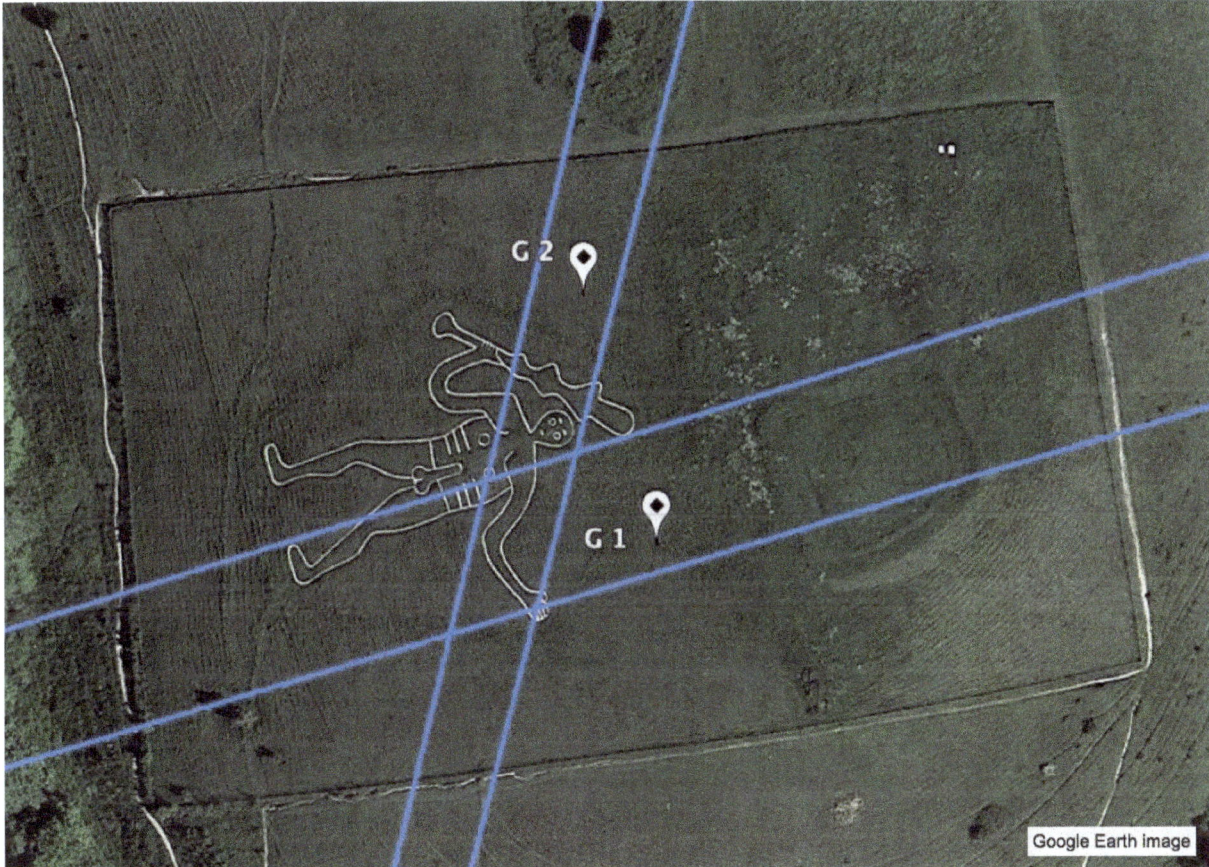

These observations are characteristic of the other features discussed above. They are aligned with areas of higher permeability within the groundwater, and so is the Giant. Based on these observations, the persons who originally constructed the Cerne Abbas Giant appear to have been aware of the two concentrated flows and orientated the giant accordingly. This observation suggests the origin of the figure may coincide with the construction of the hillfort or earlier. This figure reminded me of the Blythe figures located along the southern

Figure 73: Ometecuhtli / Orion / Male & G 1 - G 3, Blythe, CA

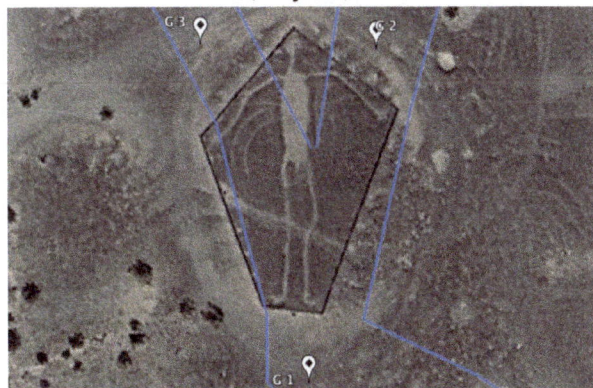

Colorado River Valley in the United States, as shown in Figure 73. The body of the figure is orientated along the trend of one concentrated flow, and the arms extend across the other two flows. In Peru, some of the biomorphic figures are also located along the trend of concentrated flows, for example, the whale.(Johnson 2009, 2019 and Papers on Ceremonial Landscapes 2018)

Petroglyphs

Cup

The cups I observed in England are basically the same type of feature referred to as cupules in the United States. Basically, their meaning remains a mystery, however all of cupolas I have documented are located on one or more areas of higher permeability. (Johnson 2009, 2019 and Papers on Ceremonial Landscapes 2018)

Tregiffian Burial Chamber

WIKIPEDIA describes Tregiffian Burial Chamber as follows:

The Tregiffian Burial Chamber (Cornish: *Hirvedh Treguhyon*)[1] is a Neolithic or early Bronze Age chambered tomb. It is a rare form of a passage grave, known as an Entrance grave . It has an entrance passage, lined with stone slabs, which leads into a central chamber. This type of tomb is also found in the neighbouring Isles of Scilly. The large stone grave, half of which was covered by a road in 1846, was, unlike Cornish quoits, for the most part covered with soil, with only the entrance exposed. From the edge of the site a passage, covered by four 3 m long stones, led to the 4-metre deep grave chamber. In front of the chamber, a cross-lying ornate stone, with cup-and-ring markings, formed a barrier. The original stone is in Truro, in the Royal Cornwall Museum, the local stone is a replica. Inside the tomb there was the chamber grave, which consisted of upright stones and a cover slab. Tregiffian probably formed a holy place with the Merry Maidens and other sites. (WIKIPEDIA 2018)

Figure 74: Tregiffian Burial Chamber

Figure 75: Tregiffian Burial Chamber & T 1

The burial chamber is located along the trend of T 1 which was 13 ft / 3.9 m wide trending at 7° N. (Figures 74 & 75) The width of the cross-lying ornate stone with cup and ring markings is nearly the width of T 1. In the United States, similar petroglyphs often extend across the width of the concentrated flow they are located on. (Johnson 2009, 2019 and Papers on Ceremonial Landscapes 2018)

Mounds And Barrows

The following is the definition for these terns provided by WIKIPEDIA.

A tumulus (plural tumuli) is a mound of earth and stones raised over a grave or graves. Tumuli are also known as barrows, burial mounds or kurgans, and may be found throughout much of the world. A cairn, which is a mound of stones built for various purposes, may also originally have been a tumulus. Tumuli are often categorized according to their external apparent shape. In this respect, a long barrow is a long tumulus, usually constructed on top of several burials, such as passage graves. A round barrow is a round tumulus, also commonly constructed on top of burials. The internal structure and architecture of both long and round barrows has a broad range, the categorization only refers to the external apparent shape. The method of inhumation may involve a dolmen, a cist, a mortuary enclosure, a mortuary house, or a chamber tomb. (WIKIPEDIA 2018)

All of the mounds I investigated are located along one or more area of higher permeability. (Figures 4 - 6, 24 - 25, 38 - 41) Like the other features discussed above, they share the similar characteristics with Native American great cairns and mounds. (Johnson 2009, 2019 and Papers on Ceremonial Landscapes 2018) However, in England, in some cases the mound's diameter is equal to the width of one of the concentrated flows, while others are wider or narrower than the width of the flow they are located on. For example:

Ballowall Barrow

WIKIPEDIA describes Ballowall Barrow as follows:

Ballowall Barrow (Cornish: *Krug Karrekloos*)[1] is a prehistoric funerary cairn (chambered tomb) which Ashbee (1982) and Hencken (1902–81) [2] state contains several phases of use from the Neolithic to the Bronze Age. It is situated on the cliff top at Ballowall Common, near St Just in Cornwall, England, UK. It is also known as Carn Gluze Barrow.[3]

It was first excavated in 1878 by William Copeland Borlase,[4] when it was discovered under mining debris. A report by Sharpe (1999)[3] states that there are several discrepancies in the accounts of the excavation work, some of the finds were lost and interpretation of the site is difficult. Reconstruction work which was done after the excavation to make the inside more accessible has further complicated the site. The site today is a confused mix of original and reconstructions introduced by Borlase.[5] The finds from excavations are in stored in museums at Truro, Cambridge and the British Museum. [6]

The barrow is 72 feet (22 m) in diameter. The Cornwall and Scilly Historic Environment Record describes it as a central domed structure, containing cists and with a pit beneath, surrounded by an outer cairn also containing cists. An entrance grave is located in the external side of the outer cairn. The construction of the site is unique in consisting of a combination of Neolithic and Bronze Age funerary rituals.[7] (WIKIPEDIA 2018)

I circled the barrow and located only one concentrated flow. (Figure 76)

B 1 - 40 ft / 12 m wide trending at 106° SE. Consistently, mounds and barrows were centrally located on the concentrated flow(s). At this site, the structure is sightly off set to the north. Perhaps this was a result of the site's reconstruction, a calculation error by those who constructed it or the concentrated flow curves slightly as it crosses the site. I did not enter the structure to determine if B 1 curves.

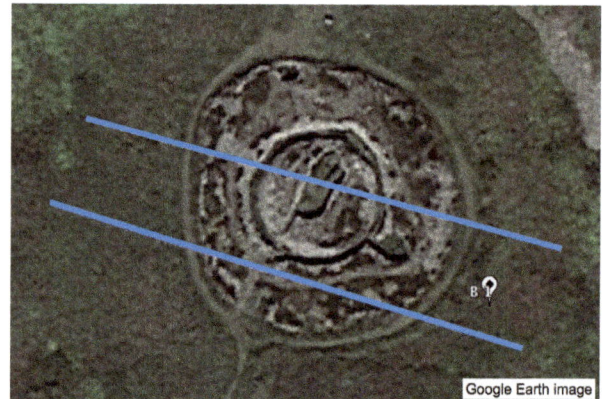

Figure 76: Ballowall Barrow & B 1

Drizzlecombe Mounds

During this survey I investigated twelve mounds that varied in size and were located on one or more concentrated flows. (Figures 4, 54, 61, 68 & 77) The results were as follows:

Mound 1 is located where A 1 and A 4 intersect. The mound's diameter is basically the width of A 1 which is 26 ft / 7.9 m; however, the width of A 4 is 20 ft / 6 m wide.

Mound 2 is located where A 3 and A 4 intersect. The mound's diameter is basically the width of A 3 which is 26 ft / 7.9 m; however, the width of A 4 is 20 ft / 6 m.

Mound 3 is located on A 4, and its diameter is basically 20 ft / 7.9 m wide which is equal to the width of A 4.

Mounds 4 and 5 are basically 15 ft / 4.57 m in diameter and are located on each width boundary of A 5 which is 50 ft / 15.2 m wide.

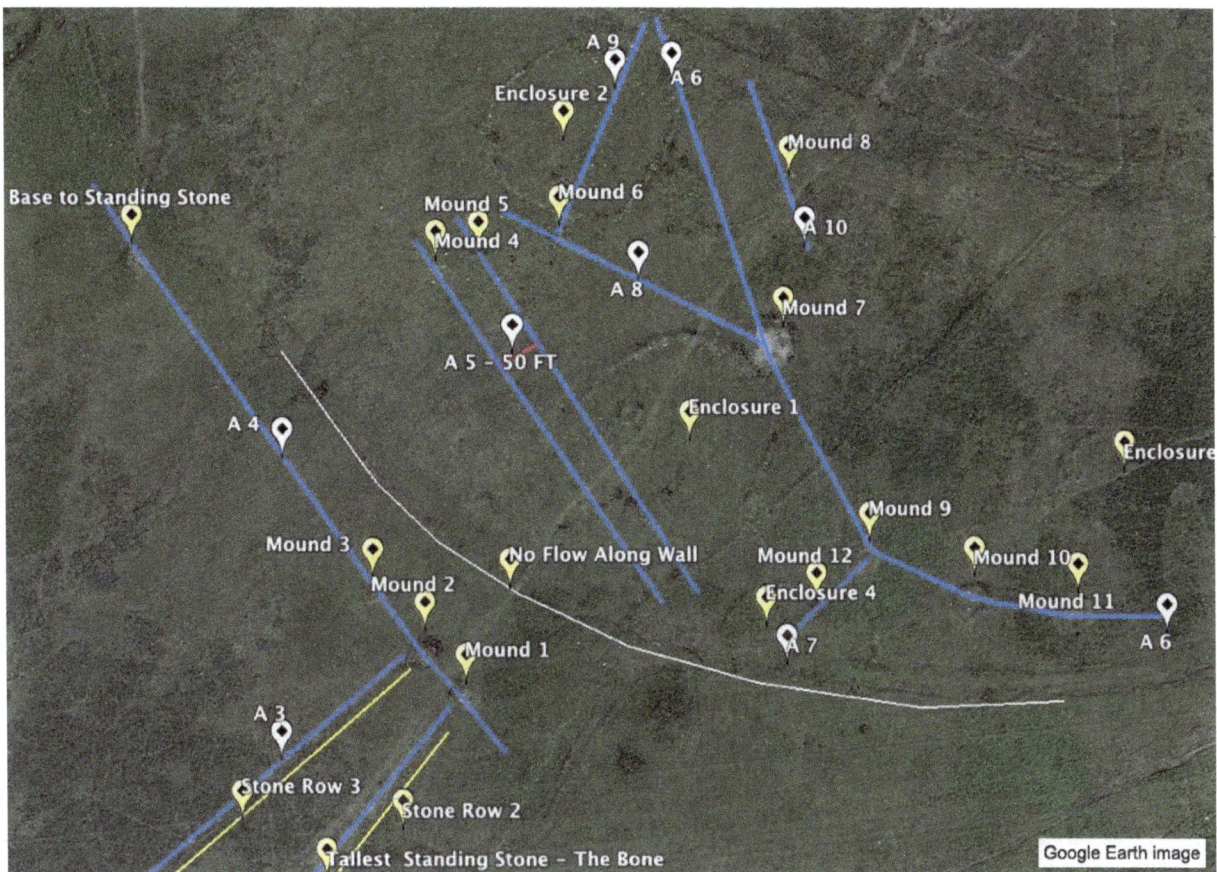

Figure 77: Drizzlecombe mounds 2 -11 & A 3 - 10

Mound 6 is located where A 8 and A 9 intersect. The diameter of mound 6 is basically equal to the widths of A 8 and A 9 which is 15 ft / 4.57 m wide.

Mound 7's diameter is approximately 50 ft / 15.2 m, which is basically the width of A 6 at that location. A 8 intersects A 6 at this mound.

Mound 8 is located on A 10, and its diameter is equal to the width of A 10 which is 26 ft / 7.9 m.

Mound 9's diameter is approximately 40 ft / 12 m, which is equal to the width of A 6. At this mound A 7 intersects A 6.

Mounds 10 and 11's diameters are basically 40 ft / 12 m wide which is equal to the width of A 6. Mounds 9 through 11 also map A 6's curving trend.

Mound 12 / Barrow / Giant Basin - This is a large mound which is located along A 2. A 2 was 76 ft / 23 m wide, which is basically equal to the diameter of mound 12.

91

In addition to cultural, spiritual and mortuary associations, mounds are located at specific locations along areas of higher permeability and indicate the following:

1. The trend of a concentrated flow(s).

2. The width of a concentrated flow(s).

3. Where concentrated flows intersect.

4. The change in a concentrated flow's width.

This is also true for mounds and great cairns in the United States. (Johnson 2009, 2019 and Papers on Ceremonial Landscapes 2018)

Throughout this research, I have been amazed at the similarity between various types of stone features and their vertical alignment with areas of higher permeability within the groundwater, in-spite of different historical periods, environments and cultures. As stated above, it is possible this was a universal human trait at that time.

Part 5

Megalithic Sites Of Carnac, France

Figure 78: Carnac's Megalithic Sites

Introduction

The region around Carnac, France contains some of the most iconic Neolithic megalithic sites in the world. In January 2020, I conducted a survey of various sites within the Carnac area. (Figure 78) I used the same methodology I have been using from the outset of this research. The focus of this preliminary survey was to determine if the megalithic sites are associated with concentrated flows / areas of higher permeability within the groundwater. Due to time restraints and the large concentration of sites in this region, I chose various sites based on their size and diversity. These sites have undergone considerable changes over thousands of years. Therefore, the remaining stones may represent only a fraction of those which existed when the site was constructed. All of the sites I documented were associated with one or more concentrated flows within the groundwater.

At Ménec, Kermario, Kerlescan and Erdeven, the areas of higher permeability are close together. Therefore, I color coded my lines to indicate the width boundaries of each flow. In-between lines with the same color, a concentrated flow was documented, and between different colored lines, I did not detect a concentrated flow. For example, Figures 86 & 92. The width of the concentrated flows are equal to the width of the standing stone lines they flow between. However, since the standing stones are located along the width boundary of the concentrated flows, I placed my lines next to the standing stones so they can be seen. At other sites, the concentrated flows' width boundaries are documented by paralleling blue lines on wide flows and a single line on narrow flows.

Since the terms associated with Carnac's megalithic sites also apply to southern England, please refer to pages 17 through 22 above. Please keep the following in mind. For menhirs, I used the term standing stone since I have used this term in other discussions in this text, as well as others. Another term to consider is cromlech. Paysages De Mégalithes discribes the term Cromlech as follows:

> CROMLECH [an English word borrowed from old Welsh: crom = bend, bent, twisted and lech = flat stone]: cromlech (sometimes written cromlec'h) is a term often used in everyday language to refer to circular enclosures of standing stones. Some scientists deem this term to be used improperly, as it is often used for quadrilaterals, ovals and semicircles as well as circles. (Paysages De Mégalithes 2020)

Within this discussion I referred to these enclosures as circles, squares, rectangles and quadrilaterals.

The following discusses my mapping of the concentrated flows associated with the megalithic sites and stone features I researched near Carnac.

The Ménec, Kermario and Kerlescan Alignments

These megalithic sites date to the Neolithic period and were constructed between 5,500 and 6,500 B.P.. (Centre des Monuments Nationaux 2020) Throughout the Neolithic period, humans favored symmetry and geometric shapes, rather than irregularity, in the construction of settlements, structures and monuments. However, when you analyze the standing stone alignments associated with the Ménec, Kermario and Kerlescan alignments, irregularity is apparent. This suggests the people who constructed these sites were aligning the standing stones with something that was not controlled by human design, but, perhaps, natural features which do not conform to symmetry. Consider the following observations.

Figure 79: Meandering stone lines

94

1. The stone lines meander along their length. (Figures 79 & 86) Since geological features, such as bedrock fractures and faults, can meander, the concentrated flows they conduct also meander.

2. Although the stone lines appear to parallel one another, the width between them is not consistent. (Figure 86) Since the width of geological features can vary, the width of the areas of higher permeability they conduct also very.

3. Some of them trend toward one another and eventually intersect. (Figure 89) Since geological features can intersect and cross one another, the concentrated flows they conduct also intersect one another.

4. Ménec, Kermario and Kerlescan are not aligned with one another. Although Ménec and Kermario trend southwestward, their trends are offset, and Kerlescan is orientated east-west. (Figure 80) This is also characteristic of geological features.

Figure 80: Ménec, Kermario and Kerlescan Alignments

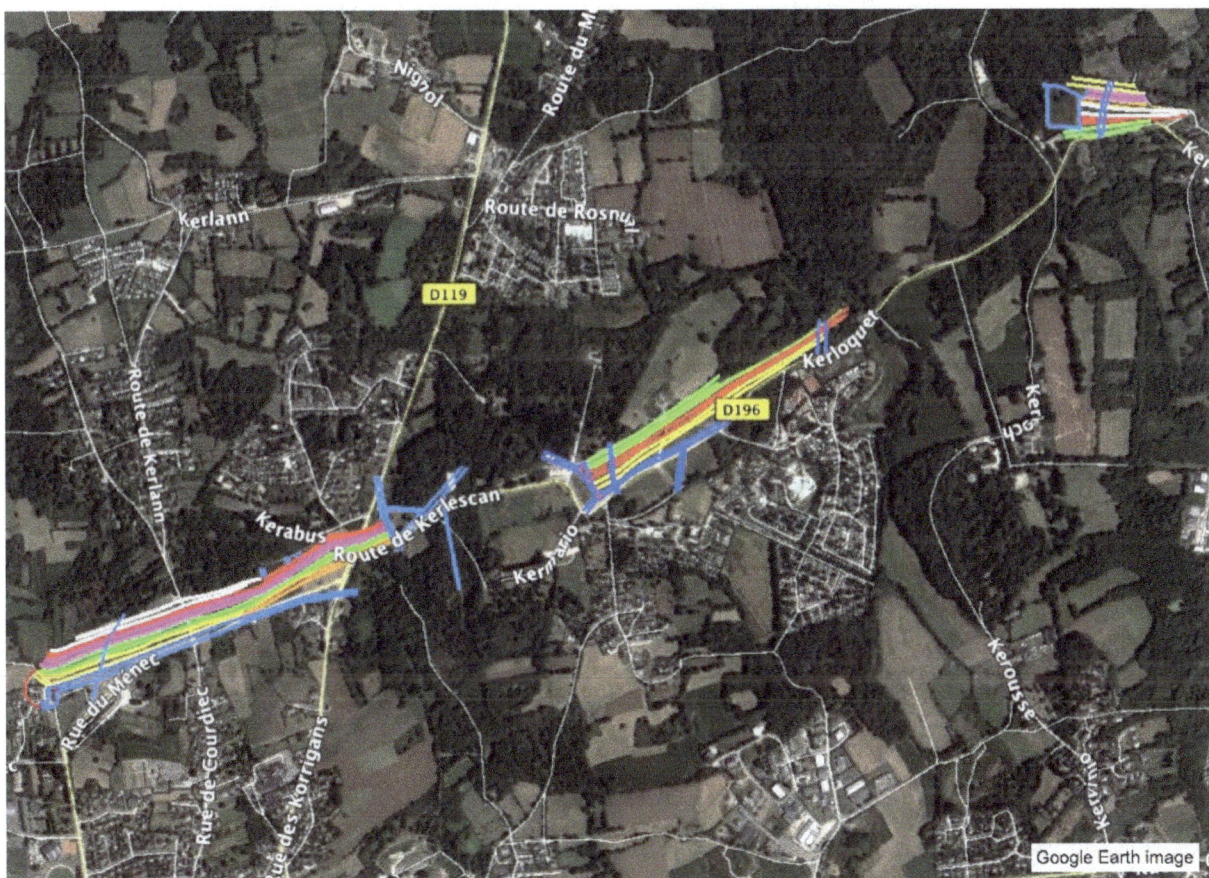

5. The standing stones and concentrated flows at Ménec and Kermario are relatively evenly spaced along the site's length and do not fan out on either end. This

suggests they may be associated with a geological feature which has a similar trend. At Kerlescan, the concentrated flows fan outward from east to west. This suggests they are transferring from one geological feature to another. For example, when a concentrated flow contained within a fault or fracture intersects a highly fractured area, it is no longer confined within a narrow feature. At Kerlescan the east-west concentrated flows may be entering a highly fractured area where two faults cross one another.

Figure 81: Tallest stones at the west end of Ménec

Within the fractured bedrock, it follows areas of least resistance and can form channels which branch from one another. (Figure 80)

6. At Ménec and Kermario and Kerlescan, the largest standing stones are on the western end with the shortest ones at the eastern end. (Figure 81) This could be indicating the flow pattern is toward the tallest concentration of standing stones.

7. Along the southwestern end of Ménec and Kermario and the east end of Kerlescan, the standing stone alignments stop abruptly; however, additional standing stones branch outward from these areas. (Figures 80, 91, 93 & 99) As mentioned above, geological features can intersect or cross one another which influences the concentrated flow pattern they conduct.

8. Outlier stone features, such as tumulus and dolmens, are orientated in various directions, and their size varies. Geological and hydrological features follow similar patterns.

These characteristics are similar to those documented at similar sites throughout the regions I have investigated. Within those regions, my data, as well as that of other researchers, has demonstrated an alignment between geological, hydrological and archaeological features

Before discussing the Ménec, Kermario and Kerlescan alignments, some observations need to be discussed regarding the local geology, the alignment's orientation with one another and the areas of higher permeability I documented.

Carnac is located just south of the South Armorican Shear Zone where a group northwest-southeast trending regional faults cross Brittany as shown in Figure 82. (WIKIPEDIA 2020) Within the Morbihan region, faults trend northwest-southeast and northeast-southwest. When their trend is extended, these faults cross the area near Carnac where the Ménec, Kermario and Kerlescan alignments are located as shown in Figure 83. (WIKIPEDIA 2020, Kreisberg 2018)

Figure 82: Geology of Brittany, France

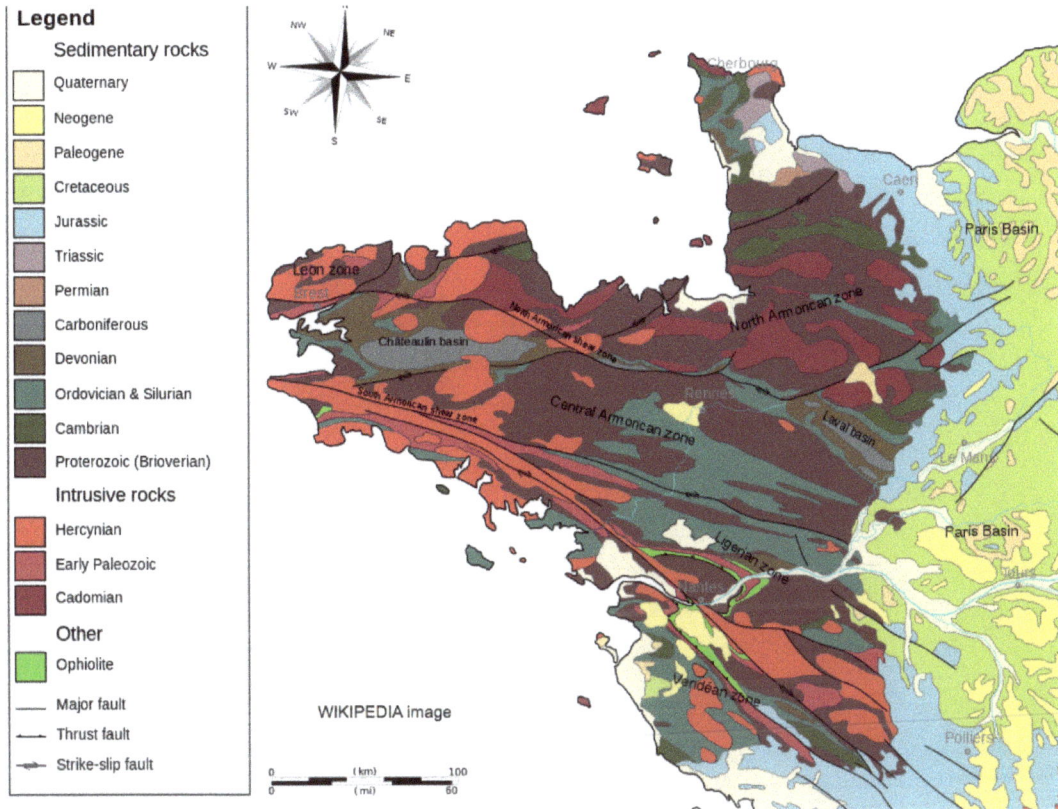

Legend

Sedimentary rocks
- Quaternary
- Neogene
- Paleogene
- Cretaceous
- Jurassic
- Triassic
- Permian
- Carboniferous
- Devonian
- Ordovician & Silurian
- Cambrian
- Proterozoic (Brioverian)

Intrusive rocks
- Hercynian
- Early Paleozoic
- Cadomian

Other
- Ophiolite
- Major fault
- Thrust fault
- Strike-slip fault

WIKIPEDIA image

Figure 83: Faults near Carnac, France

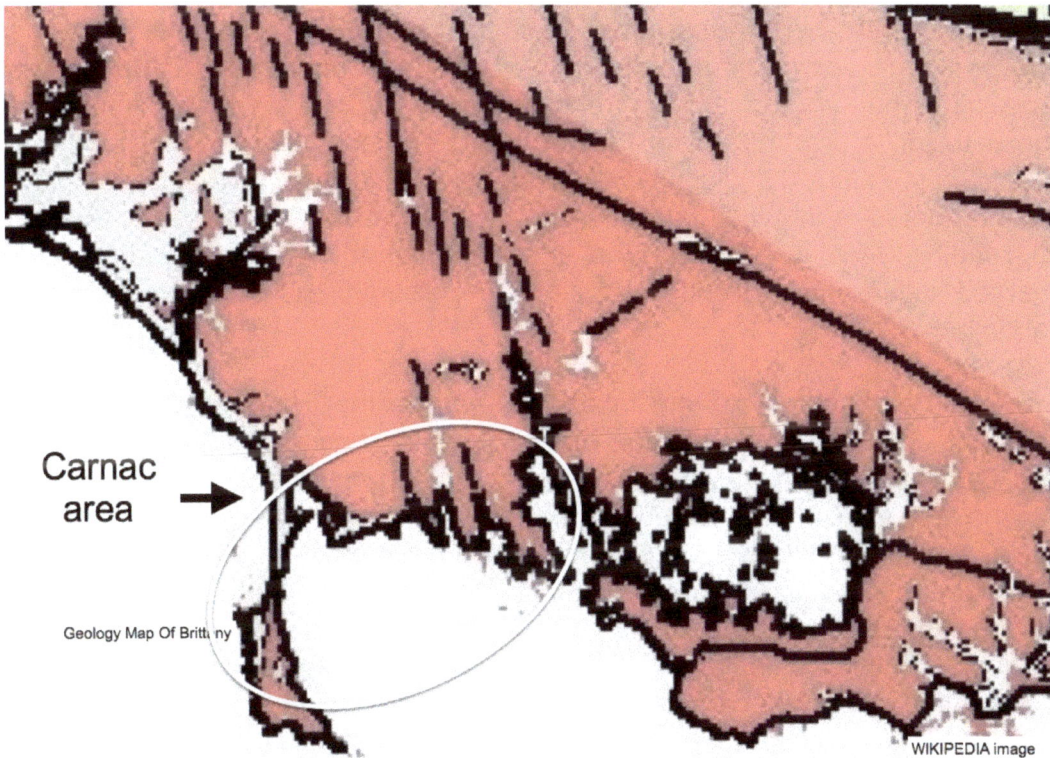

Carnac area

Geology Map Of Brittany

WIKIPEDIA image

97

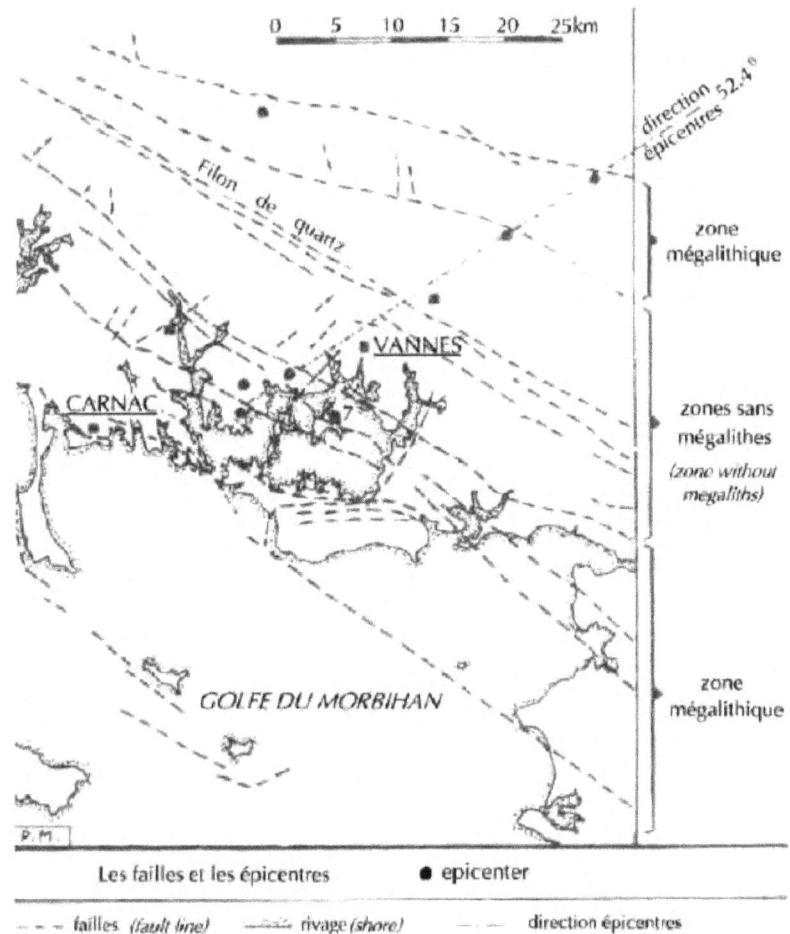

Figure 84: Faults & seismic activity near Carnac & Morbihan region,

(Kreisberg 2018, p. 259)

In Pierre Mereaum's publication, *Carnac: Stones For The Living*, his map, Figure 84, shows seismic activity and faults in the Morbihan region near Carnac. (Kreisberg 2018, p. 259) When you project the trend of the faults in Figure 83, some of them are very close to, or in alignment with, Ménec and Kermario. The only east-west trending fault identified in Figure 83 is located northeast of the Kerlescan alignment. It is possible an undocumented east-west fault crosses Kerlescan and intersects a north-south trending fault. When I compare the area of higher permeability flow patterns I documented with the fault trends and stone alignments, the data suggests there is a correlation between them.

The following five faults are inferred based on the trends of the faults identified on the geological maps for this region that I was able to access. I did not find any maps showing faults within the immediate area around Carnac. Therefore, I extended the trend of the fault lines on the accessed maps into the area where the Ménec, Kermario and Kerlescan alignments are located, thus they are inferred faults. I realize I have not provided specific scientific data regarding the existence of these faults. As mentioned above, the purpose of this text is to present my data which discusses another explanation for the stone feature's locations near Carnac. Then archaeologists, geologists and hydrologists can apply this data to their research.

To simplify the Ménec, Kermario and Kerlescan discussion, I have labeled the inferred faults associated with these sites as follows:

Fault 1 - northeast-southwest trend - extends along Ménec and Kermario
Fault 2 - northwest-southeast trend - crosses the circle at the southwest end of Ménec
Fault 3 - northwest-southeast trend - crosses between Ménec and Kermario
Fault 4 - east-west trend - crosses along the length of Kerlescan
Fault 5 - northwest-southeast trend - crosses the west end of Kerlescan

These inferred faults are identified by gray lines which are labeled faults 1 through 5. The lines for faults 1 and 5 are located along the north side of the standing stone alignments and concentrated flow lines to avoid confusion. Otherwise, they would be centered on the alignments. The lines for faults 2, 3 and 5 are located along their inferred trend. (Figures 86, 87, 92, 93, & 99)

1. The Ménec and Kermario standing stone alignments are very similar in appearance; however, they are not in alignment with one another. When you consider the fault patterns indicated on the geological maps of Brittany and Morbihan, there may be an explanation for this. (Figures 85 - 87) When you project the trend of fault 1 to the southwest, the Ménec and Kermario alignments appear to be located along it; however, they are not in alignment. The difference in the alignment could be associated with an offset along fault 1 which was caused by fault 3 where it crosses fault 1. If this is true, concentrated flows C 21 to C 25 along fault 1 could be transferring into fault 3. It could also cause subsurface ponding where C 20 is located. Then, some of the groundwater within the ponding flows out along C 18 and C 19 and connects with C 16, and perhaps C 1, which transfers some of the groundwater back into fault 1 at the northeast end of the Ménec alignments. The groundwater then flows along C 1 through 6 and C 9 to the southwestern end of Ménec. The standing stone patterns appear to support this observation. (Figures 80, 90 - 93) For example, the standing stone alignments along C 21 though C 25 stop; however, the stones along C 18 and the dolmen on C 19 extend outward from the other stone alignments. This suggests a change in direction. The concentrated flows I documented follow this pattern. My colleagues and I documented a similar pattern along the Nasca River in Peru. (Johnson 2009, Chapter 3, Part 2, pp. 33 - 39)

2. Where the stone circle is located along the southwestern end of Ménec alignments, the standing stones along C 1 through C 6 change direction. C 1 turns southward and then westward, while C 2 through C 6 turn northwestward. (Figures 9 & 10) Southwest of this location there are no similar standing stone alignment concentrations like Ménec or Kermario. My data suggests fault 2 is crossing fault 1 and diverts C 2 through C 6 from fault 1 into fault 2. These flow patterns are discussed below.

3. The geology map in Figure 83 indicates an east-west trending fault is located northeast of the Kerlescan alignments. Considering its trend, it is possible an undocumented east-west fault is associated with the Kerlescan alignments and a

northwest-southeast fault crosses it. I placed inferred fault 4 along the alignment and fault 5 crossing the eastern end. If this is true, the east-west standing stone alignments are along fault 4, and the ponding along the western end is associated with fault 5 which crosses fault 4. This is very similar to what happens at the southwestern end of Kermario. This is discussed below.

4. The orientation of the standing stones from smallest to largest along the Ménec, Kermario and Kerlescan alignments could indicate the direction the concentrated flows are taking along the faults they are associated with.

The Ménec Alignments

The Ménec standing stone alignments consist of 1,050 standing stones which extend for .64 mi / 1.02 km. (Centre des Monuments Nationaux 2020) The western end has the tallest stones forming eleven rows, and the eastern end has shorter stones forming 8 rows. (Figures 85 - 87) On the west end, the stone lines stop where there is a large stone circle and a farm, which could have destroyed some of the original standing stones. On the east end, the lines end where there is a row of stones extending across them, which does not appear to be badly damaged.

Figure 85: The Ménec Alignments

To determine if there are concentrated flows associated with this megalithic site, I dowsed around it as much as possible, as well as, across it, within areas open to the public. During January most of the site is accessible. At the western end, I documented six concentrated flows which are shown on my map. The following discusses my observations along this section from west to east.

1. The standing stones and concentrated flows associated with this alignment appear to follow the trend of fault 1 which appears to cross this area, as shown on the mining map for Brittany. (Geological Formations Of The Main Mines in Brittany 2020, Geology Map Of Brittany 2020, Figure 83) Normally, when I dowse across the trend of a fault, I locate a single concentrated flow which is conducted along it. However, at this site, I located a group of concentrated flows which coincided with the fault's projected trend and closely paralleled one another. In comparison to other sites I have researched, this pattern is very unusual and suggests this is why those who constructed this site chose this location. As mentioned above, during this time, unique and / or unusual geological and hydrological features were documented by locating megalithic or important cultural sites on them.

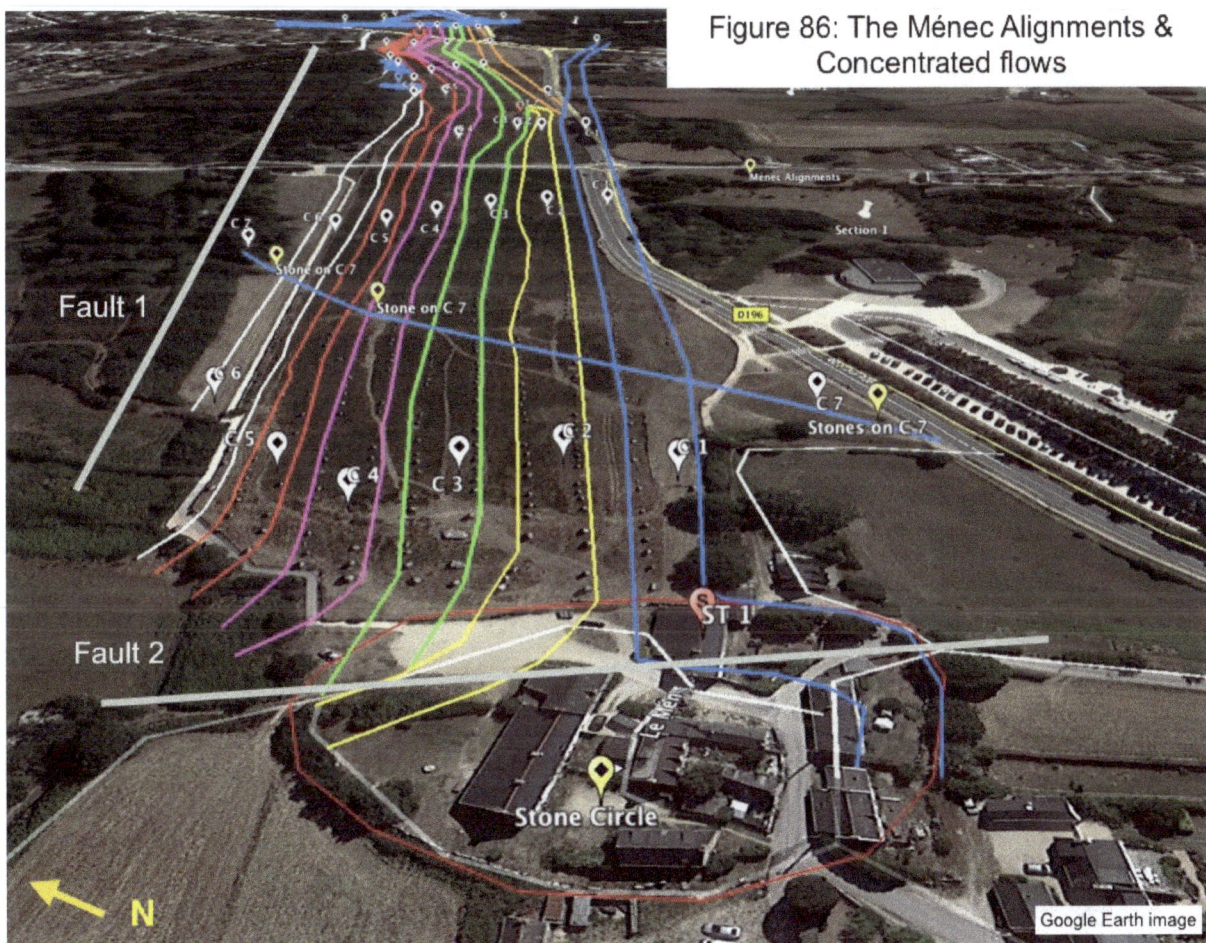

Figure 86: The Ménec Alignments & Concentrated flows

Figure 87: The western end of the Ménec Alignments & concentrated flows

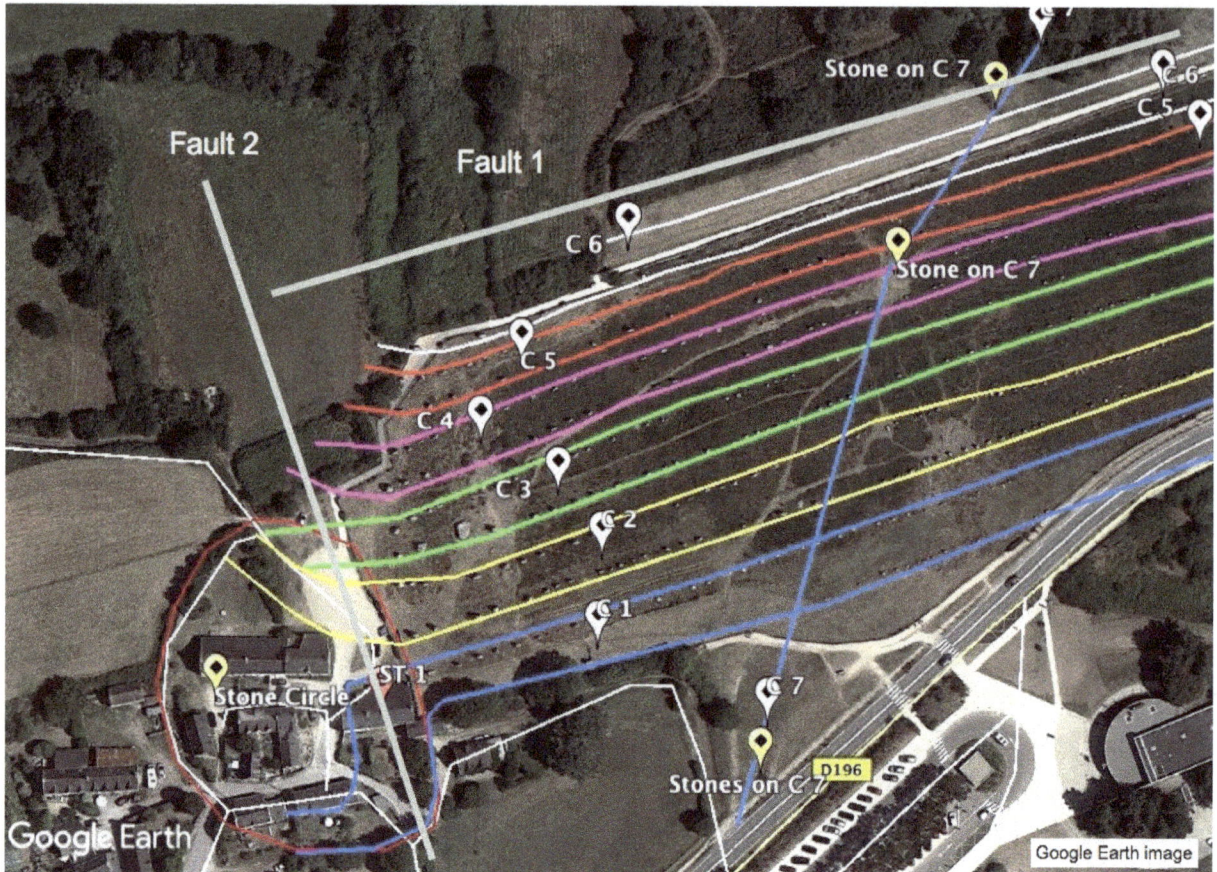

2. Along the western end of this alignment, there is a large stone circle. (Figure 87) During my research in other regions, I have encountered large circles and discussed them in my publications. Often, large stone circles are located where a concentrated flow's course curves or turns sharply. At this location, the flow pattern of C 1 through 6 begins to change direction where the stone circle is located. Unfortunately, I did not have permission to investigate the area along the west side of the circle. It is possible subsurface ponding occurs in this area which is similar to the western end of the Kermario and Kerlescan alignments, which are discussed below. In addition to this function, stone circles, depending on size and construction, document a variety of characteristics in regard to concentrated flows within the groundwater. Some are located on one or two flows, while others indicate where a group of concentrated flows merge and / or intersect.

3. At the western end the stone lines, C 1 intersects a farm structure (ST 1) and the parking lot without curving. However, immediately adjacent to ST 1's east wall, C 1 turns sharply southward and then curves back to a westerly direction. (Figures 85 - 88) This course change in C 1 follows the curvature of the lower southeast side of the stone circle. Where C 1 intersects the stone circle's perimeter, the line of stones along ST 1's east wall cross the width of C 1. At Erdeven, which is discussed below,

102

a similar pattern was observed along E 2 and E 3. At that location, a similar course change occurs along E 3, and stones extend across the width of E 3 indicating this. Where concentrated flows turn sharply, I have observed this same stone pattern in the United States within Native American ceremonial stone landscapes. Consider the following. Unlike C 2 through 6, C 1 does not flow along the length of the site. Near 494065.84 m E, 5271085.50 m N, it curves into alignment with C 2 through 6 from the

Figure 88: Southern width boundary of C 1

east, and C 9 merges with it. This suggests C 1 is at a different depth within the bedrock and / or being influenced by another geological feature other than fault 1. Then, where C 1 intersects the stone circle, it diverts to the south and then back to a westerly flow pattern within a short distance. This suggests that C 1's course is being influenced by fault 2, which is also influencing C 2 through 6. However, C 1 is not being diverted to the northwest like C 2 though C 6. Unfortunately, I was not able to follow C 1 further west to determine its trend.

4. Also, the paralleling lines of standing stones associated with C 2 through C 6 begin to curve to the northwest just before they intersect the stone circle. (Figures 85 - 87) Because of private land, I could not follow them beyond the parking lot. However, I have observed similar patterns at sites in other regions. If fault 2 is crossing fault 1, it could be redirecting the course of C 2 through C 6 northwestward along its course. It is possible ponding is occurring where the stone circle is located; however, I was unable to ground survey that area.

5. A similar geological pattern appears to be occurring along the northeastern end of this alignment where eight rows of standing stones end abruptly. (Figures 89 & 90) At this location, C 9 and C 3 through 5 intersect C 14 and do not cross it. This indicates they branch from C 14, which was 18 ft / 5.48 m wide. The western width boundary of C 14 is mapped by the standing stones at the end of the rows associated with C 9 and C 3 through 5. C 14's eastern width boundary is documented by a row of stones extending from Route de Kerlescan to the stone wall and hedge located at 494438.41 m E, 5271337.83 m N where there are three stones located across its width. From this location, C 14 trends northwestward along fault 3.

6. Along the southwest end of the Kermario alignments, the groundwater from C 21 to 25 could be entering fault 3 and ponding. Within the ponding area, the water could collect until it encounters a fault or fracture which acts as an outlet. Along the southwestern end of Kermario, the outlets are C 18 and C 19. Then, C 18 and C 19 intersect geological features which are trending towards the Ménec alignments and

intersect C 16 which contributes groundwater to Ménec. Thus, as mentioned above, groundwater flows out of fault 1 into fault 3, and then back into fault 1.The stone features appear to support this observation, as follows. (Figures 89, 90 93)

Figure 89: The eastern end of the Ménec Alignments

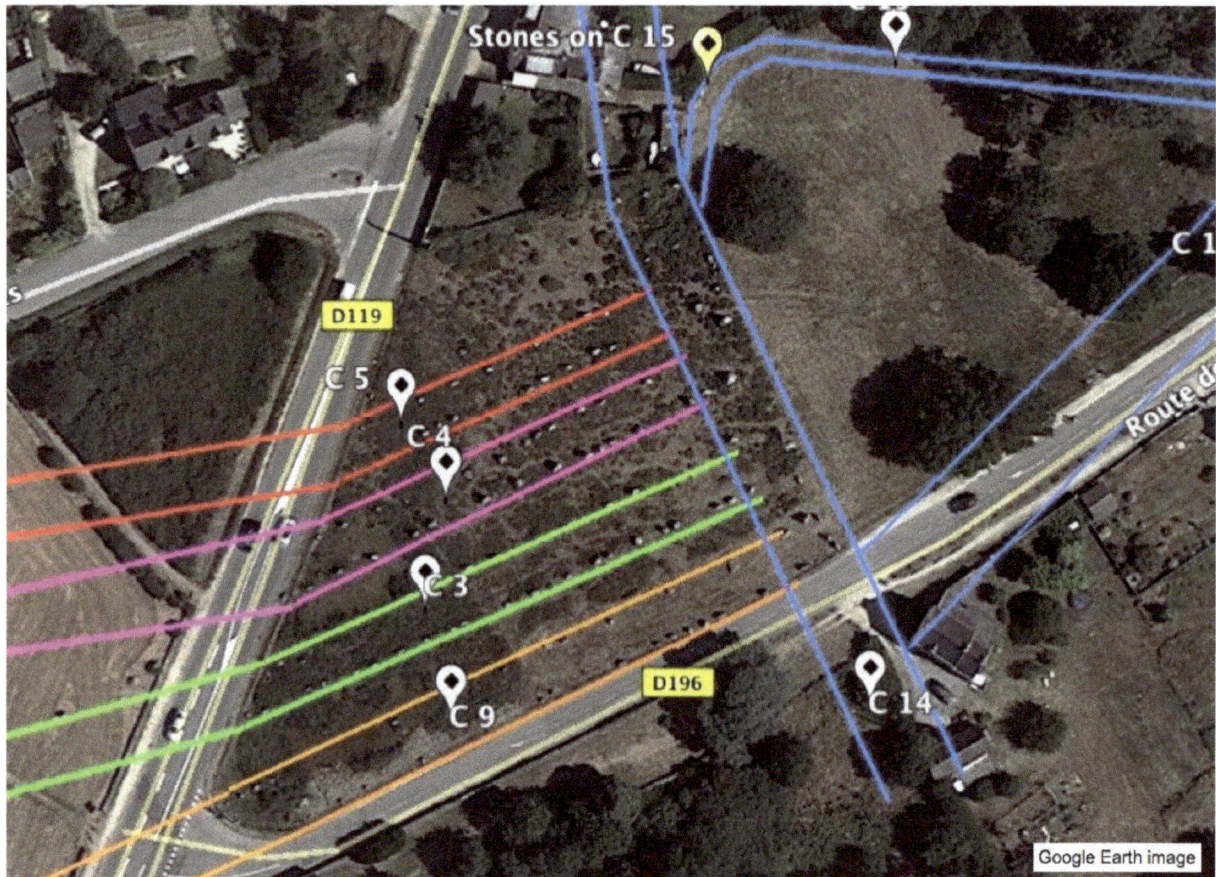

7. Along the northeastern end of Ménec, C 15, which was 20 ft / 6 m wide, intersects C 14 and merges with it. (Figures 89 & 90) Only a few standing stones are located along C 15; however, they indicate where it curves and intersects C 14. The stones are located alongside the wall and hedge located at 494443.87 m E, 5271351.75 m N. C 15 then curves sharply and intersects C 16. Some of the references suggested there is a stone circle located at this end of the site, although I am not aware of its location. The stones along the wall and hedge mentioned above appear as the partial remains of a stone circle; however, they are located along the north width boundary of C 15.

8. C 16 was 25 ft / 7.6 m wide and intersects C 14 immediately adjacent to the intersection of C 9 and C 14, but does not cross C 14. (Figures 89 & 90) I followed C 16 northeastward to the parking lot and located four standing stones along it, which I labeled L Stone 1 through 4. L Stone 1 and 2 are located on the north and south width boundaries of C 16, and L Stone 1 is also located where C 15 branches from

104

it. L Stone 3 is located along the south width boundary of C 16, and where C 17 intersects it. L Stone 4 is located on C 17. When you project the trend of C 16, it appears as though it intersects C 18. If C 16 and C 18 intersect, they connect the Ménec and Kermario alignments.

Figure 90: C 14, 15 16 & 17 along east end of the Ménec Alignments

9. The stone line along the northern width boundary of C 6 has been destroyed. At 494090.17 m E, 5271167.68 m N, C 6 merges with C 5, and the width of C 5 widens for a short distance at this location. (Figures 85 - 87 & 91)

10. C 2 merges with C 3 at 494070.56 m E, 5271102.69 m N immediately south of structure 2 (ST 2). The stone line along C 2's south width boundary curves to where it intersects C 3's southern width boundary and stone line. (Figure 91)

11. C 9 extends from C 14 on the site's eastern end to where it merges with C 1 along Rue du Ménec and immediately south of structure ST 2 at 494061.70 m E, 5271079.58 m N. (Figures 89 & 91)

12. Labels C 8 and C 13 are not included since they were a continuation of one of the previously labeled concentrated flows. Therefore, these labels were dropped.

105

Figure 91: Where concentrated flows merge within the Ménec Alignments

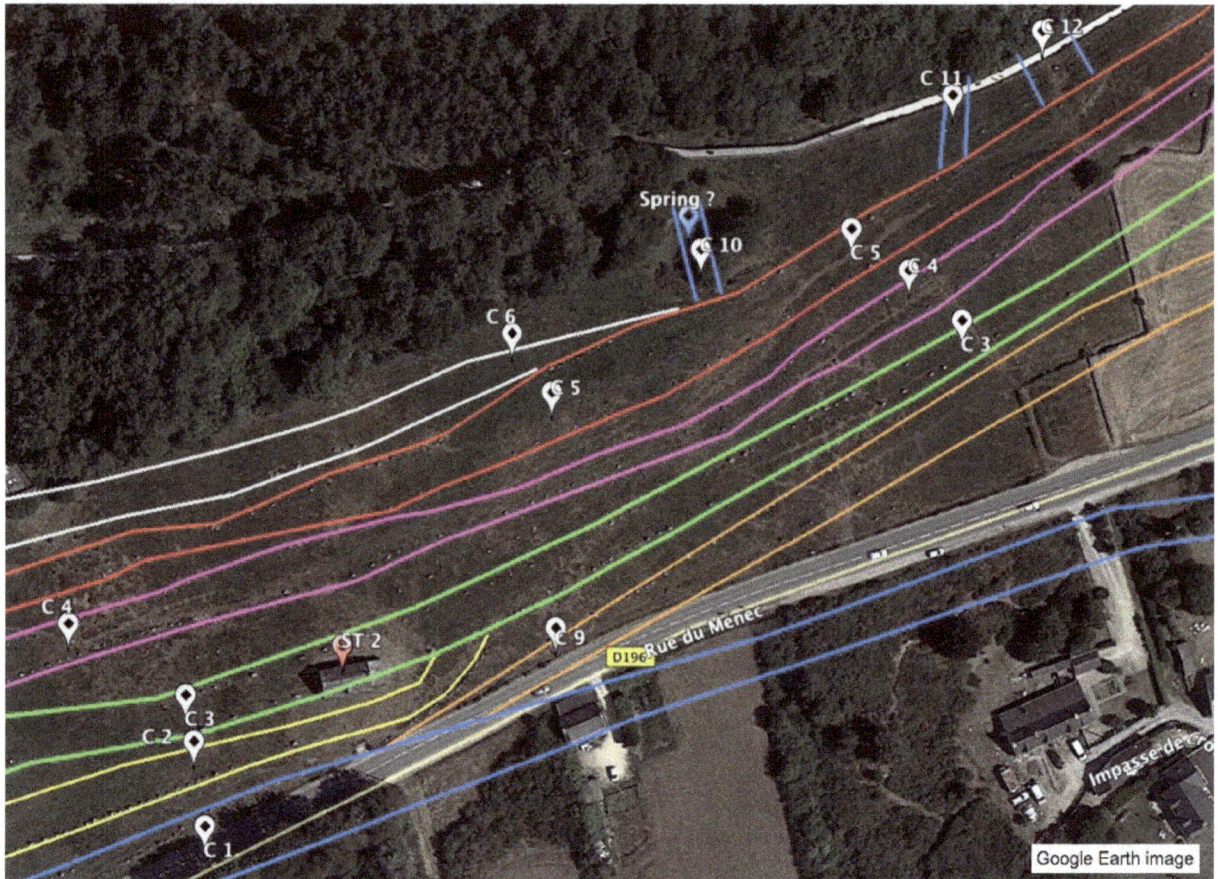

13. Between the farm and parking lot on the southwestern end and D119, I documented 4 concentrated flows which intersected or crossed the stone lines associated with C 1 through C 6. These concentrated flows are labeled C 7 and 10 through 12.

   a. C 7 was 6 ft / 1.8 m wide, crossed the site and was mapped by stone features. (Figures 86 & 87) On the south side, at 493692.59 m E, 5270889.68 m N, which is by D196, there are a few stones which appear to be a damaged marker. These stones are centrally located on C 7. Although I did not have access to the area where there is a tall standing stone at 493730.00 m E, 5271030.00 m N, the trend of C 7 suggested it is located along it. On the north side of the site, at 493758.63 m E, 5271077.86 m N, there is a stone wall with a larger stone on the end which is located on C 7. The trend of C 7 curves slightly while crossing the site. Since C 7 crosses C 1 through C 6, it suggests it is at a different depth than the other flows.

   b. C 10 intersects the site at 494131.16 m E, 5271186.91 m N, which is where C 6 branches from C 5. C 10 was 17 ft / 5.18 m wide. There is a small pond at this location, which could be a spring, and a stone on each width boundary of C 10. (Figure 91)

c. C 11 intersects C 5 at 494191.95 m E, 5271217.46 m N and was 20 ft / 6.9 m wide. I followed its trend for a short distance; however, it appears that C 11 and C 12 intersect just north of the site. (Figure 91) Three of the stones located there are on the width boundaries of C 11, and the one on the east side is just off the flow.

d. C 12 intersects C 5 at 494221.17 m E, 5271235.03 m N and was 40 ft / 12 wide. There are three stones located on C 12. Two are on the width boundaries of C 12, and one is centrally located on the flow. (Figure 91)

14. The increase in size and height of the standing stones from east to west could indicate the direction of the flow pattern is from northeast to southwest.

The Kermario Alignments

Before I discuss this alignment, it is important to mention that I was unable to ground survey the following sections: between La Petite Métairie Road and the tower located at 495366.43 m E, 5271685.00 m N, and from near the house located at 495655.37 m E, 5271828.09 m N and the horse farm at 496160.53 m E, 5272250.71 m N. However, the areas I ground surveyed provided important data which can be applied to these sections.

Figure 92: The Kermario Alignments

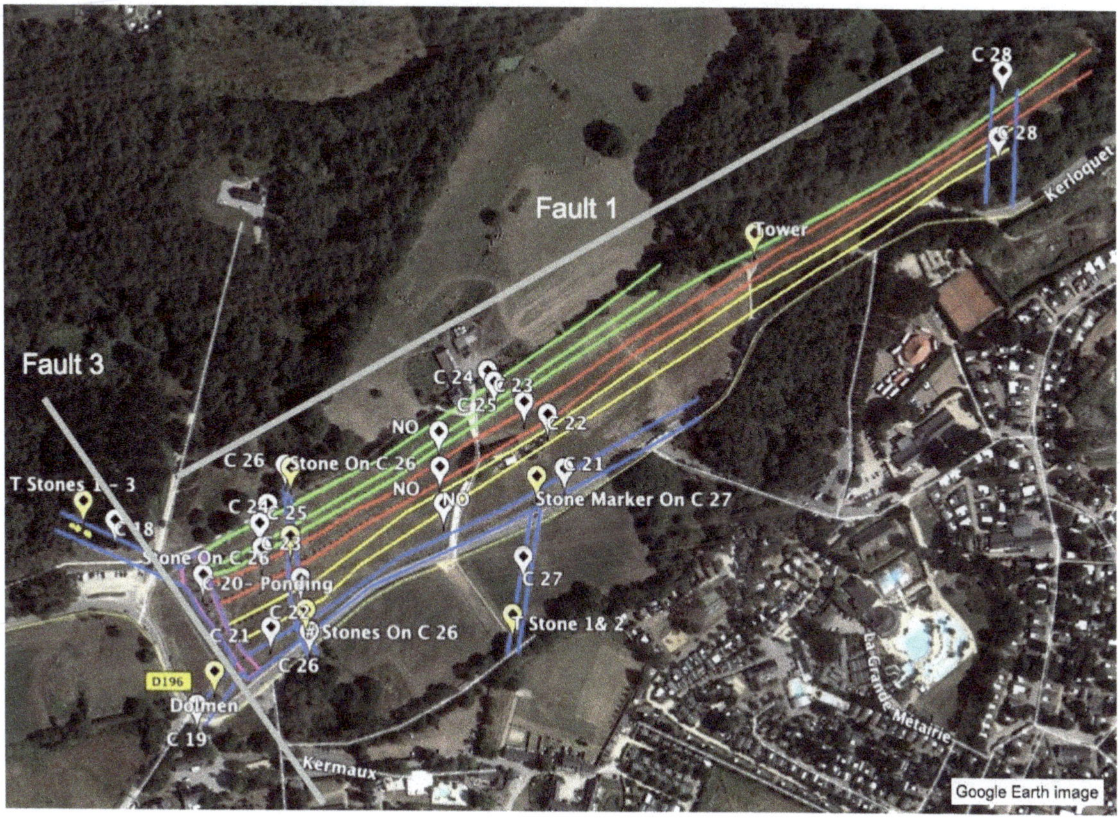

The Kermario alignments is reported to have 1029 standing stones in lines which extend for at least .67 mi / 1.08 km. (Centre des Monuments Nationaux 2020) When you observe this site in Google Earth, the western end draws your attention since the stone lines suddenly end. However, when you add the concentrated flows to this site, you realize it continues to the northwest and southwest along two concentrated flows. The following discusses the data I gathered during the ground survey of this site. (Figure 92)

1. As mentioned above, the Kermario and Ménec alignments are not in alignment with one another; however, they appear to be connected by C 16 and C 18. The offset in their alignment could be due to an offset in fault 1 which was caused by fault 3 crossing it. (Figure 80)

2. Along the standing stone alignments, I documented five concentrated flows which are labeled C 21 through C 25. Each flow has a line of stones along each width boundary indicating their width and course. These alignments appear to correspond to the trend of fault 1. (Figures 92 & 93)

Figure 93: West end of the Kermario Alignments

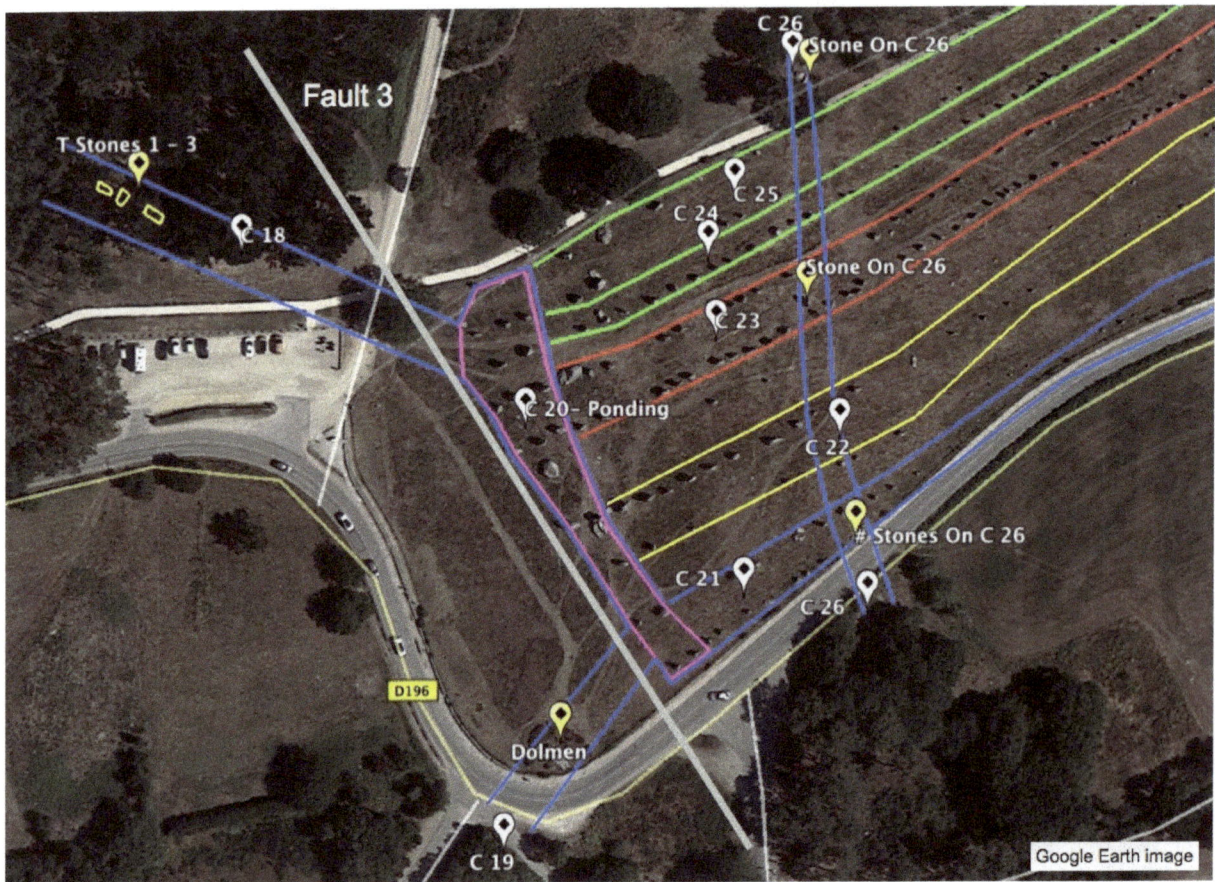

108

3. C 24 and 25 are unusual since they are located along a single concentrated flow; however, there is a line of stones separating them. (Figures 92 & 93) The southern and northern green lines are the width boundaries of the flow, and the middle line marks the center of the flow. I divided this flow into two separate ones since it is possible one side of the flow is intermittent. I have seen this before where I had the opportunity to survey a similar concentrated flow during different seasons. During the dry season, one section of the flow can dry up while the other section continues to conduct water.

4. I labeled the area along the southwestern end of the site C 20 for the following reason. (Figures 92 & 93) As indicated by the width boundary markers of C 21 through 25, the area between them did not have a concentrated flow. However, at the west end of these lines, the area labeled C 20 indicated there is a concentration of groundwater, as indicated on my map. This suggests the groundwater being conducted along C 21 through C 25 is intersecting a geological feature which appears to be fault 3, which is causing subsurface ponding in this area. Then, there are two outlets for the ponding, C 18 and C 19.

5. C 18 was 59 ft / 18 m wide and extends from C 20 thus serving as an outlet. (Figures 92 & 93) Within a short distance there are three large stones which are centrally located on it. I did not follow C 18 beyond these stones. It appears that C 18 intersects C 16, as mentioned above.

6. C 19 also serves as an outlet for C 20. It was 32 ft / 9.75 m wide and trends to the southwest. (Figures 92 - 94) The dolmen located on it, at 494956.91 m E, 5271355.93 m N, is orientated across the width of C 19, and its length is equal to the width of C 19. Dolmens are discussed below.

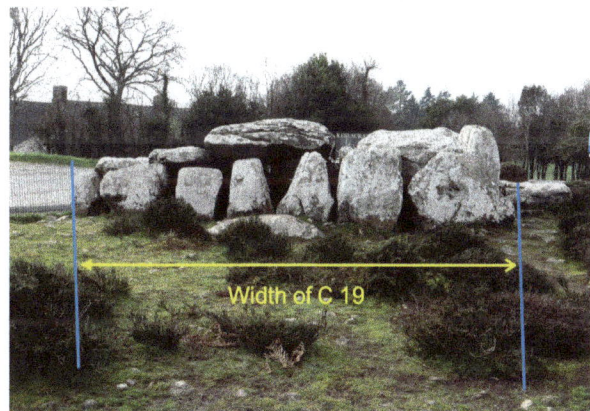
Figure 94: Kermario Dolmen & C 19

7. C 26 was 15 ft / 4.5 m wide and crosses the site. (Figures 92 - 93) While researching sites in other regions, I realized where concentrated flows intersect an important site, like this one, there are stone features identifying that location. Then, if it crosses the site, there are additional stones mapping its trend across the site. Where C 26 intersects the site, there is a large stone at 495013.84 m E, 5271509.67 m N, which is centrally located on C 26. This is by the wood platform. Then, at 495015.96 m E, 5271460.00 m N, there is a large tall stone that appears to be out of alignment; however, it is centrally located on C 26. On the south side of the site, at 495027.73 m E, 5271405.57 m N, there is a stone on each width boundary of C 26, and one centrally located on it. When you know what to look for, this type of pattern clearly indicates where flows intersect or cross one another.

8. Another example of an intersection marker is located at 495203.00 m E, 5271505.00 m N along the south width boundary of C 21. At this location, C 27 intersects C 21. (Figures 92, 95 - 96) This group of tall standing stones is not in alignment with the south width boundary of C 21. It is located next to it and centrally located on C 27. Then, when you follow the trend of C 27, it takes you to the two tall standing stones located at 495185.00 m E,

Figure 95: Tall standing stones where C 27 intersects C 1

5271403.00 m N, which are located on the width boundaries of C 27. I could not determine whether or not C 27 crosses the site since this section was closed to the public on that day, and I could not walk along the northern boundary of the site due to private land.

Figure 96: Intersection of C 21 & C 27

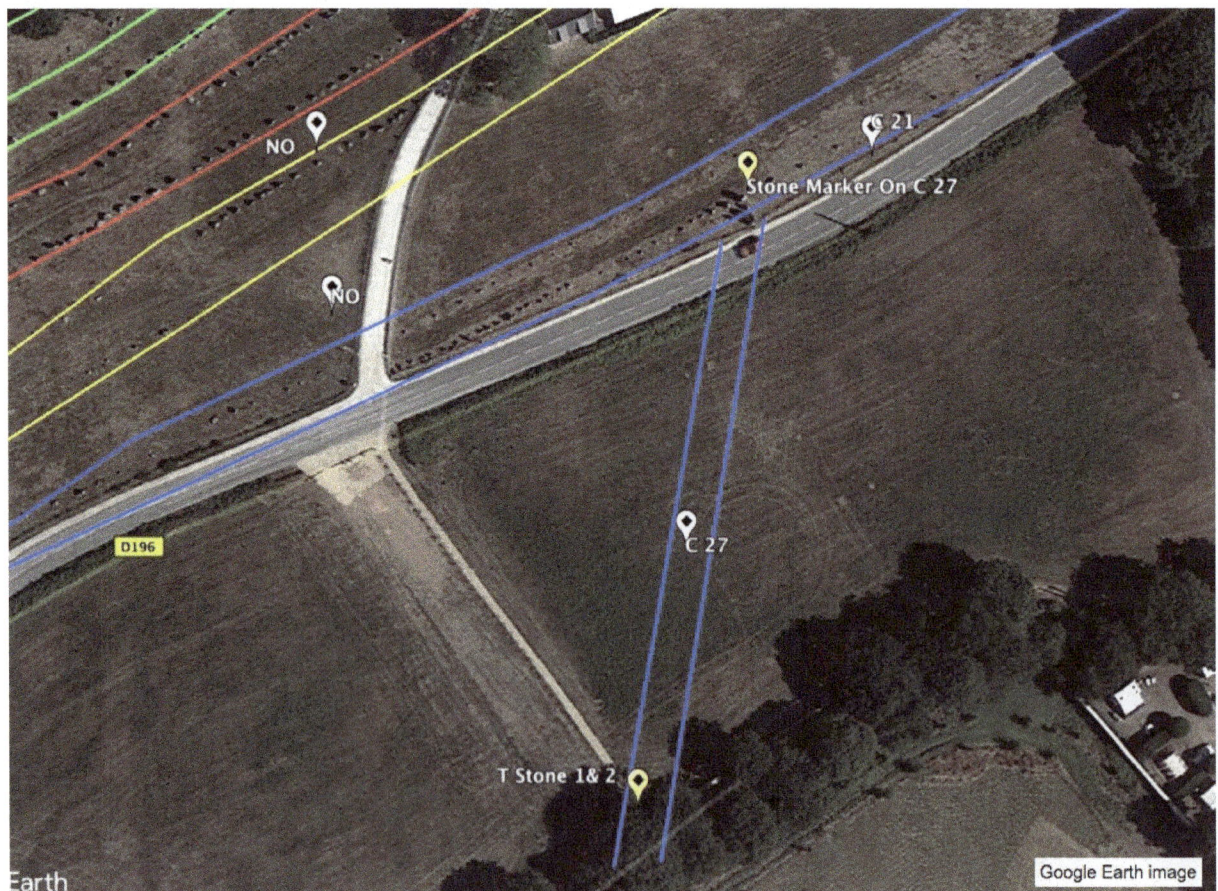

110

9. C 28 was the only other area of higher permeability I located that crossed the site. It was 65 ft / 19.8 m wide, on average, while narrowing on the site's south side. Where it intersects the site's north boundary, there is a line of stones across its width at 495558.00 m E5271809.00 m N. (Figures 92 & 97)

Figure 97: Where C 28 crosses the Kermario Alignments

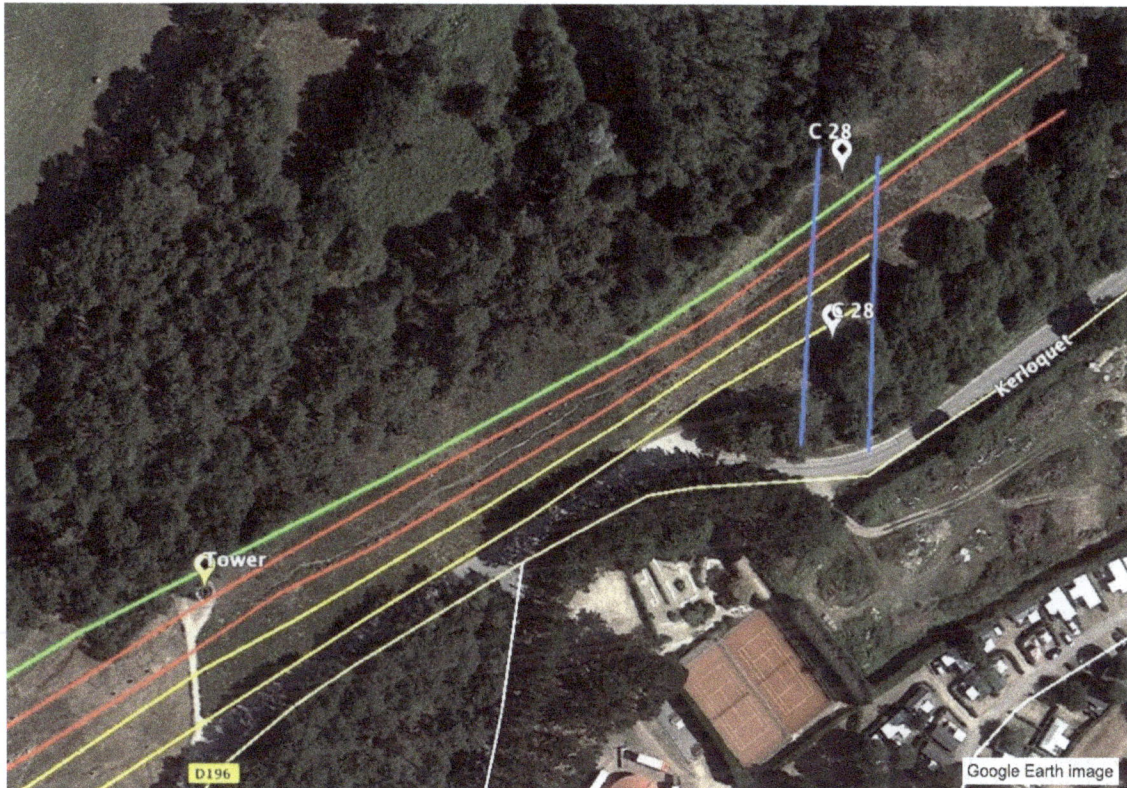

10. When you project the trend of C 22 through 25 to the northeast, they appear to intersect C 36, thus connecting Kermario with the Kerlescan alignments. (Figures 80 & 96)

The Kerlescan Alignments

The Kerlescan alignments were open to the public, and I was able to ground survey the site. This is an amazing site, and I am very glad I had access to it. Figures 98 and 99 show the site without and with the concentrated flows.

1. The standing stones increase in size from east to west. As mentioned above, this may be indicating the direction of flow from east to west. (Figure 98)

Figure 98: The Kerlescan Alignments

Figure 99: The Kerlescan Alignments, concentrated flows & inferred faults

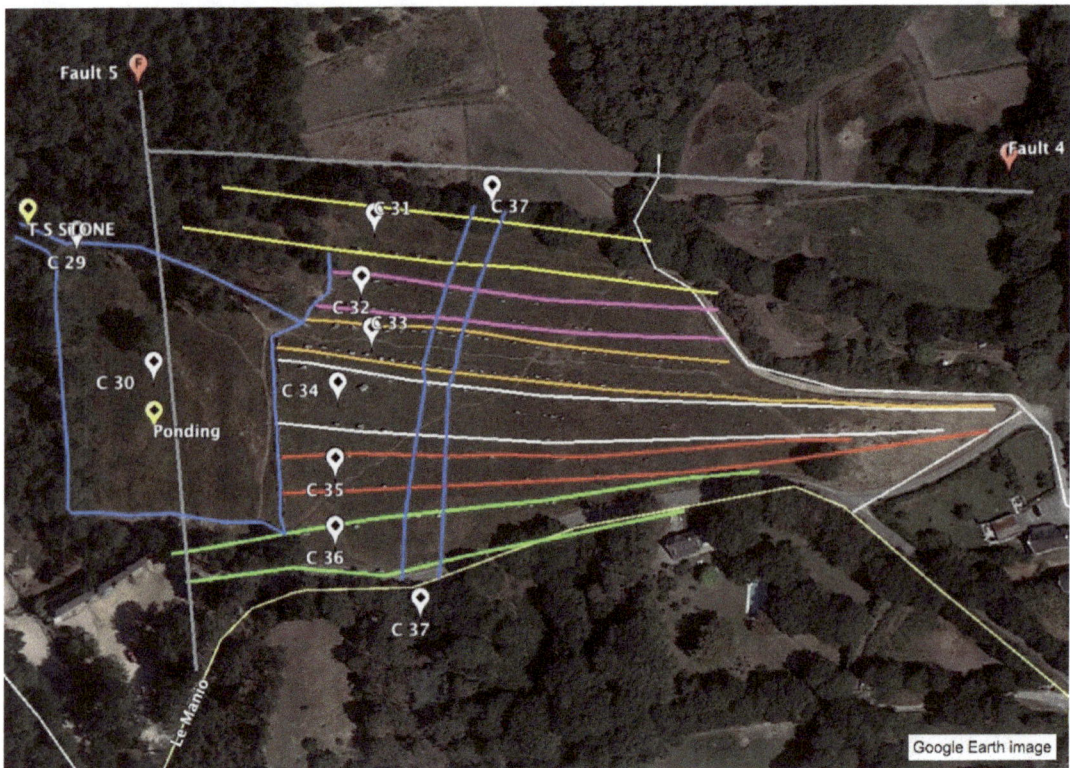

2. C 31 through C 36 and the stone alignments extend across the site in an east-west direction and could be associated with fault 4. At the eastern end, C 31 through C 36 trend toward one another, which suggests they merge just east of the site. They appear to intersect the Le Petit Ménec Alignments, which I did not have time to investigate. (Figures 98 & 99) This suggests they could be transferring from one geological feature to another, for example, fault 4 to fault 5.

Figure 100: C 30, Ponding and Kerlescan Alignments

Google Earth image

3. Based on the geology map of Brittany in Figure 83, the ponding (C 30) is located where fault 5 may be crossing fault 4. (Figures 98 - 101) The ponding was definitely identified by the people who constructed this site since its perimeter is defined by large tall standing stones. Although this enclosure is not a circle, it functions like the stone circle located on the southwest end of the Ménec alignments. I dowsed across the area in various directions, and the rods continued to cross indicating there is a concentration of groundwater. C 32 through 35 intersect this feature and contribute water to it. C 31 crosses the north boundary of the site and does not appear to contribute water to it. C 29 is an outlet for the ponding, and, based on the trends of C 29 and C 31, they intersect just west of the site. On the south side, C 36 touches the southeastern corner of the ponding and could be contributing water to it and / or

113

serving as an outlet. As mentioned above, ponding also occurs at the western end of the Kermario alignments.

Figure 101: C 30, Ponding & C 29 - 37 Kerlescan Alignments

4. C 29 was 50 ft / 15.24 m wide and is the main outlet for C 30. There is a tall standing stone centrally located on C 29 just northwest of where it begins. (Figure 101)

5. C 36 touches the southeast corner of C 30 and may be contributing to, or drawing some water from, C 30. When you extend the trend of C 22 through C 24 northeastward, they appear to intersect C 36, which can contribute groundwater to them. (Figures 99 & 101)

6. C 37 is the only concentrated flow I documented which intersected or crossed the site. It crosses the site and was 27 ft / 8.2 m wide on the site's north boundary and 44 ft / 13.4 m wide on the south boundary. (Figures 99 & 101)

When compared to the other sites I have investigated, including the Nasca Lines, the Ménec, Kermario and Kerlescan alignments contain the greatest concentration of stones features and concentrated flows within a relatively small area.

114

Following my investigation of the Ménec, Kermario and Kerlescan alignments, I surveyed additional sites within the area to determine if they replicated the patterns I documented at the larger sites, and if they are associated with concentrated flows within the groundwater.

Erdeven Alignments and Kerzerho les Géants

This site is located along Route D781 / Rue des Menhirs, approximately 5 mi / 8 km northwest of Carnac and divided into two sections, the Erdeven alignments and Kerzerho les Géants. Interestingly, the Kerlescan and Erdeven alignment areas of higher permeability flow patterns are very similar.

Figure 102: The Erdeven Alignments

Google Earth image

Erdeven Alignments

Unfortunately, the highway crosses the site's western section, and it is surrounded by agricultural fields which indicate several of the standing stones have been destroyed. Currently, the southern site consists of ten lines of standing stones.

115

(Figures 102 & 103) In spite of the damage, important data was documented during this survey.

Figure 103: The Erdeven Alignments with concentrated flows

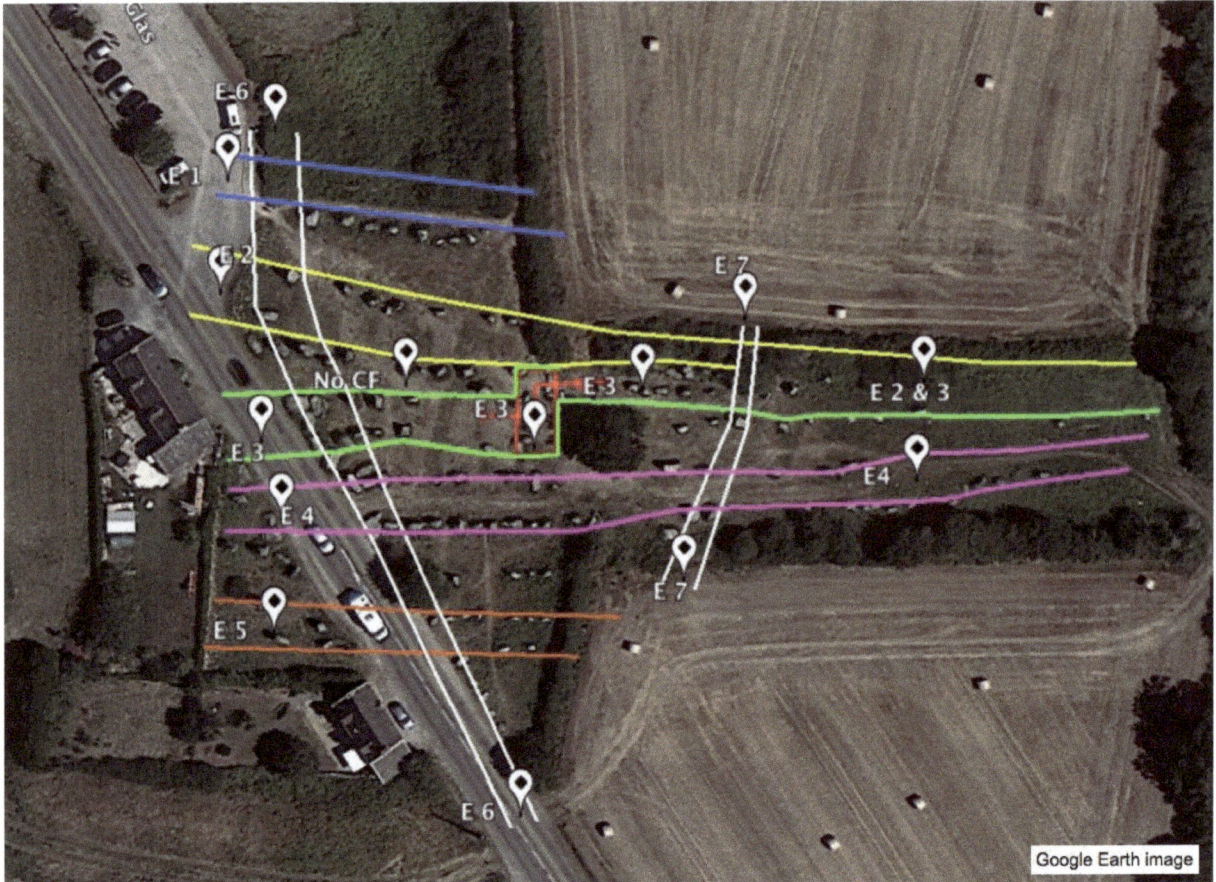

The standing stone pattern is very similar to the Ménec and Kermario, and especially, the Kerlescan alignments. As I crossed the site from north to south along the road, I located five concentrated flows and, with the exception of E 6, they had lines of standing stones along each width boundary. (Figures 102 & 103) As I continued eastward, some of the flows merged with or branched from one another. It is important to remember that the standing stone alignments along E 1 and E 5 most likely extended eastward into the fields.

1. With the exception of E 2 and E 3, which are discussed below, all of the concentrated flows were separated by an area where I did not detect a concentrated flow.

2. The north width boundary of E 1 is missing a line of stones, and only a small portion of the south width boundary still exists. (Figures 102 & 103)

116

3. Along the east end of the site, E 2 and E 3 are a single concentrated flow. Then, at 488841.30 m E, 5275704.75 m N, E 3 branches from E 2. At that location, there is a line of stones orientated north-south across E 3 which indicates it turns sharply. (Figures 104 - 105) The second line of stones located at 488838.46 m E, 5275699.27 m N indicates it turns sharply again. Thus, E 3 makes two right angle turns within this short distance where it branches from E 2, as shown within the red rectangle on my map. This can be caused by a variety of geological features, for example, an offset in a fault or bedrock fracture, where two faults or fractures cross one another or a blockage in alluvium. On the west side of these short stone lines, E 3 continues to flow westward. This is similar to the deviation along C 1 where it intersects the stone circle at Ménec.

Figure 104: Stones across E 3, Erdeven Alignments

Figure 105: Stones across E 3, The Erdeven Alignments

4. Although I did not detect a concentrated flow between E 4 and E 5, there is a line of 4 stones centered on this area. They could be indicating something associated with these two concentrated flows is happening in the field immediately east of them. (Figures 102 & 103)

5. E 6 crosses the site along the east side of the road. (Figure 103) Since this is so close to the road, some of the stones may have been moved from their original positions. Therefore, it is difficult to determine which ones mapped E 6's width boundaries. With that said, I have mapped the course and width of E 6 with white lines.

6. E 7 was 12 ft / 3.65 m wide and crosses the site. (Figure 103) E 7 intersects the north side of the site at 488870.70 m E, 5275711.76 m N where there are three stones with one on each width boundary and one centrally located on it. The south side is located at 488863.91 m E, 5275686.66 m N where there is a large standing stone on each width boundary.

7. Along the site's eastern end, E 2 and E 4 trend toward one another and will merge just east of the site. (Figures 102 & 103)

Kerzerho les Géants

Figure 106: The Kerzerho les Géants

118

Within the site's northern section, nine concentrated flows were documented. With the exception of L 6, the stones were aligned across the width of L 1 through L 9. The stones associated with L 5 through L 9 were also aligned along L 6's trend. Figure 106 shows the site's location, but, unfortunately, most of the stones are covered by vegetation. Some of these standing stones are the largest in the area.

Figure 107: L 1, Kerzerho les Géants

Figure 108: L 2, Kerzerho les Géants

L 1 - 40 ft / 12 m wide with a stone on each width boundary. The stone on the south boundary has fallen down. (Figure 107)

L 2 - 18 ft / 5.48 m wide with a stone on each width boundary, as shown in Figure 108

There is a stone next to the south width boundary stone on L 2 which is not on a concentrated flow. (Figure 108)

L 3 - 8 ft / 2.4 m wide with a tall stone on the north width boundary and a short stone on the south boundary. (Figure 109)

Grooved Stone - It is located between L 3 and L 4 and is not located on a concentrated flow. It has either fallen down or is in its original position. (Figures 109 & 110)

Figure 109: L 3 & L 4, Kerzerho les Géants

Figure 110: Stone with cupules & not on flow, Kerzerho les Géants

L 4 - 6 ft / 1.8 m wide with a tall stone on the north width boundary and a small pointed stone on the south boundary. (Figure 109)

Figure 111: L 5 & L 6, Kerzerho les Géants

Figure 112: L 6 & L 7, Kerzerho les Géants

L 5 and L 6 - L 5 was 12 ft / 3.65 m wide and L 6 was 8 ft / 2.4 m wide. At this location L 6 intersects L 5. Then L 6 trends southward. There is a stone on each width boundary of L 5, and one centrally located on it. The alignment of these three stones are also along the trend of L 6. (Figure 111)

L 7 - 60 ft / 18 m wide and has a concentration of large stones, including the tallest standing stones, on it. The stones are across the width of L 7 and along the trend of L 6. The tallest standing stone appears to be at least 25 ft / 7.6 m tall. (Figure 112)

Figure 113: L 6 & L 8, Kerzerho les Géants

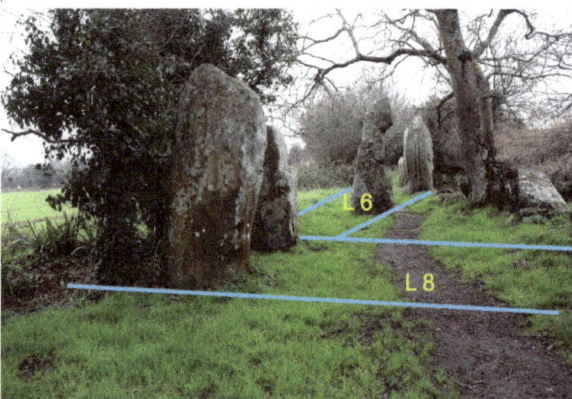

Figure 114: L 9 & L 6, Kerzerho les Géants

L 8 - 8 ft / 2.4 m wide with a stone on each width boundary. They are also orientated along the trend of K 6. (Figure 113)

L 6 - There is a stone centrally located on L 6 which is located between the stones on L 8 and L 9. (Figure 113)

L 9 - 14 ft / 4.26 m wide with a stone on each width boundary, and they are orientated along the trend of K 6. (Figure 114)

Although I did not ground survey L 6 from L 9 southward, its trend indicates it intersects the southern site. If it does, L 6 and E 6 could be the same concentrated flow.

It is possible additional stones, which were in alignment with L 1 through L 9, extended to the east and west; however, they were destroyed.

In addition to these standing stone alignments, I also ground surveyed several individual standing stones, all of which were located on an area of her permeability. Some were the width of the flow, while others were centrally located on a wider flow.

The Vieux-Moulin Alignment

This site is located just north of D781 in an active agricultural field. Fortunately, I received permission to ground survey this site. At this site, some of the areas of higher permeability have a standing stone located on each width boundary, while others have one centrally located on it.

Figure 115:The south Vieux-Moulin Alignment

Figure 116: The south Vieux-Moulin Alignment

The southern site consists of six stones which document four concentrated flows labeled V 1 through 4, as shown in Figures 115 & 116. V 1 and 2 have a standing stone on each width boundary, while V 3 and 4 have a single stone centrally located on them. The single stone's width on V 3 and 4 is equal to the flow's width. These flows are very narrow, for example, V 2 which was only 8 ft / 2.4 m.

The northern site has three concentrated flows labeled V 5 through V 7. Each concentrated flow is mapped by a single, very large stone whose width is equal to the flow's width. (Figures 117 & 118) These flows are also very narrow. The widest is V5 which is 12 ft / 3.65 m.

Figure 117: The north Vieux-Moulin Alignment

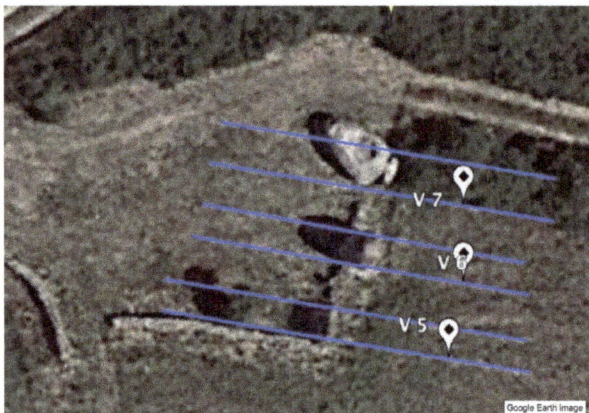

Figure 118: The north Vieux-Moulin Alignment

Kerbougnec Cromlech And Alignments

Figure 119: Kerbougnec Cromlech & Standing Stone Alignments Survey

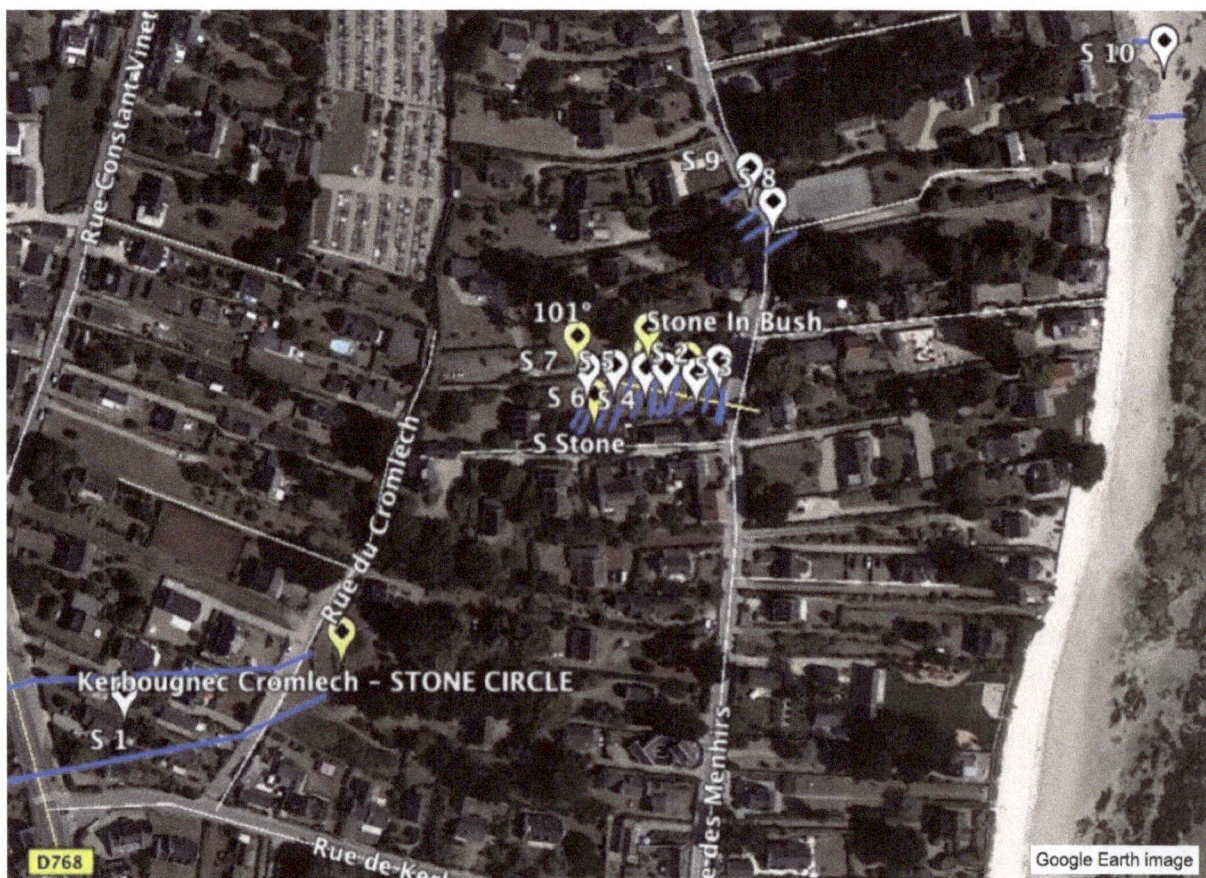

This site is located in St Pierre-Quiberon and consists of a stone circle and a standing stone alignment. Only a small section of the circle remains, and the alignment appears to be missing some standing stones. In spite of this, it is an interesting site since the circle and alignments are located very close to one another. I was able to document the flow pattern by dowsing along the streets that cross and surround these sites. (Figure 119)

Stone Circle - One concentrated flow, S 1, intersected the circle along the southwest side. S 1 was 55 ft / 16.7 m wide where it intersects the circle, however, along Avenue Des Druides, it was 115 ft /35 m wide. (Figures 119 & 120) On the northeast side of the circle, I located six concentrated flows trending towards the circle, which are clearly mapped with standing stone alignments. This suggests that S 1 branches into S 2 through 7 within or near the northeast side of the circle. It is not unusual for a group of concentrated flows to intersect a stone circle, for example, Stone Henge discussed above. However, I have not documented a stone circle where a wide concentrated flow intersects it and then branches into several flows like it does at this site. This flow pattern is similar to the one I documented at Silbury Hill, England, which is discussed above.

Figure 120: Kerbougnec Cromlech

Figure 121: Kerbougnec Standing Stone Alignments

Standing Stone Alignments - My map of the concentrated flows associated with this alignment is shown in Figures 119 through 123. The width of S 2 through 7 is indicated by the distance between the standing stones, which are on the width boundaries of these flows, and the blue line associated with them.

S 2 through S 7 all trend toward the stone circle, and S 2 and S 3 curve towards S 4, indicating they merge with it. As I followed these concentrated flows northeastward, I located two concentrated flows, S 8 and 9, which cross the Rue Marthe Delpirou and were 28 ft / 8.5 m and 38 ft / 11.58 m wide. (Figure 119) There were no other flows within the area. This indicates S 2 through S 7 merged into these two flows. Then, I followed S 8 and S 9 to the beach where I located one flow, S 10, which was 100 ft / 30.48 m wide. This is an unusual flow pattern and suggests this is why they documented it. Consistently, my data indicates sites like these are connected to one another by concentrated flows within the groundwater.

Astronomical alignments are another component which needs to be considered when researching megalithic sites. I realize that these sites have undergone considerable modifications and may represent only a fraction of their original size. However, although fragmented, at some sites enough data can be obtained to evaluate whether or not an astronomical alignment is present.

Another point to consider is one's modern perception of these sites. At sites like Ménec, Kermario and Kerlescan, or this one, one can easily be misled by the number of stone alignments they visualize at the site or draw on the site's map by connecting two or more stones, and then finding something in the sky or some place on earth that they can align it with or point to. However, I do not think this is what the people who constructed these sites considered or intended. Several factors need to be considered when verifying an astronomical alignment as discussed on page 21. Consider the following.

Figure 122: Kerbougnec Standing Stone Alignments, concentrated flows & 101 Az

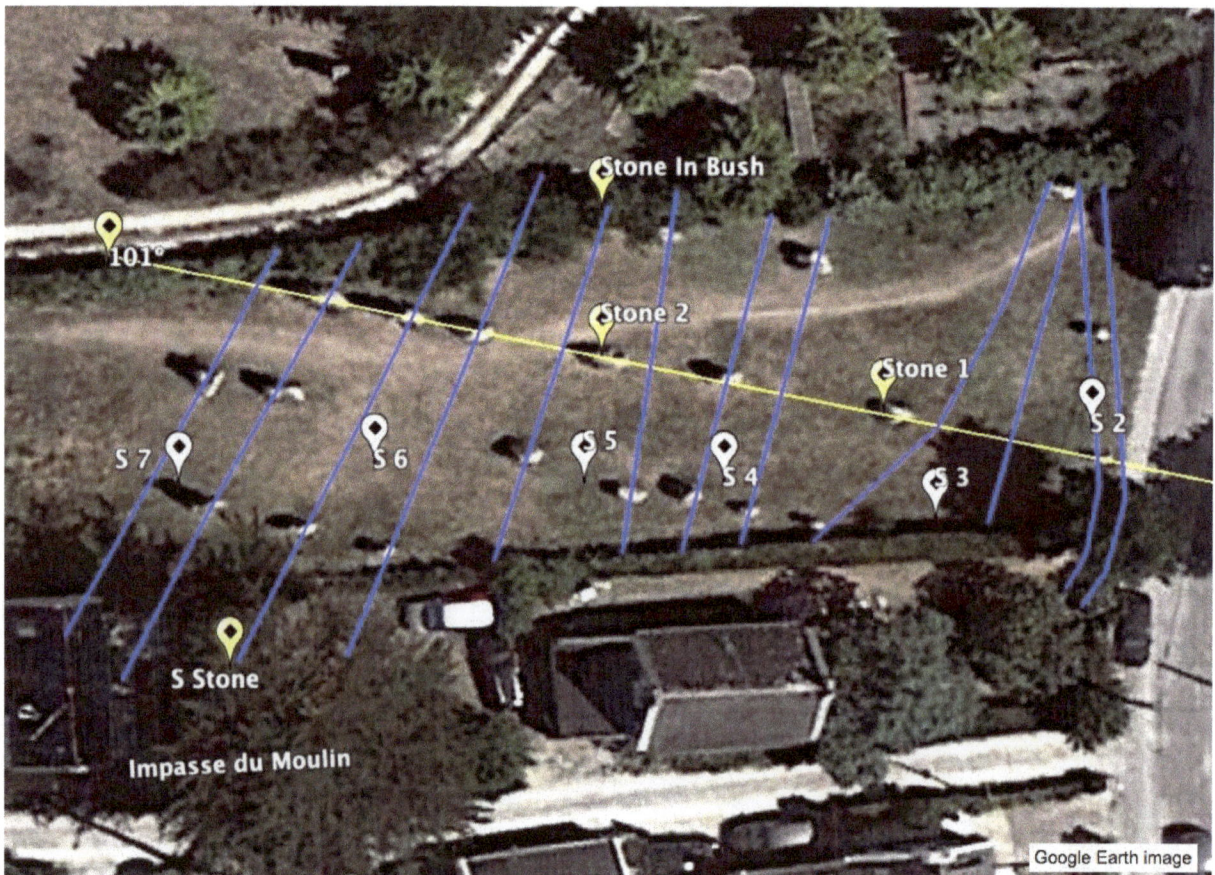

Within this group of standing stones, there is a distinctive row of seven stones with an azimuth of 101° SE from true north, as shown by the yellow line in Figures 121-123. Five of the stones are located on the width boundary of the various concentrated flows; however, stones 1 and 2 are not. Stone 1 is located between S 3 and S 4 and is not on a concentrated flow. Stone 2 is centrally located on S 5. All seven of the standing stones appear to be in their original position. However, stones 1 and 2 were out of place since

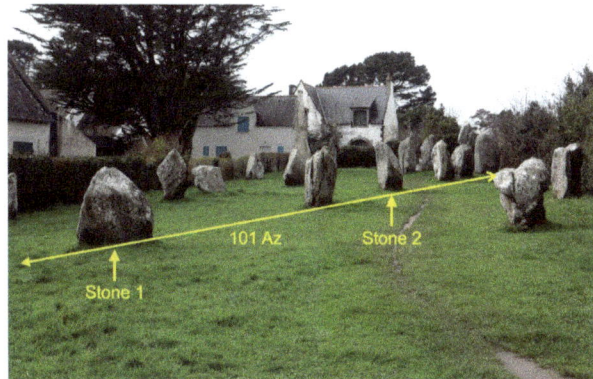

Figure 123: Six of the seven standing stones along the 101 Az

they were not located along the width boundaries of the concentrated flows. When I observe something like this, I wonder if those who constructed the site were documenting something other than groundwater. Consistently, these sites incorporate components which are associated with the three worlds. Since I had a vertical alignment between the standing stones in the present world and the concentrated flows within the groundwater of the underworld, I wondered if the 101° Az was associated with an astronomical event, thus completing the alignment of the three worlds. If the 101° Az alignment was constructed around the time the site was constructed, it could be pointing to an astronomical event that coincided with their placement. To determine this, several factors have to be considered. Therefore, I asked Ivy Merriot, PhD, archeoastronomy, to assist me with this issue. Using the 101° Az alignment I had made at the site and the site's latitude and longitude from Google Earth, she found three sky events worthy of mentioning. The seven stones are aligned with the star group called Pleiades, the vernal equinox and the Milky Way. Just before dawn on the vernal equinox of 4000 BC (+/- seventy-five years), the heliacal rise of Pleiades occurs in the night sky. Then, on the same evening at midnight when the Sun reached its lowest point in its daily journey, far below the earth and most distant from the visual horizons, the night sky's largest visual feature, the Milky Way, stood straight up in alignment with the stones, its galactic center visually tagged to the top of the stones. This would have visually created one long alignment of stones and sky advancing across the entire celestial sphere, horizon to horizon, splitting the sky and earth in half. The coinciding of heliacal Pleiades, and the Milky Way's galactic center aligning with these stones on the vernal equinox, happens only once in over 20,000 years. Interestingly, Pleiades is also referred to as the Seven Sisters, which corresponds to the number of standing stones along this alignment.

125

Crucuno Cromlech And Dolmen

Crucuno Cromlech

Figure 124: Crucuno Cromlech & Dolmen survey

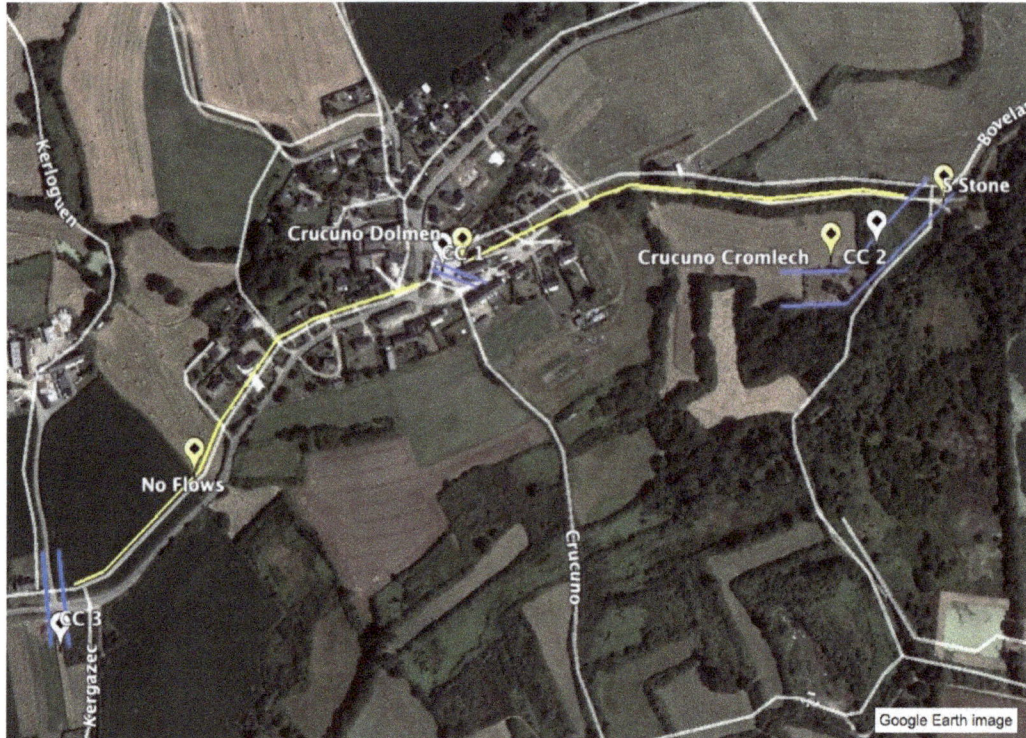

Figure 125: Crucuno Cromlech

Figure 126: Crucuno Cromlech east with boundary marker

My ground measurements for the Crucuno Cromlech were 110 ft / 33.5 m from east to west and 100 ft / 30.48 m from north to south. In Google Earth it measures 115 ft / 35 m by 90 ft / 27.4 m. Either way, it is a quadrilateral / rectangle with right angle corners and not a circle. (Figures 124 & 128) I measured CC 2 at three different locations, and it averaged 100 ft / 30.48 m wide. This is an impressive megalithic site

126

which documents the width of the widest concentrated flows I documented during my investigations of sites near Carnac. I did not have time to visit all the sites in the area, thus there may be others which are associated with concentrated flows wider than CC 2 at Crucuno Cromlech.

Figure 127: Crucuno Cromlech

I did not follow CC 2 westward due the private land, however I was able to document its trend northeast of the site. Interestingly, at 490943.00 m E, 5274611.00 m N, where CC 2 crosses the road, there is a small pointed standing stone located on the east width boundary of CC 2. (Figures 124 - 125 & 127) It is in a precarious location with dirt roads passing on each side. However, it appears to be at its original location since it is located precisely on the width boundary of CC 2.

Since CC 2 flowed in the direction of the village and the dolmen located there, I dowsed along the road from the pointed standing stone to the village, and then along the road to the intersection with Kerloguen Road, indicated by the yellow line in Figure 124, to determine if CC 2 crossed through this section. The only concentrated flows I located was the one associated with the dolmen, CC 1, and another, CC 3, at the intersection of the main road with Kerloguen Road. CC 3 was 50 ft / 15 m wide. This suggests the course of CC 2 curves to the southwest or south.

127

Crucuno Dolmen

It is orientated along the trend of CC 1, which was 18 ft / 5.4 m wide trending at 111° SE which suggests it intersects CC 2. (Figure 128) The width of the dolmen is equal to the width of CC 1.

Crucuny Cromlech

Crucuny Cromlech is a stone circle located within Crucuny village. Unfortunately, most of the circle has been destroyed. What remains is a small section along the road, however, it defines where the circle was located. I was able to dowse around half of the circle and located one concentrated flow intersecting it, C 1, which was 35 ft / 10.66 m wide and trended towards the standing stone in the backyard of the house on the other side. (Figure 126)

Figure 128: Crucuno Dolmen & CC 1

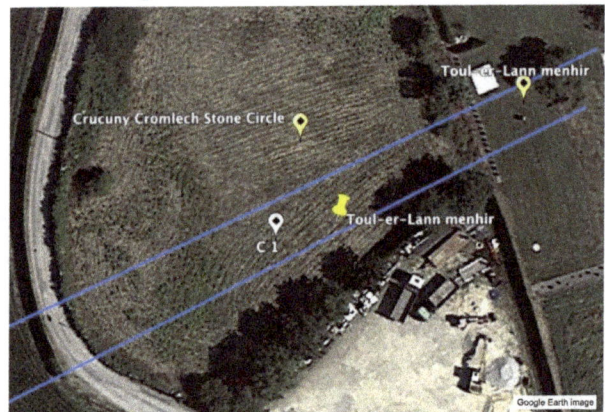

Figure 129: Crucuny Cromlech

The Locmariaquer Megalithic Complex
Including
La Table des Marchands Dolmen, Grand Menhir Er-Grah and Er-Grah Tumulus

This site consists of the largest standing stones, petroglyphs and structures within the area which strongly suggest it was an important Neolithic site dating back to 6,700 B.P.. This site has been heavily damaged since it was used as a stone quarry by the Romans and has undergone extensive reconstruction. By 1870, when the government purchased the property, La Table des Marchands Dolmen was reduced a the cap stone with a few supporting stones (WIKIPEDIA 2020). It is important to mention that the area where the main features are located was closed to the public. So I circled the site along the public walkway and documented the concentrated flows I encountered. Therefore, there may be additional concentrated flows within the closed area that I did not document. (Figure 130)

Figure 130: The Locmariaquer Megalithic Complex including La Table des Marchands Dolmen, Grand Menhir Er-Grah and Er-Grah Tumulus

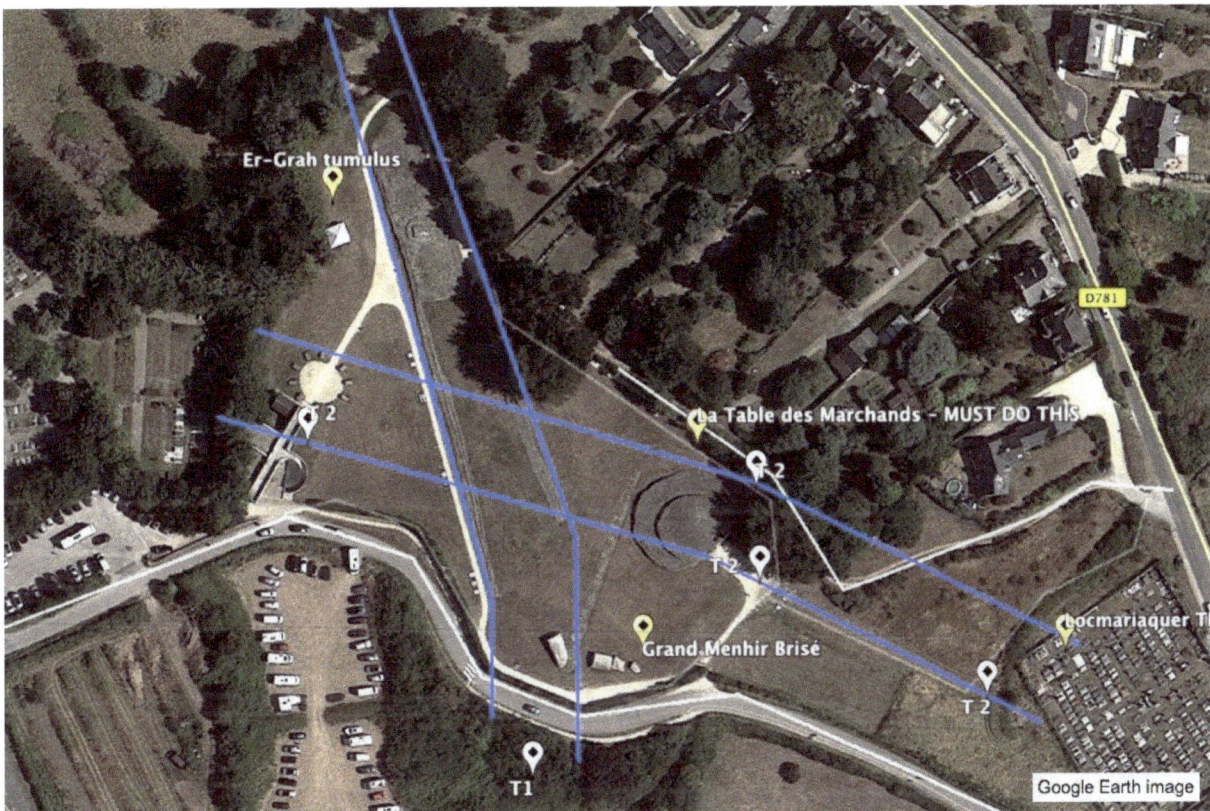

Figure 131: Er-Grah Tumulus

Figure 132: La Table des Marchands Dolmen as it appears today

T 1 - crosses the site along Er-Grah Tumulus at 162° SE and then curves to approximately 178° S. T 1 was 60 ft / 18.28 m wide on the north end of the tumulus and 75 ft / 22.86 m wide where it crosses the road immediately south of the Grand Menhir. (Figures 130 & 131) If the tumulus' shape has not been modified, it maps the width and course of T 1 at that location.

T 2 - crossed the site at 105.5º SE between the visitor center and La Table des Marchands Dolmen. Then, from the dolmen it curved to 116º SE. I took the width of T 2 at three locations, and it averaged 75 ft / 22.86 m. (Figures 130, 132 & 133) The inner dolmen / chamber of La Table des Marchands appears to be centrally located on T 2.

During my site surveys in the Carnac area, T 1 and T 2 were two of widest concentrated flows I documented. The only concentrated flow that I documented in the Carnac area which was wider was located at the Crucuno Cromlech site, which was 100 ft / 30.48 m wide. As mentioned throughout this text, as well as, my other publications on this subject, ancient cultures located important cultural sites on unusual geological and hydrological features. The width of these two concentrated flows could have influenced those who chose this location.

Figure 133: La Table des Marchands Dolmen's inner chamber back supporting stone

Figure 134: Grand Menhir Er-Grah, 67.6 ft tall & weighs 330 tons, erected 4,700 BC

Grand Menhir Er-Grah is the largest single block of stone to have been transported and erected by Neolithic people in this region. It was erected around 6,700 B.P. and in alignment with eighteen additional standing stones. (Figures 130 & 134) It was 67.6 ft / 20.60 m long and weighted of 330 tons. The stone is from a bedrock outcrop located several kilometers away from Locmariaquer. It is worked over its entire surface and has a hatchet-plough / plow design on it. Unfortunately, the Grand Menhir fell over and broke into four sections, and the other standing stones have been removed. (WIKIPEDIA 2020) Its base is located on the east width boundary of T 1. The other eighteen standing stones appear to have been located along the line extending from the base of Grand Menhir. I did not ground survey that area.

Tumuli Near Carnac

While in Carnac I ground surveyed some of the tumuli in the area. Interestingly, with the exception of Er-Grah Tumulus, all of them were on one concentrated flow that was less than 21 ft / 6.4 m wide. Although I investigated only four tumuli, their alignments along an area of higher permeability were not similar, and most did not align with the trend of the northeast-southwest and northwest-southeast trending faults.

Saint Michel Tumulus

Saint Michel Tumulus is located in Carnac and was the largest tumulus I researched in this region. It is a mound of earth and stones that is 410 ft / 125 m long, 160 ft / 50 m wide and 33 ft / 10 m high with a central chamber. (WIKIPEDIA 2020) S 1 was the only concentrated flow that crossed the site. It was 18 ft / 5.48 m wide and crosses along the tumulus' length. There is a modified standing stone on the west end of the tumulus' summit which is centrally located on S 1. (Figure 135)

Figure 135: Saint Michel Tumulus & S 1

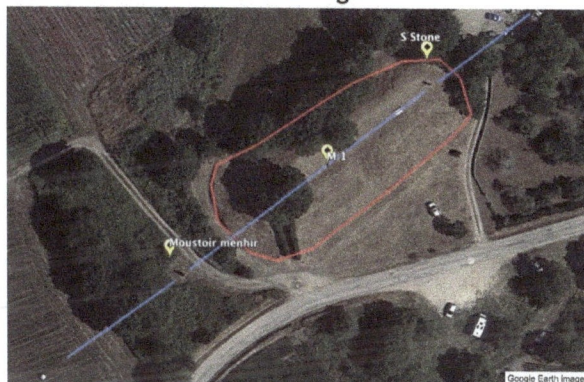
Figure 136: Moustoir Tumulus & two standing stones along M 1

Figure 137: Kercado Tumulus & two standing stones along K 1

Figure 138: Crucuny Tumulus & standing stone

Moustoir Tumulus

The Moustoir Tumulus is 295 ft / 90 m long, 131 ft / 40 m wide and 26 ft / 8 m high with chambers along its length. M 1 crosses the site along its length and was 21 ft / 6.4 m wide. The standing stone on top of the tumulus' east end and the one at its base on the west side are both centrally located on M 1. (Figure 136)

Kercado Tumulus

This tumulus is located just south of the Kermario alignments and is very interesting as it has a circle of low standing stones that appear to surround it. (Figure 137) The tumulus' entrance is centrally located on K 1, which is 12 ft / 3.65 m wide. There are three standing stones located on K 1. One is in front of the tomb's entrance, another on top of it and the third is a slightly taller standing stone within the stone circle along the back of the tomb.

Crucuny Tumulus

It is located immediately north of Crucuny, and near Crucuny Cromlech. It is centrally located on CT 1 which was 12 ft / 3.65 m wide. The standing stone on top is also centrally located on CT 1, as well as, the stones at its base on the south side. (Figure 138)

Dolmens Near Carnac

All of the dolmens are located along one or two concentrated flows. Individual dolmens are located on a single concentrated flow and orientated along its trend or across its with. Groups of dolmens were located where two of more concentrated flows crossed or intersected a site, and they are all in alignment with one or two of the flows.

The orientation of the dolmens I surveyed did not align with the northeast-southwest and northwest-southeast trending faults. They could be orientated along smaller undocumented faults or bedrock fractures.

Dolmens de Mane Keriaval

The site has been damaged by Route D768 which goes through it. Currently there are three dolmens and a few standing stones at the site. Some of the standing stones are on the southeast side of the road. In spite of the damage, some interesting data was documented. (Figure 139)

Dolmen 1 - is located along the west side of the site. Its length is equal to the width of D 1, which is 30 ft / 9 m wide. (Figure 140)

Dolmen 2 - is located along the northern width boundary of D 1, and its length is orientated along the trend of D 1. However, it is also located where D 3 intersects D 1, and its length is also equal to the width of D 3, which is 15 ft / 4.5 m. (Figure 141)

Standing Stone 1 - is centrally located on D 3 and a few feet north of Dolmen 2. The combination of Dolmen 2's orientation and the standing stone literally marks the location where D 1 and D 3 intersect. (Figure 139)

Figure 139: Dolmens de Mane Keriaval & standing stones

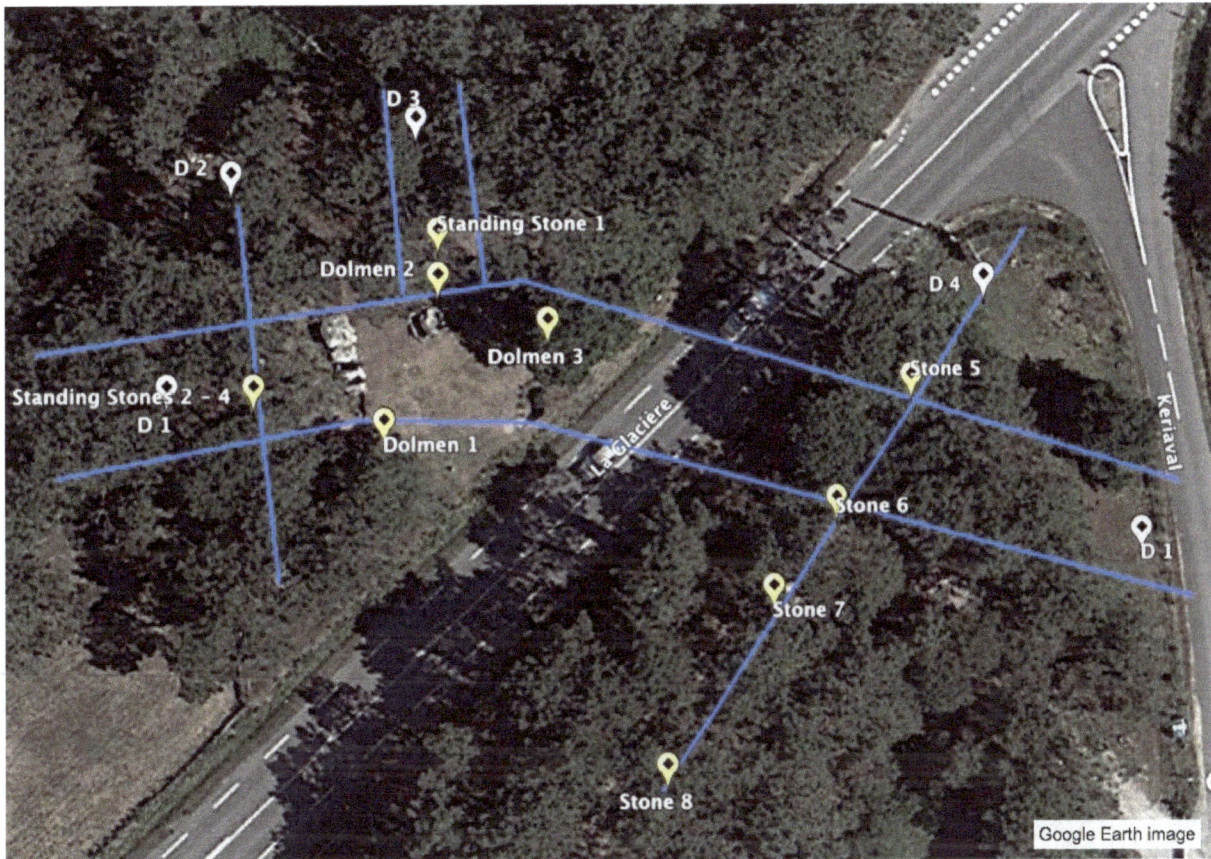

Dolmen 3 - is located along the east side of the site, and it is still buried underground. Its length is equal to the width of D 1, which is 30 ft / 9 m wide. It is also located where D 1 begins to curve from northeast to southeast. (Figure 139)

Figure 140: Dolmen 1 & standing stone, Dolmens de Mane Keriaval

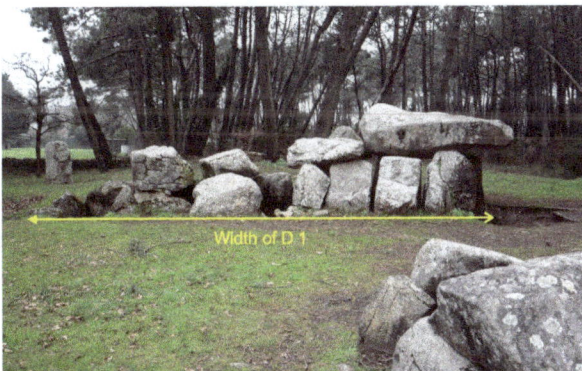

Figure 141: Dolmen 1 & standing stone 1, Dolmens de Mane Keriaval

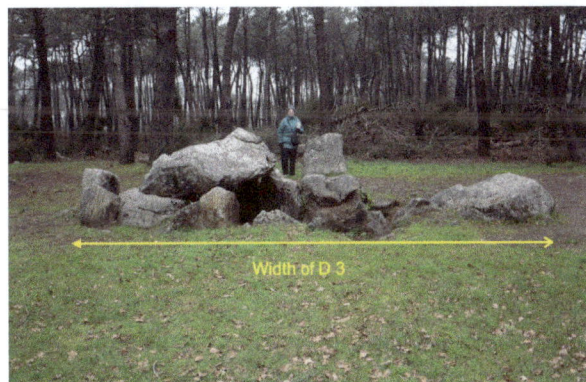

Low Standing Stones 2 - 4 - They are centrally located on D 2, which is 10 ft / 3 m wide trending north-south and on the west side of the site. (Figure 139)

Four Standing Stones 5 - 8 - They are located across the road and are centrally located on D 4. Stones 5 and 6 are also located on the north and south width boundaries of D 1. (Figure 139)

The combination of these features clearly map the concentrated flows crossing this site.

Rondossec Dolmens

Figure 142: Rondossec Dolmens

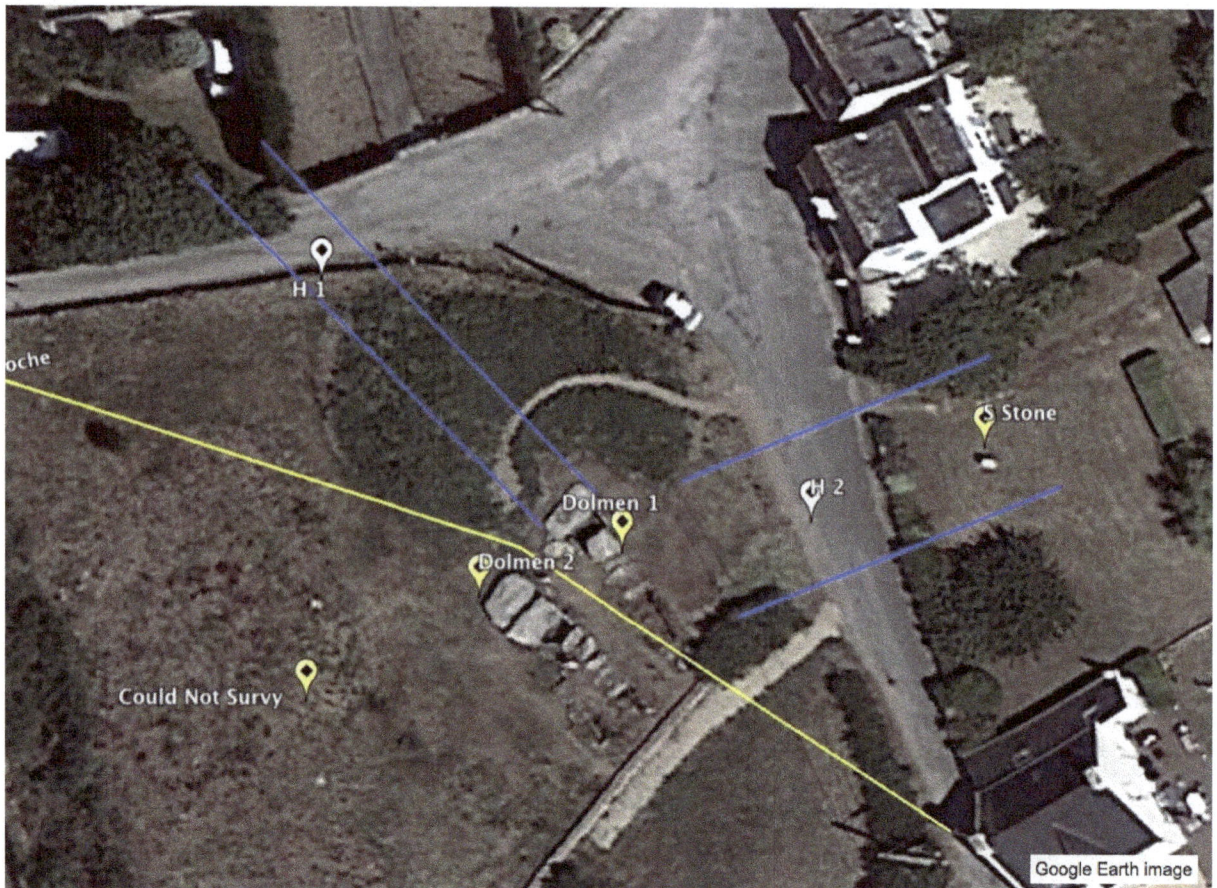

Although most of this site was closed to the public, I was able to walk around half of it and half way across it on the public access path. The orientation of the two dolmens map the location of the two concentrated flows which intersect this site. This is similar to the pattern at the Dolmens de Mane Keriaval site. (Figure 142)

Dolmen 1's length extends across the width of H 2, which is 45 ft / 13.7 m. Dolmen 1 is also located along the trend of H 1, and its width is equal to the width of H 1, which is basically 15 ft / 4.57 m.

Dolmen 2's length is equal to the width of H 2, which is 45 ft / 13.7 m.

Kergevat Dolmen

It is located along D781, and its width is equal to the width of K 1, which is 15 ft / 4.57 m wide. (Figure 143)

Kerroc'h Dolmen

It is located along a single concentrated flow, K 1, which is 10 ft / 3 m wide, and its width was equal to K 1. (Figure 144)

Figure 143: Kergavat Dolmen

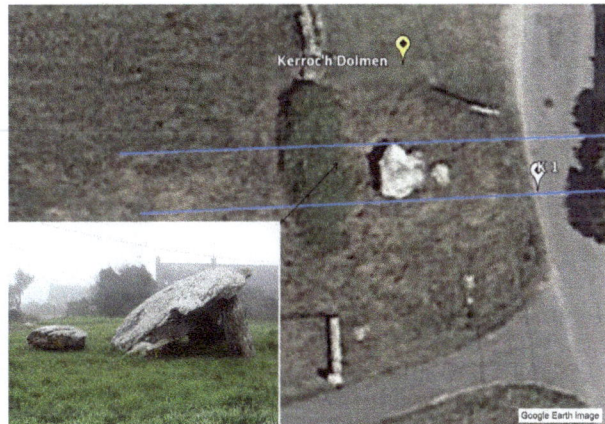
Figure 144: Kerroc'h Dolmen & K 1

Figure 145: Mane-Rethuel Dolmen & R 1

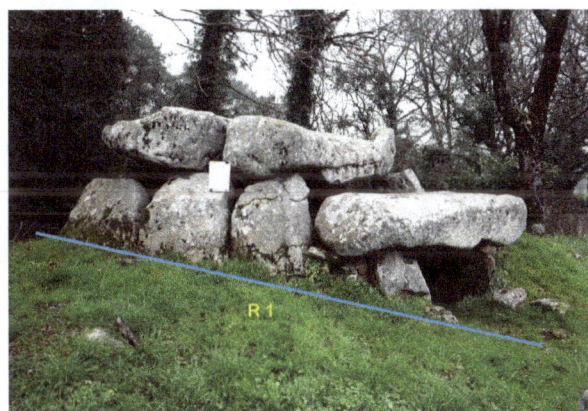
Figure 146: Dolmen Er Roc'h Feutet & R 1

Mane-Rethuel Dolmen

It is located just south of the Locmariaquer Megalithic Complex. The dolmen's length extends across the width of R 1, which is 75 ft / 22.86 /m wide. (Figure 145) Although R 1 does not trend toward the complex, its width is basically equal to T 1 and 2. These three concentrated flows are among the widest I documented during the Carnac survey.

Dolmen Er Roc'h Feutet

It is located on a shallow hill and on R 1. It is the width of R 1, which is 8 ft / 2.4 m.(Figure 146)

Hourel Dolmen

This dolmen was of special interest to me since it is located at the end of a narrow peninsula with the ocean on three sides and in a grove of evergreen trees. It is a small dolmen and has been damaged. It is located on HD 1, which is 7 ft / 2 m wide, and is equal to the width of HD 1. HD 1 trends along the west side of the peninsula and along its length. (Figure 147)

Figure 147: Hourel Dolmen & HD 1

The purpose of this initial investigation was to research another region of the world, which has a concentration of megalithic sites containing a variety of features, to determine if they are associated with areas of higher permeability within the groundwater. All of the sites I ground surveyed near Carnac were aligned with one or more areas of higher permeability, which corresponds to the data I have documented in other regions.

Conclusion

During this research, the tourist information signs and site reports consistently commented the reason for the location of various features is unknown, and several theories are proposed. However, when you apply the methodology discussed throughout this book and compare the data with other regions, a reasonable explanation emerges. The alignment of the under, present and upper worlds was paramount in the minds of ancient cultures. To achieve this alignment you need to begin with the under world, which is more elusive.

This data strongly suggests specific varieties of stone features were used to map areas of higher permeability within the groundwater during different historical periods and cultures, as well as, in a variety of environments in different regions of our planet. In different regions, a feature may incorporate a modification that is representative of the culture that constructed it, however the basic shape, as well as its function, indicates it is mapping the concentrated flows within the groundwater. For example, lines of standing stones in England and France, parallel lines of stone piles or etched lines in Peru and Chile and cairns in the United States and Canada have the same function, which is mapping the trend of an area(s) of higher permeability and aligning the site's features with them. This can be compared to choosing a font to write with on a computer. For example, an A in Arial, Times and Courier fonts all mean the same, even though they are shaped somewhat differently. Then, in addition to mapping the concentrated flows, the stone features are also associated with cultural and spiritual concepts.

Applying this methodology to site surveys leads you to the various features more quickly than conducting standard site surveys. When a standard archaeological ground survey is conducted, some of the features can be associated with one another while others appear to be randomly placed. However, when the areas of higher permeability are added to the investigation, all of the features are connected. By following the concentrated flows, they take you to the features that are visible on the surface, as well as, those that have been buried. For example, compare Figures 85 & 86, 98 - 103, and 121 and 122.

When I apply this methodology to sites which predate modern religions, such as Christianity, the features are located on areas of higher permeability. As modern religions spread, communities, structures and monuments were not aligned with areas of higher permeability within the groundwater. Those that are aligned with concentrated flows were constructed on ancient sites that predate them indicating their placement was coincidental.

When you incorporate a survey of the concentrated flows / areas of higher permeability within the groundwater into an archaeological survey, you add a third dimension that has been neglected by modern archaeologists; however, it was an integral component within the concepts of ancient civilizations.

Part 6

David Johnson's Dowsing Methodology

Site And Stone Feature Analysis

As discussed in Part 1, it is important to consider the following. When researchers learn that dowsing is included in my methodology, they conclude that this is the only method I use to reach my conclusions. Actually, this is not the case. In addition to dowsing, geological, hydrological, archaeological and ethnographic studies are included. Within each region, Native American First Nation archaeological, spiritual, cultural and elder authorities are consulted and collaborate with this research. All of these diverse disciplines are considered prior to writing a final report.

This section discusses my dowsing methodology since many researchers are not familiar with it or have simply dismissed it as unscientific. However, once they apply this methodology they tell me it changed the way they analyze archaeological sites. By adding another layer, the areas of higher permeability within the groundwater, to their investigation the placement of various features becomes more clear, as well as their association with one another.

Johnson's Dowsing Methodology

I developed the following methodology over the course of twenty years beginning with my research on the Nasca Lines and other coastal geoglyphs in Peru and Chile, South America, and the Native Americans' Ceremonial Landscapes throughout North America. Consistently, the same methodology was used for each site.

Johnson's Methodology

*AHP = Areas of Higher Permeability
A. **Tools**

1. Dowsing rods
2. GPS unit
3. Compass

4. Notebook
5. Measuring devices for both long and short distances.
6. When possible, use satellite images of the site to assist in mapping it.
7. It helps if you have one or two people helping you.

B. Using Dowsing Rods

1. Dowsing Rod Description

a. Various types of dowsing can be used to obtain the same results. My methodology uses two right angle metal rods which are 12 in / 30.4 cm by 5 in / 12.7 cm. The short end is inserted into a plastic tube. My hands hold the plastic tubes and do not touch the rods. This allows the rods to swing freely. (Figure 148) If you are learning to use metal rods, it is advisable to

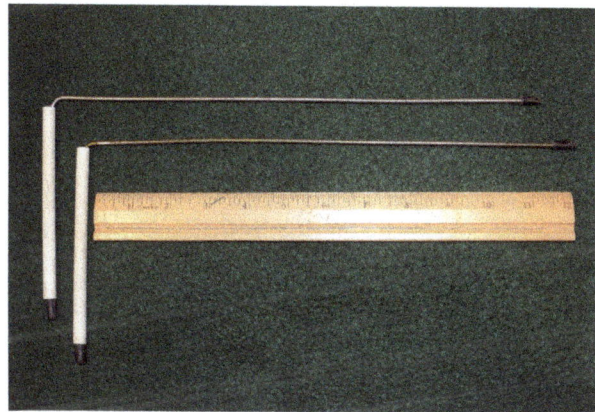

Figure 148: Johnson's dowsing rods

begin by practicing on known concentrated flows first, such as water pipes. I make my dowsing rods out of items found around the house or in a community. Then, when I am in remote arid regions, where communities need water, I teach them how to make dowsing rods and use them.

2. Man-Made Features Can Influence The Rods

a. When passing under or over electrical lines the dowsing rods will cross. If the electrical line is a single cable, the rods will cross briefly as you walk over or under it. If it is a major power line the rods will cross while you are under it and indicate the width of the power lines above you.

b. When crossing over or under water or oil pipes the dowsing rods will cross. The pipes are usually less than 3 ft / .914 m wide.

3. Natural Features Can Influence The Rods

a. Recent precipitation, both rain and snow, can soak into the ground and create ponding or flows near surface which the rods will detect. This water tends to dry up in a few days. Therefore, it is wise to wait until the ground dries out.

139

b. The rods will cross wherever snow covers the surface. Wait until it melts and the ground dries out.

c. Magnetite deposits will cause the rods to cross. If this happens the rods will cross over a broad area, and you will have difficulty locating the AHPs.

C. Procedure For Conducting A Site Survey

1. Documentation
a. Flag, label and GPS every point of interest during the survey

b. Take detailed notes

c. Thoroughly document the areas of higher permeability

d. Describe each surface feature and measure it

e. Determine if the feature is associated with the width or trend of an AHP

2. Surface Flows Versus Subterranean Flows

a. Observing surface flows while dowsing can mislead you. When mapping AHPs using dowsing, it is important to ignore the topography. Most of the time the AHPs within the groundwater do not correspond to surface features which can conduct water, such as streams and rivers.

b. Once you complete mapping the AHPs, compare their flow pattern to surface flows. If they are similar, both may be following the same geological feature.

c. Also, compare them to geological features which may be visible at the site.

3. Beginning A Site Survey

a. Whenever possible, establish a grid line along two sides of the site. For example, the south and east sides of a site.

b. Dowse along each grid line and flag the width of each concentrated flow intersecting it.

c. From the grid lines follow each area of higher permeability across the site while flagging the width boundaries frequently, as well as where other concentrated flows intersect it. Also flag any archaeological features observed along the AHP.

d. Flag where two AHPs intersect or cross one another, however continue to document the one you are currently following. Then once it is completed, document the other AHPs one at a time.

4. Interpreting The Dowsing Rods

a. Locating AHP near you

1. If you are not following a grid line

a. Stand still while keeping the rods parallel and perpendicular to one another and watch which way the rods turn, left, right, straight forward or back towards you. This indicates the direction you should walk to locate the AHP.

b. While walking towards the AHP, the rods will not swing back and forth until you are close to the AHP. The closer you get to the AHP, the more the rods will swing back and forth. If the rods swing slowly it usually indicates a narrow AHP, and if they swing rapidly it indicates a wide AHP.

c. When the rods stop moving and remain crossed you are standing above an AHP.

2. If you are following a grid line

a. Follow the grid line. When the rods cross, document both width boundaries of the AHP.

3. Interpreting the rods when crossed

a. Rate of flow

1. The rate of flow is the number of gallons / liters per minute an AHP conducts. The geology of an area affects the rate of flow. Therefore, it is difficult to determine the rate of flow using dowsing within a given location without researching the scientific geological and hydrological data.

2. If there are wells with high capacity pumps within the area which operate regularly, they can affect the rate of flow by drawing large amounts of groundwater from the water table and / or AHPs.

3. Barely cross - weak rate of flow and could also indicate near surface water, usually from recent precipitation.

4.   Middle cross - moderate rate of flow.

5.   Complete cross - high rate of flow.

6.   Just because an AHP is wide, for example 100 ft / 30.48 m, it does not mean the rate of flow is high.

b. **Determining the width and trend of an AHP**

1.   The trend of an AHP can meander, and its width can vary.

2.   To obtain the best results, map an AHP completely across a site to determine its average width and trend.

3.   When you encounter an AHP, flag the width boundary.

4.   Then, follow that width boundary for at least 50 ft / 15.24 m, and flag it frequently. The line of flags indicates the trend of the concentrated flow.

5.   When you stand on a width boundary of an AHP, the rods will point away from each other. This also indicates the trend of the flow at that location.

6.   Go back to the first flag and then cross the AHP perpendicular to the trend. Then, flag the opposite width boundary. The distance between them is the width of the AHP at that location.

7.   The trend of some AHPs can change abruptly. For example, when one fault intersects another at a right angle, the AHP can change course by 90 degrees.

8.   If two AHPs intersect one another, move off the flows and dowse around the intersection to determine if they merge or cross one another.

9.   If they merge or branch from one another, they will not cross one another.

10. If they cross one another and their width and trend are the same on both sides of the intersection, it indicates they are located at different depths within the ground.

11. If two cross, their trends can be the same on both sides of the intersection, however its width may be narrower on one side.

This usually indicates one of the concentrated flows is either loosing or gaining water to the other AHP.

c. Dowsing while riding in a vehicle

1. Once you master dowsing while walking, it is possible to use this technique while riding in a vehicle.

2. While someone else drives, sit in the passenger seat and hold the rods as if you were walking with them.

3. Make sure there are no water bottles under the rods.

4. Operate the rods as if you are walking.

5. On very rough roads it is difficult to hold the rods parallel and perpendicular.

d. Determining the depth of an AHP

1. Based on my experience, it is very difficult to learn how to determine the depth of an AHP. With that said, here is the procedure I was taught by another dowser.

2. This works best for AHPs wider than 15 ft / 4.57 m and have a high rate of flow as indicated when the rods crossed completely.

3. Stand in the middle of the AHP with the rods crossed and walk in a circle within the width boundaries of the concentrated flow.

4. Then, walk away from the flow at a right angle.

5. The rods will try to turn back toward the AHP.

6. To prevent this, tilt the ends of the rods slightly downward to keep them from turning back.

7. Continue walking until the rods turn back even though they are tilted downward.

8. Measure the distance from the point where they turned back to where you started.

9. This should be the approximate depth to the AHP.

10. Warning: If you cross another AHP, water pipe or electrical line, this procedure will not work.

D. Feature Identification

These features include culturally modified trees, petroglyphs, pictographs, structures and stone formations, for example, cairns, circles, crescent shaped cairns and snake walls .

1. Johnson's book titled <u>Native Americans' Sacred And Ceremonial Landscape's Correlation With Groundwater</u> can assist in identifying the features associated with North American and South American sites. The book titled Megalithic Features of Southern England and Groundwater can assist you in identifying the features in England.

2. GPS the location of each feature.

3. If they are large, such as large roomblocks, GPS each corner.

4. Determine if a structure's walls and features are aligned with the width and / or trend of one or more AHPs that intersect or cross it.

5. For circular structures, GPS the diameter on two opposite sides of the perimeter and compare its diameter with the width of the AHP. Frequently they are the same.

6. For square or rectangular structures, GPS each corner, measure the width and length. Compare the structure's width and length with the AHP. Often, the structure's width or length is equal to the width of the AHP.

E. Artifacts Documentation

1. At some sites the sheer number of artifacts, such as pottery shards, makes it impossible to document every item, however their distribution is important in relation to the AHP. Our data strongly suggests 85% or more of all the artifacts are located along the AHPs.

2. GPS the location of projectile points and tools to determine if they are located along an AHP.

3. For large accumulations of artifacts, such as pottery shards, estimate the percentage of artifacts on and off the AHP.

F. Hydrological Features Associated With The Site

1. Once you complete mapping the AHPs, document the hydrological features present.

   a. **Springs**

      1. Estimate the rate of flow.

      2. If possible, ask local residents or the area's water department for data on the spring. For example, rate of flow and seasonal changes.

      3. In some cases, springs have been drilled and a pump installed.

      4. In some cases, springs have been drilled, however they do not require a pump since they are artesian.

      5. Also keep in mind that some springs have dried up.

   b. **Wells**

      1. If possible, obtain when it was dug / drilled, well depth, depth to water and seasonal changes.

      2. For wells with pumps, obtain the pump's capacity, average rate of flow, pipe diameter and seasonal changes.

      3. If there are two or more wells close together, they can affect each other's rate of flow.

      4. In some cases, wells do not require a pump since they are artesian.

      5. Research USGS hydrological maps of the area.

G. Geological Features Associated With The Site

1. Some of the features which can conduct AHP include faults, bedrock fractures, dikes, contact zones between two different bedrock types and alluvial deposits which have larger grains concentrated within smaller grain deposits.

2. Document the geological features.

3. Research USGS geological maps of the area.

H. Entering Mapping Data

1. Enter the GPS points into your mapping program.

2. Categorize the features, use a different icon for each category and consecutively number each feature within that group.

3. I use blue lines to indicate each width boundary of an AHP wider than 15 ft / 4.57 m and a single line for the narrower ones.

I. Final Site Map

1. Once all the data is mapped, you should be able to determine the following:

    a. How many AHPs bring water into the site.

    b. How many AHPs are located within the site.

    c. The correlation between the AHPs' trends and widths to the location and size of stone features and structures.

    d. Percent of features on and off AHPs.

    e. Artifact distribution on and off AHPs.

Conclusion

My colleagues and I have used this methodology throughout the regions we have researched. Consistently, the late Neolithic sites I ground surveyed in southern England and near Carnac, France, are located on areas of higher permeability within the groundwater. This strongly suggests those who constructed these sites were mapping the concentrated flows and locating their habitation, ceremonial and sacred sites along them. By implementing this methodology, you can conduct a more efficient and comprehensive investigation of an archaeological site. Researchers who are replicating this methodology and I agree that this procedure is paramount in developing a more in depth understanding of late Neolithic sites and the features associated with them.

REFERENCES

I realize the following list of references does not follow the standard format, however please consider the following. To research the English sites I used WIKIPEDIA and its reference sources for the history of each site. These references can be accessed by bringing up each site in WIKIPEDIA. Therefore, I have copied each reference as it appears in WIKIPEDIA. All of the English sites were accessed October 6 - 28, 2018.

ARCHI The Archaeological Sites Index
   2018 *United Kingdom National Grid Reference*, accessed May 2018, http://www.archiuk.com/archi/archi_more_info.html.

Atlas de L'environnement du Morbihan
   2020 https://csem.morbihan.fr/dossiers/atlas_env/etat/geologie.php

Brosnan, Tanya, Matthew W. Becker, Carl P. Lipo
   2018 "Coastal groundwater discharge and the ancient inhabitants of Rapa Nui (Easter Island), Chile", *Hydrogeology Journal*, Published online: 04 October 2018, https://doi.org/10.1007/s10040-018-1870-7.

Brun, Jean-Pierre, J. Chantraine, Denis Gapals, Charles Gumlaux
   2004 *Tectonic history of the Hercynian Armorican Shear belt (Brittany, France)*, https://www.researchgate.net/publication/250199766_Tectonic_history_of_the_Hercynian_Armorican_Shear_belt_Brittany_France

Burnham, Andy
   2020 *The Megalithic Portal*, https://www.megalithic.co.uk/article.php?sid=9313

Centre des Monuments Nationaux
   2020 *Paysages De M'egalithes*, http://www.megalithes-morbihan.com/sites/megalith-site.html

Cunliffe, Barry
   1991 *Iron Age Communities in Britain: An account of England, Scotland and Wales from the Seventh Century BC until the Roman Conquest*, Routledfge, Chapman and Hall Inc., New York, New York.

DiNapoli Robert J., Carl P. Lipo, Tanya Brosnan, Terry L. Hunt, Sean Hizon, Alex E. Morrison and Matthew Beaker
   2018 "Rapa Nui (Easter Island) monument (ahu) locations explained by Freshwater sources", research article, PLOS one, 2018.

Dorn, Caroline, Tanguy Le Borgne, Joseph Doetsch, Niklas Linde
2010 *GPR borehole reflection experiments constrain fracture geometry in a crystalline rock aquifer*, Ploemeur, Brittany, France, https://www.researchgate.net/publication/252081930_GPR_borehole_reflection_experiments_constrain_fracture_geometry_in_a_crystalline_rock_aquifer_Ploemeur_Brittany_France

Feininger, Tomas
1978 "The Extraordinary Striated Outcrop at Saqsaywamàn, Peru", *Geological Society of America Bulletin*, v.89, P. 494-503, April 1978, doc. No. 80402.

Gantley, Michael J.
2017 "Europe's Mighty Megaliths "Rock" the Winter Solstice", *National Geographic*, https://www.nationalgeographic.com/archaeology-and-history/magazine/2017/11-12/history-europe-megaliths-solstice/

Geological Formations Of The Main Mines In Brittany
2020 Accessed February 2020, https://upload.wikimedia.org/wikipedia/commons/b/b8/Géologie_bretagne.jpg

Geology Map Of Brittany, France
2020 WIKEPIDIA, https://fr.wikipedia.org/wiki/Massif_armoricain#Le_domaine_sud_armoricain_ou_domaine_hercynien

Geology of the Surface of France
2020 Accessed February 2020, https://upload.wikimedia.org/wikipedia/commons/8/8b/France_geological_map-fr.svg

Hoare, Sir Richard Colt
1821 *The Ancient History of Wiltshire*, Vol. II, published by Lackington, Hughes, Harding, Mavor and Lepard, London.

Johnson, David W.
1998 "The Water Lines of Nasca", *Rumbos* 3(11), 50-56. Lima.
1999 "The Correlation Between the Lines of Nasca and Water Resources", pp. 157-164, in *Geheimnisvolle Zeichen im Alten Peru*, edited by Herausgegeben von Judith Rickenback, Rietberg Museum, Zurich, Switzerland.
2000 "The Lines of Nasca: Clues To The Origin Of Groundwater In Southern Peru", in *Geological Society of America*, November 2000, Dr. Steve Mabee, Dr. Donald Proulx, David Johnson and Janna Levin co-authors.
2002 "The Correlation Between Geoglyphs and Subterranean Water Resources in the Rio Grande de Nasca Drainage", (with Donald Proulx and Stephen B. Mabee) in *Andean Archaeology II – Art, Landscape and Society,* edited by Helaine Silverman and William H. Isbell, pp. 307-332, Oxford: Kluwer Academic/Plenum Publishers.

2003 "The Nasca Lines: Geoglyphs Reveal An Ancient Water Map", in *Permaculture Activist*, Winter 2003-04, No. 51.

2009 *Beneath the Nasca Lines and Other Coastal Geoglyphs of Peru and Chile*, Global Learning Inc, Poughkeepsie, NY.

2017 "The Ancestral Native Americans' Sacred Landscape and Features Associated with Areas of Higher Permeability Within the Groundwater", *Occasional Papers, Number IV*, 27 - 95, The Incorporated Orange County Chapter Of The New York State Archaeological Association, Goshen, N.Y.

2018 "The Ancestral Native Americans' Sacred Landscape", in *Spirits In Stone: The Secrets on Megalithic America*, Chapter 10, edited by Glenn Kreisberg, Bear & Company, Rochester, Vermont.

2018 Papers on Ceremonial Landscapes, No. 2018-14, National Anthropological Archives, Smithsonian Institution, Washington, D.C..

2020 *Native Americans' Sacred and Ceremonial Landscapes Correlation with Groundwater*, Hudson House Publishing, Poughkeepsie, New York.

Kreisberg, Glenn M.
2018 "Carnac: Stones For The Living", Chapter 11, Pierre Mereaux's Classic Work, translation and commentary by Ros Strong, fault map, pp. 259, in *Spirits In Stone: The Secrets on Megalithic America*, edited by Glenn Kreisberg, Bear & Company, Rochester, Vermont.

K. Manchuel, P. Traversa, D. Baumont, M. Cara, E. Nayman & C. Durouchoux
2018 "The French Seismic CATalogue (FCAT-17)", *Bulletin of Earthquake Engineering,* volume 16, pages 2227-2251, 2018, https://link.springer.com/article/10.1007/s10518-017-0236-1

Martin, Larry
2005 *A General Description of the Hydrogeology, Water Supply Wells, Groundwater Monitoring, and Potential Threats to Groundwater Resources of Chaco Culture National Historical Park*, New Mexico, *Technical Report NPS/ NRWRD/NRTR-2—5/325,* Water Resources Division, Fort Collins, Colorado, http://www.nature.nps.gov/water/technicalReports/Intermountain/chcu.pdf

Menier, David, Raynaud Jan-Yves
2006 *Basement Control on Shaping and Infilling of Valleys Incised at the Southern Coast of Brittany*, France, https://www.researchgate.net/publication/ 236661906_Basement_Control_on_Shaping_and_Infilling_of_Valleys_Incised _at_the_Southern_Coast_of_Brittany_France

Centre des Monuments Nationaux
2020 *Paysages De M'egalithes*, http://www.megalithes-morbihan.com/sites/ megalith-site.html

Stone, William J.
   2006   *Hydrogeology of the Gallup Sandstone, San Juan Basin*, Northwest New Mexico, online. http://info.ngwa.org/gwol/pdf/810600286.PDF

Stukeley, William, M.D.
   1743   *Abury, A Temple of the Britifh Druids*, With Some Others, Described, Second Volume, printed for the Author: and sold by W. Innys, R. Manby, B. Dod, F. Brindley, and the Booksellers in London.

Urton, Gary
   1985   "Animal Metaphors and the Life cycle in an Andean Community", in *Animal Myths and Metaphors in South America*, edited by Gary Urton. University of Utah Press, Salt Lake City, 1985. P. 251-284.

Vergnaud-Ayraud, Verginie, Luc Aquillina, T. Labasque, Helene Pauwels
   2008   *Compartmentalization of physical and chemical properties in hard-rock aquifers deduced from chemical and groundwater age analyses*, https://www.researchgate.net/publication/223833603_Compartmentalization_of_physical_and_chemical_properties_in_hardrock_aquifers_deduced_from_chemical_and_groundwater_age_analyss

WIKIPEDIA
   2020   *Brittany geological map*, https://upload.wikimedia.org/wikipedia/commons/6/63/Carte_géologique_de_Lorient.gif
   2020   *Brittany geological map*, https://en.wikipedia.org/wiki/Armorican_Massif#/media/File:Geologic_map_Armorican_Massif_EN.svg
   2020   *Saint-Michel tumulus*, https://en.wikipedia.org/wiki/Saint-Michel_tumulus

Wood, John Edwin
   1978   *Sun, Moon And Standing Stones*, Oxford University Press, Oxford, London.

WIKIPEDIA's References For England

Avebury
   WIKIPEDIA
   https://en.wikipedia.org/wiki/Avebury
   1. Burl 2002, p. 154 and 300.
         https://en.wikipedia.org/wiki/Avebury#Bur02
   2. Gillings and Pollard 2004, P. 6 and 26.
         https://en.wikipedia.org/wiki/Avebury#Gil04

Boscawen-Un stone Circle
   WIKIPEDIA
   https://en.wikipedia.org/wiki/Boscawen-Un
   4. Peter Herring, (2000), *Boscawen-Un – An Archaeological Assessment*, Historic Environment Service, Cornwall County Council.

5. Carolyn Kennet, (2018) *Celestial Stone Circles of West Cornwall: Reflections of the sky in an ancient landscape.*

Sanctuary Stone Circle

WIKIPEDIA
https://en.wikipedia.org/wiki/The_Sanctuary
1. "Avebury: The Sanctuary". *The Heritage Journal.* 28 February 2010. Retrieved 5 March 2018.
   https://heritageaction.wordpress.com/2010/02/28/avebury-the-sanctuary/
2. *History of the Sanctuary, Avebury*, english-heritage.org.uk. 2006. retrieved 5 March 2018.
   https://www.english-heritage.org.uk/visit/places/the-sanctuary/history/
4. *"The Sanctuary: HER id 4743"*, Wiltshire and Swindon Historic Environment Record. Retrieved 5 March 2018.

Carwynnen Quoit

WIKIPEDIA
https://en.wikipedia.org/wiki/Carwynnen_Quoit

Carn Euny

WIKIPEDIA
https://en.wikipedia.org/wiki/Carn_Euny
2. Craig Weatherhill *Cornovia: Ancient Sites of Cornwall & Scilly* (Alison Hodge 1985; Halsgrove 1997, 2000).
3. http://www.english-heritage.org.uk/daysout/properties/carn-euny-ancient-village/
4. Sites Managed and Cared for by Cornwall Heritage Trust for English Heritage Archived 12 March 2011 at the Wayback Machine.
5. http://www.stonepages.com/home.html

Castle an Dinas

WIKIPEDIA
https://en.wikipedia.org/wiki/Castle_an_Dinas,_St_Columb_Major

Cornwall Heritage Trust
http://www.cornwallheritagetrust.org/our-sites/castle-an-dinas/

Cerne Abbas Giant

WIKIPEDIA
https://en.wikipedia.org/wiki/Cerne_Abbas_Giant
2. *"Historic England, Hill Figure Called The Giant (1003202"*, National List for England, retrieved 14 October 2012.
   https://en.wikipedia.org/wiki/Historic_England
3. Haughton, Brian, *Hidden History: Lost Civilizations, Secret Knowledge, and Ancient Mysteries*, publisher Read, HowYouWant.com, 2009, ISBN 1442952601, 9781442952607, page 258.

4. William Holloway, "The Giant of Trendle Hill", The minor minstrel: or, Poetical pieces, chiefly familiar and descriptive, Printed for W. Suttaby, 1808, 182 pages, page 140.

5. Hutchins, John (1973) [1742]. *The History and Antiquities of the County of Dorset*. Robert Douch (Contributor). Oxford: *Rowman & Littlefield Publishers. ISBN 0-87471-336-6.*

6, 9 & 16. Hy. Colley March M.D. F.S.A., "The Giant and the Maypole of Cerne", *Proceedings*, Dorset Natural History and Archaeological Society, Vol.22, 1901, pages 104, 107 - 108.

7. Stuart Piggott, "The Hercules Myth—beginnings and ends", *Antiquity* Vol.12 No.47, September 1938, Page 327.

8. Timothy Darvill, "Cerne Giant, Dorset, England", in *Concise Oxford Dictionary of Archaeology*, publisher: Oxford University Press, 2009, ISBN 0199534047, 9780199534043, 544 pages.

10. Koch, John T. (2006). *Celtic Culture: A Historical Encyclopedia*. ABC-CLIO. p. 395. ISBN 1-85109-440-7.

11. "Cerne Abbas Giant & Cerne Abbas, Dorset", Weymouth & Portland Borough Council. Archived from the original on 30 March 2009. Retrieved 2010-10-03.

12. Chris Court, "Nose Job for Chalk Giant", Press Association, Sunday 11 April 1993, Home News.

13. Raphael Samuel, *Theatres of Memory: Past and Present in Contemporary Culture*, Publisher: Verso Books, 2012, ISBN 1844678695, 9781844678693, 508 pages, page 172.

14. Paul Edwards, "Campaigning Couples to Gather at Ancient Fertility Symbol", Press Association, Sunday 2 May 1993.

15. Temple Willcox, "Hard times for the Cerne Giant: 20th-century attitudes to an ancient monument" (abstract), *Antiquity*, Vol.62 No.236, September 1988, page 524.

17. Eugene Monick, *Phallos, Sacred Image of the Masculine*, Volume 27 of Studies in Jungian psychology, publisher Inner City Books, 1987, ISBN 0919123260, 9780919123267, 141 pages, page 36.

18. Antony Barnett, "Bishop tried to gird the giant's loins", *The Observer*, 5 March 2000.

19. "Editorial, regarding the Home Office file, Obscene Publications, "The Cerne Abbas Giant" (PRO HO 45/18033)", *Antiquity*, Vol. 50 No. 198, June 1976, pages 93–94.

20. Grinsell, Leslie (1980), "The Cerne Abbas Giant: 1764–1980", *Antiquity*. **54** (210): 29–33.

Chun Quoit

WIKIPEDIA
https://en.wikipedia.org/wiki/Chûn_Quoit

1. Pevsner, N. (1970) *Cornwall*; 2nd ed., revised by E. Radcliffe, Penguin; p. 121.

Chysauster Ancient Village

WIKIPEDIA

https://en.wikipedia.org/wiki/Chysauster_Ancient_Village
1. *Chysauster*, prices and opening times, English Heritage, retrieved 11 April 2011
   http://www.english-heritage.org.uk/daysout/properties/chysauster-ancient-village/prices-and-opening-times
2. *Chysauster Settlement*, Pastscape, retrieved 11 April 2011.
3. *Chysauster Iron Age Village*, Britain Express, retrieved 11 April 2011.
4. *Chysauster Iron Age Village*, English Heritage, retrieved 11 April 2011.
   http://www.english-heritage.org.uk/daysout/properties/chysauster-ancient-village/

Chun Castle

WIKIPEDIA
https://en.wikipedia.org/wiki/Chûn_Castle
1. Craig Weatherhill Cornovia, *Ancient Sites of Cornwall & Scilly,* Alison Hodge 1985; Halsgrove 1997, 2000.

Drizzlecombe

WIKIPEDIA
https://en.wikipedia.org/wiki/Drizzlecombe
1. *The Dartmoor Trust Drizzlecombe Menhir And Stone Row,*
   http://www.dartmoortrust.org/archive/307
2. *The Dartmoor Trust Drizzlecombe Menhir, Sheepstor,*
   http://www.dartmoortrust.org/archive/12338
Drizzlecombe map with stone row insert, from WIKIPEDIA
   https://commons.wikimedia.org/wiki/File:Stone-Rows,_Drizzlecombe_-_A_Book_of_Dartmoor.jpg
Map from Esas Cosds Este Mundo, a veces insolito,
   http://www.esascosas.com/drizzlecombe-stone-rows/

Fogou

WIKIPEDIA
https://en.wikipedia.org/wiki/Fogou
1. *Fogou - Merriam Webster,*
   https://www.merriam-webster.com/dictionary/fogou
2. *Fogou - Order of Bards and Druids,*
   http://www.druidry.org/library/fogous Lanyon Quoit

Lanyon Quoit

WIKIPEDIA
https://en.wikipedia.org/wiki/Lanyon_Quoit
1. *The Dartmoor Trust Drizzlecombe Menhir And Stone Row,*
   http://www.dartmoortrust.org/archive/307
2. *The Dartmoor Trust Drizzlecombe Menhir, Sheepstor,*
   http://www.dartmoortrust.org/archive/12338

Longstones Cove
WIKIPEDIA
https://en.wikipedia.org/wiki/The_Longstones
1. Historic England, "Avebury Long Stone (1008104)", National Heritage for England. Retrieved 11 September 2015.
https://en.wikipedia.org/wiki/National_Heritage_List_for_England

Maiden Castle
WIKIPEDIA
https://en.wikipedia.org/wiki/Maiden_Castle,_Dorset
2. Sharples (1991a).

Men-an-tol
WIKIPEDIA
https://en.wikipedia.org/wiki/Mên-an-Tol
1. *Pastscape*, retrieved 9 November 2013,
http://www.pastscape.org.uk/hob.aspx?hob_id=424271
2. William Borlase, (1769), *Antiquities Historical and Monumental of the County of Cornwall*, Bowyer and Nichols, London.
3. John Thomas Blight, (1864), *A week at the Land's End, 1861, Churches of West Cornwall.*
4. William Copeland Borlase, (1872), *Naenia Cornubiae*, Longmans.
5. Hugh O'Neill Hencken, (1932), *The Archaeology of Cornwall and Scilly*, Metheun.
6. Ann Preston-Jones, (1993), *The Men-an-Tol. Management and Survey*, Historic Environment Service, Cornwall County Council.

Merry Maidens Stone Circle
WIKIPEDIA
https://en.wikipedia.org/wiki/The_Merry_Maidens
2. William Borlase, *Antiquities Historical and Monumental of the County of Cornwall.* Bowyer and Nichols, London 1769.
3. William Copeland Borlase, *Naenia Cornubiae.* Longmans 1872.
4. Hugh O'Neill Hencken, *The Archaeology of Cornwall and Scilly.* Metheun 1932.
5. John Barnatt: *Prehistoric Cornwall: The Ceremonial Monuments*, Turnstone Press Limited 1982.

Hurlers Stone Circles
WIKIPEDIA
https://en.wikipedia.org/wiki/The_Hurlers_(stone_circles)
5. *English Heritage*,
http://www.english-heritage.org.uk/daysout/properties/hurlers-stone-circles/history-and-research/

Oldbury Castle
WIKIPEDIA
https://en.wikipedia.org/wiki/Oldberry_Castle

1. Gathercole, Clare, "Dulverton" (PDF), *English Heritage Extensive Urban Survey*, Somerset County Council, Archived from the original (PDF) on 17 July 2011, Retrieved 5 March 2011.
2. *Exmoor National Park Historic Environment Record*, English Heritage, Retrieved 16 January 2011,
   http://www.heritagegateway.org.uk/Gateway/Results_Single.aspx? uid=MSO11210&resourceID=1022
3. *Fortified England,* Archived from the original on 11 July 2011, Retrieved 15 January 2011,
   https://web.archive.org/web/20110711020616/http://www.fortifiedengland.com/Home/Categories/ViewItem/tabid/61/Default.aspx?IID=1485

Old Sarum
WIKIPEDIA
https://en.wikipedia.org/wiki/Old_Sarum

English Heritage, *Old Sarum*, p. 24. (London), 2003,
https://www.english-heritage.org.uk/visit/places/old-sarum/history/sources/

Passionate about British Heritage!
https://www.britainexpress.com/History/prehistoric_monuments.htm

Stonehenge Circle
WIKIPEDIA
https://en.wikipedia.org/wiki/Stonehenge
1. Christopher Young, Amanda Chadburn, Isabelle Bedu (July 2008), "Stonehenge World Heritage Site Management Plan". *UNESCO*: 18.
2. Morgan, James (21 September 2008), "Dig pinpoints Stonehenge origins", BBC. Retrieved 22 September 2008.
3. Kennedy, Maev (9 March 2013),"Stonehenge may have been burial site for Stone Age elite, say archaeologist", BBC, Retrieved 22 September 2008,
   https://www.theguardian.com/science/2013/mar/09/archaeology-stonehenge-bones-burial-ground
4. Legge, James (9 March 2012), "Stonehenge: new study suggests landmark started life as a graveyard for the 'prehistoric elite'", *The Independent*. London. Retrieved 11 March 2013,
   https://www.independent.co.uk/news/uk/home-news/stonehenge-new-study-suggests-landmark-started-life-as-a-graveyard-for-the-prehistoric-elite-8527686.html
5. Stonehenge builders travelled from far, say researchers", *BBC News*, 9 March 2013, Retrieved 11 March 2013,
   https://www.bbc.co.uk/news/uk-21724084
6. Scott, Julie; Selwyn, Tom (2010). *Thinking Through Tourism*, Berg. p. 191.

Stonehenge Cursus

WIKIPEDIA

https://en.wikipedia.org/wiki/Stonehenge_Cursus

3. *shef.ac.uk*. Archived from the original on 24 December 2008, https://web.archive.org/web/20081224125415/http://www.shef.ac.uk/archaeology/research/stonehenge/stonehenge07-05.html

4. Souden, David (1997). *Stonehenge, Mysteries of the Stones and Landscape*, Swindon: English Heritage, pp. 46 and 47, ISBN 1-85585-291-8.

5. Richards, Julian (2007). *Stonehenge, The Story so Far*, Swindon, English Heritage, pp. 37& and 38. ISBN 978-1-905624-00-3.

6. *Operation Stonehenge: What Lies Beneath*, BBC.

Stonehenge Great Cursus Barrows Burial Mounds

WIKIPEDIA

https://en.wikipedia.org/wiki/Cursus_Barrows

2. Historic England, *PastScape*. Retrieved 17 March 2016, https://en.wikipedia.org/wiki/Cursus_Barrows

   2. *Cursus barrow Group* (219681)

   3. *Twin bell barrow and a bell barrow* (1012586)

   4. *Amesbury 43* (942691)

   5. *Amesbury 44* (942696)

   6. *Amesbury 45* (942703)

   7. *A bowl barrow and three bell barrows* (1012401)

   8. *Amesbury 47* (942705)

   9. *Amesbury 47* (942709)

   10. *Amesbury 48* (942712)

   11. *Amesbury 49* (942659)

   12. *Two bowl barrows* (1012400)

   13. *Amesbury 114* (1119431)

   14. *Amesbury 50* (942661)

   15. *Bowl barrow* (1012399)

16. Gaffney, C.; Gaffney, V.; Neubauer, W.; Baldwin, E.; Chapman, H.; Garwood, P.; Moulden, H.; Sparrow, T.; Bates, R.; Löcker, K.; Hinterleitner, A.; Trinks, I.; Nau, E.; Zitz, T.; Floery, S.; Verhoeven, G.; Doneus, M. (2012), "The Stonehenge Hidden Landscapes Project". *Archaeological Prospection*. **19** (2): 147. doi:10.1002/arp.1422.

17. "A new 'henge' discovered at Stonehenge", University of Birmingham, 22 July 2010, Archived from the original on 11 July 2012, Retrieved 2010-07-22.

18. Kennedy, Maev (2010-07-22). "Stonehenge twin discovered stone's throw away". London: The Guardian. Retrieved 2010-07-22.

19. "Archaeologists unearth Neolithic henge at Stonehenge". BBC News. 2010-07-22. Retrieved 2010-07-22.

20. Owen, James (2010-07-23), "Stonehenge Had Neighboring, Wooden Twin—More to Come?". National Geographic, Retrieved 2014-08-2.

21. "How significant is the 'new henge'?". BBC News. 2010-07-22. Retrieved 2011-05-10.

22. Historic England. *"Amesbury 51 (942662)"*, *PastScape,* Retrieved 17 March 2016.
23. Historic England. "Bell barrow situated south of The Cursus and east of Fargo Plantation (1012398)". *National Heritage List for England*, Retrieved 17 March 2016.
24. Historic England. *PastScape*. Retrieved 17 March 2016.
https://en.wikipedia.org/wiki/Cursus_Barrows
    24. *Amesbury 52 (942672)*
    25. *Bowl barrow (1012397)*
    26. *Amesbury 53 (942674)*
    27. *Bowl barrow (10112396*
    28. *Amesbury 54 (219678)*
    29. *Bowl barrow (1012377)*
    30. *Amesbury 112 (1066498)*
    31. *Disc barrow (1012403)*
    32. *Fargo Hengiform (219510)*
    33. *Hengi-form monument (1012402)*

Tregiffian Burial Chamber

WIKIPEDIA

https://en.wikipedia.org/wiki/Tregiffian_Burial_Chamber

1. *Place-names in the Standard Written Form (SWF)*, List of place-names agreed by the MAGA Signage Panel. Cornish Language Partnership.
2. Sites Managed and Cared for by Cornwall Heritage Trust for English Heritage Archived 2012-06-13 at the Wayback Machine.
3. William Copeland Borlase, *Naenia Cornubiae*, Longmans 1872.
4. Hugh O'Neill Hencken, The Archaeology of Cornwall and Scilly, Metheun 1932.
5. Glyn Edmund Daniel, *The Megalith Builders of Western Europe*, Harmondsworth, Penguin 1963.

Tumulus / Barrow / Mound

WIKIPEDIA
https://en.wikipedia.org/wiki/Tumulus

West Kennet Long Barrow

WIKIPEDIA
https://en.wikipedia.org/wiki/West_Kennet_Long_Barrow

Woodhenge Cahokia

WIKIPEDIA
https://en.wikipedia.org/wiki/Cahokia_Woodhenge

Woodhenge

WIKIPEDIA
https://en.wikipedia.org/wiki/Woodhenge

1. "Woodhenge", *World Heritage Site*, English Heritage, Retrieved 7 October 2012.

2. "History and Research: Woodhenge". *www.english-heritage.org.uk*. English Heritage. Retrieved 7 October 2012.\

Index